W9-ASJ-378

*N*OTE TO THE READER

How many times have you lamented during tax-paying time, "If only I started planning sooner . . ." or "If I had only known about this, I would have done things differently so I could have paid less tax . . ." or "There's got to be another deduction I could take . . ." or "I really don't understand what information the IRS needs here; I wish I had an example." To help individuals gain valuable insight and to offer practical answers to a variety of tax-planning issues quickly and easily are some of the reasons why we decided to publish the *Personal Tax Adviser*—to help *you* save both time and money.

Written in simple English by experienced tax professionals, the *Adviser* has the up-to-the-minute information you need about a wide variety of tax-planning areas—deductions, exemptions, rates . . . even how to cope with the dreaded IRS audit. Wondering if a rule applies to your situation? There are numerous **Tax Tips**, **Examples**, and **Cautions** to clarify the issue. Stumbling over a tax term? Our **Glossary** will translate it for you. Want to find something fast? Our comprehensive, easy-to-use **Index** will make your search less "taxing."

Remember, the more you know about taxes, the greater the savings you can achieve. Let the *Price Waterhouse Personal Tax Adviser* provide you with valuable tax tips and planning ideas to save you money now and in the years to come!

Price Waterhouse LLP

About Price Waterhouse

Price Waterhouse is committed to providing the ideas, information, and advice that will help our clients make better business decisions. Through a global network of firms practicing in 118 countries and territories, Price Waterhouse professionals work together to provide accounting, auditing, tax planning and compliance, management and technology consulting, litigation support, and business advisory services to corporations, individuals, nonprofit organizations, and government departments and agencies.

Through more than 100 offices and its legislative monitoring service in Washington, DC, our US firm—Price Waterhouse LLP—advises businesses and individuals nationwide on the planning and compliance implications of the tax law. Our professionals frequently consult on tax issues with the Treasury Department and the Internal Revenue Service on behalf of clients. The firm also offers seminars and publishes a variety of periodicals and booklets on tax and personal financial planning.

THE

PRICE WATERHOUSE

PERSONAL TAX ADVISER

1995-1996 EDITION

THE

$\mathcal{P}$RICE WATERHOUSE

PERSONAL TAX ADVISER

1995-1996 EDITION

IRWIN
Professional Publishing

Chicago • Bogotá • Boston • Buenos Aires • Caracas
London • Madrid • Mexico City • Sydney • Toronto

Tennessee Tech Library
Cookeville, TN
WITHDRAWN

© Price Waterhouse LLP, 1995

Price Waterhouse LLP is referred to herein as Price Waterhouse.

All rights reserved. No part of this publication may be reproduced, stored in a retrieval system, or transmitted, in any form or by any means, electronic, mechanical, photocopying, recording, or otherwise, without the prior written permission of the publisher.

This publication is designed to provide accurate and authoritative information in regard to the subject matter covered. It is sold with the understanding that neither the author or the publisher is engaged in rendering legal, accounting, or other professional service. If legal advice or other expert assistance is required, the services of a competent professional person should be sought.

From a Declaration of Principles jointly adopted by a Committee of the American Bar Association and a Committee of Publishers.

Irwin Professional Book Team

Publisher:	Wayne McGuirt
Executive editor:	Amy Hollands Gaber
Senior marketing manager:	Tiffany Dykes
Project editor:	Beth Cigler
Production supervisor:	Carol Klein/Lara Feinberg
Assistant manager, desktop services:	Jon Christopher
Compositor:	Kramer Communications
Typeface:	10/12 Palatino
Printer:	R.R. Donnelley & Sons Company

Times Mirror
Higher Education Group

ISBN 0-7863-0500-2

ISSN 1076-9625

Printed in the United States of America

1 2 3 4 5 6 7 8 9 0 DO 2 1 0 9 8 7 6 5

Tennessee Tech Library
Cookeville, TN

CONTENTS

As We Went to Press . . .

C ongress was developing a package of tax cuts—up to $245 billion over seven years—to be included in massive deficit-reduction legislation aimed at balancing the budget by the year 2002. Significant tax reductions for individuals have been approved by House and Senate tax-writers. If enacted, some of these provisions would affect 1995 tax returns. Key changes primarily affecting individuals could include the following:

- **Family tax credit** The House proposal would create a $500-per-child tax credit for children under age 18, effective beginning in 1996; the credit would begin to be phased out for married couples with adjusted gross income (AGI) above $200,000. The Senate version would begin phasing out the per-child tax credit for married couples with AGI above $110,000.

- **50-percent capital gains exclusion** Both House and Senate proposals would allow individuals to exclude 50 percent of long-term capital gains from income. Under the House version, the exclusion would be effective for sales or exchanges made after December 31, 1994, while Senate tax-writers are considering making the exclusion effective for dispositions after October 13, 1995. Other open issues are whether amounts excluded would be subject to the alternative minimum tax, and whether a loss on sale of a personal residence should be deductible.

- **Capital gains "indexing"** For purposes of measuring gain on sales of assets acquired after 1994, the House proposal would allow the basis of certain capital or business assets (if held for three years) to be adjusted to account for inflation occurring after 1994.

- **Expanded IRA incentives** Both House and Senate proposals would allow individuals to make nondeductible contributions up to $2,000 a year to a new "back-loaded" IRA. Income earned and withdrawn would be tax-free if attributable to contributions held in the IRA for at least five years and the IRA holder is at least 59 ½. The Senate proposal also would increase the current-law income limits on making deductible IRA contributions.

Related changes under consideration would allow non-employed spouses to make IRA contributions, permit penalty-free IRA withdrawals for certain qualified purposes, and create new 401(k) savings arrangements for smaller employers.

- **Estate tax changes**   Both House and Senate proposals would increase the unified estate and gift tax credit from $600,000 to $750,000 over a period of years. The Senate version would provide additional relief for a qualified family-owned business.

- **Venture capital incentives**   The Senate proposal would expand capital gains incentives enacted in 1993 for investment in qualified small business stock by increasing the amount of gains that may be excluded from 50 percent to 75 percent, among other changes; the House version would repeal the 1993 provision.

- **Social Security benefits**   The House bill would repeal, over a period of years, the 1993 provision which increased the taxation of Social Security benefits.

- **Marriage penalty relief**   Both House and Senate proposals would seek to mitigate the "marriage penalty" under current law that requires a married couple to pay more in federal income taxes than they would pay if they were not married.

- **Adoption tax credit**   A tax credit up to $5,000 would be provided for qualified adoption expenses after 1995, but would be phased out for families with AGI between $60,000 and $100,000.

- **Eldercare tax credit**   The House proposal would provide a tax credit up to $500 for taxpayers providing custodial care to a parent living in their households.

- **Student loan tax credit**   The Senate proposal would provide a tax credit equal to 20 percent of interest paid on a student loan for the first five years of repayment. The credit would be capped at $500 per year per borrower, and would be phased out at specified AGI levels.

- **Home office deductions**   The House proposal would liberalize the current-law rules for determining whether individuals may claim a home office deduction.

- **Educational assistance**   Both House and Senate proposals would reinstate the exclusion for employer-provided educational assistance retroactively to January 1, 1995.

- **Medical savings accounts**   Both House and Senate proposals would allow tax-favored medical savings accounts to be maintained for individuals covered only by a catastrophic health plan.

- **Tax "simplification"**   Numerous provisions included in the House proposal would simplify tax rules relating to individuals, pension plans and distributions, partnerships, international taxes, S corporations, estate and gift taxes, and excise taxes. Changes affecting individuals would relate, for example, to the gain on the sale of a personal residence and the payment of taxes by credit card.

The outlook for ultimate enactment of deficit-reduction legislation—and thus for tax changes just described—was unclear as we went to press. President Clinton has vowed to veto the deficit reduction bill being developed by congressional Republicans because of the size and nature of changes that would be made to Medicare, Medicaid, and other programs. The White House also has argued that any tax cuts should be targeted more toward lower-income individuals. *Any final compromise between Congress and the White House could change the substance or effective dates of the proposals summarized here.*

You should consult with your tax adviser to determine how any of these or other pending tax proposals—if enacted into law—may affect you.

1

⚜️HY TAX PLANNING?

The only way to make absolutely sure that you pay no more in taxes than you should is to devise and use effective tax strategies.

This book will help you plan strategies to use for the remainder of 1995 and throughout 1996. It's not a line-by-line guide to preparing your tax return. Instead, it will help you ensure that when preparation time does roll around, the number on the "total tax" line of your Form 1040 is as small as it legally can be.

With the enactment of the Omnibus Budget Reconciliation Act of 1993, taxable income for higher-income individuals is subject to an incremental tax rate as high as 39.6 percent. Individuals may now be taxed at five different rates—15, 28, 31, 36, and 39.6 percent. Tax rates exceeding 15 percent apply to 1995 taxable income at the following thresholds:

Filing Status	Taxable Income Threshold			
	28%	31%	36%	39.6%
Married filing jointly	$39,000	$94,250	$143,600	$256,500
Single	23,350	56,550	117,950	256,500
Head of household	31,250	80,750	130,800	256,500
Married filing separately	19,500	47,125	71,800	128,250

Net long-term capital gain income is subject to a maximum tax rate of 28 percent.

As a result of indexing or adjustments for inflation, the amount of your income subject to the preceding rates has increased—it takes a little bit more income than last year to reach each tax bracket. The levels of income subject to these tax rates will be adjusted again in 1996 and future years.

The phase-out of personal exemptions and the limits on itemized deductions for certain high-income taxpayers may effectively increase your marginal tax rate to an even higher level. For example, a taxpayer claiming four exemptions who is in the personal exemption phase-out range (1995 adjusted gross income [AGI] between $172,050 and $294,550) could have an effective marginal tax rate about three percentage points higher than the statutory tax rate. Furthermore, itemizers with AGI above applicable thresholds face an increase in the effective marginal tax rate of approximately one additional percentage point.

The combined effect of this year's rates, the personal exemption phase-out, and the itemized deduction limitation could increase the effective marginal federal tax rate for a taxpayer in the 36 percent tax bracket to approximately 40 percent. Other taxpayers will be comparably affected.

What other changes will affect 1995 returns?

- The standard deduction has gone up due to indexing.

Filing Status	1995 Standard Deduction
Married filing jointly	$6,550
Single	3,900
Head of household	5,750
Married filing separately	3,275

- The personal exemption amount you may claim on your tax return for 1995 has increased to $2,500. (See Chapter 3.)
- The threshold amounts that determine when total itemized deductions are limited have also been indexed. In general, certain upper income taxpayers must reduce the total of most itemized deductions— including qualified mortgage interest, charitable contributions, state and local income taxes, unreimbursed employee expenses, and certain other miscellaneous expenses—by an amount equal to 3 percent of the amount by which AGI tops certain thresholds.

Filing Status	1995 Itemized Deduction Limitation Threshold
Married filing jointly, single, or head of household	$114,700
Married filing separately	57,350

Deductions for investment interest, medical expenses, casualty and theft losses, and gambling losses are not subject to this 3 percent reduction. (See Chapter 4.)

- Indexing also increases the amounts used to determine the phase-out of personal exemptions. The deduction for personal exemptions is phased out by 2 percent for each $2,500 or fraction of $2,500 ($1,250 if you're married and file separately) by which your AGI exceeds certain amounts. (See Chapter 3.)

Filing Status	1995 Personal Exemption Phase-Out
Married filing jointly	$172,050
Single	114,700
Head of household	143,350
Married filing separately	86,025

- The dollar cap on wages and self-employment income subject to the OASDI portion of the Social Security tax has been increased from $60,600 in 1994 to $61,200 in 1995. All wages and self-employment income are subject to the Medicare Hospital Insurance (HI) tax. (See Chapter 24.)

Now you know some basic facts affecting 1995 returns. How do you go about trimming your personal tax liability?

What about deferring income and accelerating deductions? If you expect your marginal tax rate in 1996 to be the same as in 1995 or lower, you will probably benefit from these traditional year-end tax planning strategies.

But not everyone should follow these strategies. For example, if in 1995 your taxable income is abnormally low, the opposite tactic—accelerating income and deferring deductions—might work best depending on your anticipated top federal tax rate for 1995 and 1996. You should also be sure to consider your alternative minimum tax (AMT) situation.

It's always worthwhile to run the numbers and consider whether accelerating income or deferring deductions (or vice versa) will be beneficial. By looking at your individual circumstances, you can determine which strategy may produce tax savings for you, taking into account the time value of money and the impact of the tax rates that apply to you in each year. Then you can choose the strategies that will benefit you most.

How about capital gains? Keep in mind that when it comes to capital assets, the economic aspects of selling or holding should be your primary concern. If the economics make sense, you should develop a tax strategy to enhance your gain. Now, on to Chapter 2.

2

$\mathscr{H}$OW THE TAX RATES AFFECT YOUR BOTTOM LINE

- What are taxable income, marginal tax rate, and effective tax rate?
- When should you defer income and accelerate deductions?
- What other taxes impact your bottom line?

To help you understand the tax rate system and its impact on your bottom line, you need to know the meaning of some basic tax jargon. Three phrases are used frequently throughout this book. The first, *taxable income,** is the amount of income on which you actually pay taxes. This amount is calculated by adding up your income from all sources and subtracting all of the deductions the tax law allows you to claim.

The most common type of income you receive is compensation from your employment. This includes salary, wages, tips, commissions, fees, or business profits. Other common types of income are interest, dividends, alimony, capital gains (see Chapter 14), pensions, rents, and income from partnerships, S corporations, and trusts.

What are allowable deductions? They include adjustments to income, for example, a Keogh contribution (see Chapter 22); itemized deductions or the standard deduction (see Chapter 4); and the deductions allowed for personal exemptions (see Chapter 3).

The second phrase, *marginal tax rate*, is the rate of tax paid on the last dollar of income. Take a purely imaginary tax system with two rates. Income up to $10,000 is taxed at 5 percent; income in excess of $10,000 is taxed at 10 percent.

If a taxpayer earned $12,000 in salary and $1,000 in bonus, the marginal tax rate on the bonus is 10 percent—that is, the rate on the last dollar you received.

Marginal tax rate is also used to determine the tax benefit of a deduction. If a taxpayer's marginal tax rate is 10 percent, a $1,000 deduction saves $100 in income taxes.

---

* Terms that appear in bold italic are defined in the Glossary.

4

Finally, *effective tax rate* is the average rate at which a taxpayer's income is taxed. Assume the same two-rate system and an income of $15,000.

The tax on the first $10,000 in income is $500 ($10,000 times 5 percent), and on income exceeding $10,000, the tax is $500 ($5,000 times 10 percent).

So the taxpayer's total tax comes to $1,000 ($500 plus $500). The top marginal tax rate is 10 percent, but the effective tax rate is only 6.7 percent ($1,000 divided by $15,000).

HOW IT WORKS

The law contains five regular tax brackets: 15 percent, 28 percent, 31 percent, 36 percent, and 39.6 percent. The following tax rate schedule illustrates these rates.

1995 Tax Rate Schedule			
	Taxable Income	Tax	% on Excess
Married filing jointly*	$0	$0	15
	39,000	5,850	28
	94,250	21,320	31
	143,600	36,619	36
	256,500	77,263	39.6
Single	$0	$0	15
	23,350	3,503	28
	56,550	12,799	31
	117,950	31,833	36
	256,500	81,711	39.6
Head of household	$0	$0	15
	31,250	4,688	28
	80,750	18,548	31
	130,800	34,063	36
	256,500	79,315	39.6
Married filing separately	$0	$0	15
	19,500	2,925	28
	47,125	10,660	31
	71,800	18,309	36
	128,250	38,631	39.6

* The joint return rates can be used by a qualifying surviving spouse.

The income levels at which the tax rate brackets begin are adjusted annually for inflation.

◆ℰXAMPLE

Here's how the tax rate system works. Say you're married, file a joint return, and your 1995 taxable income comes to $200,000. Your federal income taxes for the year add up to $56,923.

Here's how the taxes are calculated. Your first $39,000 in income is taxed at 15 percent. That comes to $5,850. Your income from $39,001 to $94,250 falls in the 28 percent bracket, generating a tax of $15,470. Your income from $94,251 to $143,600 falls in the 31 percent bracket, generating a tax of $15,299. The remaining $56,400 of your income is taxed at 36 percent, so tax on this income is $20,304. The total comes to $56,923.

Instead of "working through" each bracket this way, simply use the table above. The tax on the first $143,600 of taxable income is $36,619. The tax on the "excess" over $143,600 (which is $56,400) is taxed at 36 percent, giving a tax of $20,304. The total comes to the same $56,923.

These tax rates are also affected by a special 28 percent maximum tax rate on long-term capital gains. See Chapter 14 for more information on how this special rate may affect the tax you'll owe.

Although your income may be taxed at the stated rate of 36 or 39.6 percent, your *effective marginal tax rate* may actually be higher because of two wrinkles in the tax law—the phase-out of personal exemptions and the floor on certain itemized deductions.

While neither of these two items actually increases the tax rate that is applied to your income, they both decrease the amounts you may deduct in calculating your taxable income. By doing so they increase the taxes you pay, causing your effective marginal tax rate to exceed the stated rate.

For 1995, the Medicare hospital insurance (HI) tax is paid by both the employer and the employee at a rate of 1.45 percent on all wages. Self-employment income is subject to the combined rate of 2.9 percent.

There is no dollar limit on wages and self-employment income subject to the HI tax, thus serving to further increase the effective tax rate for higher income taxpayers.

QUESTIONS AND ANSWERS

Q.   In the past, I have heard my accountant say that the best tax strategy is to defer income and accelerate deductions. Does this advice apply to 1995?

A.   In any year, making the decision to defer income and accelerate deductions involves some fortune-telling.

You have to project your income and deductions for 1995 and 1996 and decide whether you will save tax dollars by deferring income or accelerating deductions.

In short, you have to estimate your tax liabilities as best you can. You probably will want to enlist your tax adviser to help you in this process.

In spite of the top marginal rate of 39.6 percent brought about by the 1993 Tax Act, you should note that from a historical perspective, 1995 tax rates are not that high when compared to rates in previous years. For instance, the top marginal tax rate came to 50 percent in 1986 and was a whopping 70 percent in 1981.

Given our country's current deficit problems, however, most tax experts predict that if rates change again, they're still more likely to rise than fall.

Some items you and your accountant should pay close attention to are the impact of the alternative minimum tax; passive losses and passive income; the phase-out of personal exemptions; the floor on itemized deductions; and deductions (miscellaneous deductions, for example) that are subject to a threshold amount.

All of these tax issues are discussed in the chapters that follow, and tax-saving strategies are presented for dealing with them.

Q.   I have estimated my 1995 tax liability and think it makes sense for me to postpone receiving some of my income until 1996. Do you have any ideas for doing so?

A.   If your tax planning shows you would be better off postponing income until 1996, consider the following techniques to achieve that goal:

- Deferred compensation. Find out whether your company has a deferred compensation plan that would allow you to defer income into 1996 or later. Ask if your company will pay you any interest on your deferred earnings. If it does, see if it will pay a competitive interest rate. Also, weigh the risks. When you defer compensation, you become a creditor of your company. If it goes bankrupt, you stand to lose the amount owed you.

- Year-end bonuses. Ask your employer to pay your bonus in January, instead of December. Your employer will not lose its deduction by postponing payment until after year-end.

- Interest income. Consider investing in certificates of deposit or U.S. Treasury bills that mature after year-end to defer the interest income into 1996.

- Delay collections. If you are a self-employed individual who keeps the books on a cash basis, postpone billing clients or customers until near the end of the year. Why? Payment won't be received until after December 31.

- Postpone sales. Defer the sale or closing on the sale of your personal residence until 1996.

- Installment sales. If you sell real or personal property (except securities and inventory), delay receipt of part of the proceeds until next year and beyond by having the payments made in installments.

Whatever method you use to postpone income, keep in mind other considerations. Does it make economic sense for you to postpone income—can you afford to go without a portion of your earnings? How long can you go without this income?

Q.   What other types of transactions provide alternatives for deferring or accelerating income?

A.   Try to time the following transactions to best suit your tax needs, keeping in mind, of course, relevant nontax considerations:

- Selling stock that may generate gains or losses (see Chapter 14 for more information).
- Exercising taxable stock options (see Chapter 21).
- Collecting pension and profit-sharing payouts (see Chapter 23).
- Paying off bills resulting in itemized deductions—a big medical bill, for example (see Chapter 7).
- Timing the purchase and renewals of certificates of deposit and Treasury bills with maturities of one year or less.

If you own a business, you should decide whether to elect the special $17,500 write-off for equipment purchases in 1995, and you should choose the most favorable depreciation method for your equipment purchases. (See Chapter 18 for more information on depreciation.)

Q.   I've heard that I have to pay more in Social Security taxes in 1995. What will this increase mean for me?

A.   Social Security taxes (called self-employment taxes, if you're self-employed) increased in 1995.

That's because each year a component of the Social Security tax is based upon a wage cap that is adjusted for inflation. The wage cap is the maximum amount of wages subject to Social Security taxes. The wage cap on the old-age, survivors, and disabilities insurance (OASDI) component of the Social Security tax increased to $61,200 for 1995. As noted earlier, there is no wage cap on the Medicare hospital insurance (HI) component of the tax. You should note that your employer is required to "match" the amount of Social Security taxes you are required to pay.

The 1995 rate that applies to the Medicare HI portion of the tax is 1.45 percent; the rate that applies to the OASDI component is 6.2 percent. The self-employment tax rates are double these amounts—2.9 percent for the Medicare HI tax and 12.4 percent for the OASDI tax.

Self-employed taxpayers should refer to discussions in the Questions and Answers section of Chapter 24 for additional details regarding their Social Security obligations.

Q.   What is the Social Security wage cap?

A.   Wages subject to the OASDI component of the Social Security tax are "capped" at a maximum amount. That means wages over the cap are not subject to the OASDI component of the tax. All wages are subject to the HI component of the Social Security tax. The same principle applies to the earnings of self-employed individuals.

For example, say you were paid wages of $70,000 in 1995. You must pay the 1.45 percent Medicare HI tax on the entire $70,000. But you pay the 6.2 percent OASDI tax on only the first $61,200 of your earnings. The total Social Security tax withheld from your $70,000 of wages would come to $4,809 ($61,200 times 6.2 percent, or $3,794, plus $70,000 times 1.45 percent, or $1,015, for a total of $4,809).

For self-employed taxpayers, see Chapter 24 for additional details.

3

$\mathcal{M}$AKING THE MOST OF YOUR PERSONAL EXEMPTIONS

- Whom may you claim as a dependent?
- What income levels trigger the reduction of exemption amounts?
- Is there a tax advantage to failing the dependency test for your child?

In most cases, a taxpayer gets to deduct $2,500 (or more in 1996 and beyond, depending on the inflation rate) from his or her taxable income. This deduction is known as the *personal exemption.*

You can also claim a personal exemption for your spouse, if you file a joint return, as well as for each *dependent* you claim.

Deductions for personal exemptions are subject to certain qualifications and income limitations. In this chapter, we will discuss the rules regarding personal exemptions and show you how to make the best use of the personal exemptions available to you.

QUALIFYING AS A DEPENDENT

The tax law allows you to claim a personal exemption for yourself as long as you're not listed as a dependent on someone else's return. If you're married and file jointly, you're entitled to take two exemptions, one for yourself and one for your spouse.

You may also claim a personal exemption for each of your dependents.

To qualify as a dependent, a person must meet the following five tests. He or she must:

- Receive more than half of his or her support from you.
- Be a relative or live full-time in your household.
- Receive less than $2,500 a year in gross income unless he or she is your child and is either younger than age 19 or a full-time student who hasn't attained 24 years of age.

- Be a US citizen or resident of Canada or Mexico.
- Not file a joint return with someone else.

SUPPORT TEST

If you provide more than half of a person's total support during the tax year, you meet this test. Here's how you calculate how much support you provide.

First, you add up the amount you contribute toward the support of your prospective dependent. Then you compare this sum to the entire amount of support this person receives from other sources. This figure includes the individual's own funds if he or she uses them for support.

The figure will also include any tax-exempt income—such as Social Security or interest on tax-exempt municipal bonds—that the individual receives.

You may add into the total the amounts you spend for necessities— that is, food, lodging, clothing, education, medical and dental care, recreation, and transportation.

Your contribution does not include any part of the support that your dependent pays with his or her own wages, even if you're the one paying the wages.

Say, for example, that you pay your mother $100 a week to stuff envelopes. Under the law, you may not claim the amount you pay her in wages as support payments.

Money that a person receives isn't support unless the funds are actually spent on items the tax law classifies as support.

◈ ℰXAMPLE

Your father receives $2,400 in Social Security benefits and $300 in interest on his savings. He pays $2,000 for lodging, $400 for recreation, and $300 for life insurance premiums.

Even though your father received a total of $2,700, according to the rules, he spent only $2,400 for his own support. The reason? Life insurance premiums aren't considered a support item. So, assuming your father receives no support from any other sources, you provided more than half your father's support if you spent more than $2,400 to support him.

✷ ℭAUTION

It matters to the IRS whether you're supporting one parent or two. Why? Assume both of your parents spent a total of $14,000 on their own support and you contributed an additional $6,000. That's less than half (half of $20,000 in total support is $10,000), so you can't take either of them as a dependent.

But if you were contributing all of your support to just one parent, and you could substantiate this with, say, canceled checks, then your $6,000 would be more than half of that parent's total support of $10,000. And he or she could qualify as your dependent.

RELATIONSHIP OR MEMBER OF HOUSEHOLD TEST

The law defines a dependent as either a relative or someone who meets the member of household test—that is, someone who lives with you in your principal residence on a full-time basis. So a person who's related to you passes this test even if he or she isn't a member of your household. On the other hand, someone who's simply a friend may qualify as a dependent if he or she is a member of your household and meets all of the other tests.

But who qualifies as a relative?

Your natural or legally adopted children or stepchildren qualify. And so do your brothers, sisters, half brothers, half sisters, stepbrothers, stepsisters, parents, grandparents, stepfathers, stepmothers, uncles, aunts, nieces, and nephews—but not your cousins.

In the eyes of the IRS, your father-in-law, mother-in-law, brother-in-law, and sister-in-law are relatives, too. And their status as relatives doesn't change should your spouse die or you and your spouse divorce.

A person who isn't related to you for tax purposes qualifies as a dependent only if he or she lives with you at your principal residence. So if you allow a cousin to live in, say, a beach house on which you pay the rent, he or she doesn't qualify as a dependent.

A nonrelative who's temporarily absent from your home—living away at school, for example—may still meet the member of household test. The absence is considered temporary even if your dependent is in a nursing home for an indefinite period.

GROSS INCOME TEST

The law provides that the person claimed as a dependent must not report gross income that equals or exceeds the amount of the personal exemption.

For purposes of the gross income test, gross income is defined as income—in the form of money, property, and services—that is not exempt from tax. So tax-exempt income, such as municipal bond interest and some Social Security payments, isn't included in the definition. (It *does*, however, count in the support test mentioned above.)

◆ *Ɛ*XAMPLE

Your father retired five years ago, and now receives more than half of his support from you. Your father is a partner in a real estate partnership, and his share of its gross rental income is $3,000 a year before expenses. After expenses, his share of net rental income comes to $350.

> May you claim your father as a dependent? The answer is no. His share of the partnership's gross rental income constitutes gross income that exceeds the 1995 personal exemption amount of $2,500.

There are exceptions to the gross income test. If the person is your child and under age 19 or a full-time student under the age of 24, the test doesn't apply. Note: the exception for children doesn't extend to a son-in-law or daughter-in-law.

To meet the student exemption, your dependent must be enrolled for at least five months of the year in an institution in which education is the primary purpose.

For example, a hospital providing programs for interns and residents doesn't qualify. Those programs fall into the category of on-the-job training or other employee training programs. The law doesn't consider them to be qualifying educational programs. However, if your dependent is studying in a part of the hospital where the main purpose is teaching—a student nursing program, for example—he or she will qualify.

The gross income exception for full-time students is the government's way of encouraging students to work their way through school without jeopardizing the parent's dependency deduction. But keep in mind that you still must provide over half of the student's support to claim your deduction.

CITIZENSHIP TEST

This test requires that a dependent be a US citizen, resident, or national, or a resident of Canada or Mexico for some part of the tax year.

For example, you are a US citizen married to a French citizen. The two of you and your son make your home in the United States, and you file a joint return.

You may claim your child as a dependent regardless of your citizenship or your spouse's citizenship, because he's a US resident.

A special rule applies to adopted children of US taxpayers who live abroad. You may claim the child as a dependent, even if he or she isn't a US citizen or resident, as long as the child lives with you.

JOINT RETURN TEST

Even if the other tests are met, generally you're not allowed to claim an exemption for a dependent if he or she files a joint return.

◆ *E*XAMPLE

You supported your daughter for the entire year while her husband served in the armed forces. The couple files a joint return. You may not claim a dependency exemption for her, because she files a joint return with her husband.

However, there is an exception to this rule. You may claim an exemption for a dependent if neither the dependent nor the dependent's spouse is *required* to file a return, but they file a joint return to claim a refund.

MULTIPLE SUPPORT AGREEMENTS

Occasionally, no one provides more than half of the support of a person. Instead, two or more people, each of whom would be entitled to take the exemption if it weren't for the support test, together provide more than half of the dependent's support. This typically occurs when adult children support aging parents or other relatives.

In these cases of multiple support, the law allows you to agree that any one of you—but only one—who individually provides more than 10 percent of the person's support may claim an exemption for that person. You may not split the personal exemption among the supporters.

Each of the others must sign a written statement (Form 2120, "Multiple Support Declaration") agreeing not to claim the exemption for that year. The statements must be filed with the income tax return of the person who claims the exemption.

◆ ℰXAMPLE

You, your sister, and two brothers support your mother. You provide 45 percent of her support; your sister, 35 percent; and your two brothers, 10 percent each.

Either you or your sister may claim an exemption for your mother. The other must sign a Form 2120 or a written statement agreeing not to claim an exemption for her.

Because neither of your brothers provides more than 10 percent of your mother's support, neither of them may claim the exemption. Further, they don't have to sign a Form 2120 or the statement.

◆ ℐIP

The person who would benefit most from the personal exemption should claim it, even if that person doesn't contribute the most support.

IMPACT OF DIVORCE AND SEPARATION

The tax law imposes special rules for a child of separated or divorced parents or parents who've lived apart from each other for the last six months of the year.

In the case of separated parents, the parent who has custody of the child for the greater part of the year may claim the child as a dependent. It doesn't matter whether that parent actually provided any support, as long as both parents together provide at least half of the child's support and the child is in the custody of one or both parents for more than half of the year.

In the case of divorced parents, custody is usually determined either by the terms of the most recent divorce decree or separate maintenance agreement or a later custody decree.

What happens if neither a decree nor an agreement establishes custody? The law considers the parent who has physical custody of the child for the greater part of the year to have custody.

This rule also applies if the validity of a decree or agreement that awards custody is uncertain because of legal proceedings that may still be pending on the last day of the calendar year.

LIMITS ON PERSONAL EXEMPTION AMOUNTS

The law provides that the amount of the personal exemption deduction you may claim is reduced when your adjusted gross income (AGI) tops a certain amount.

The triggering levels of adjusted gross income for this reduction, or phase-out, in 1995 (these income levels are adjusted annually for inflation) are:

- $172,050 for married individuals filing joint returns and surviving spouses.
- $114,700 for single individuals.
- $143,350 for heads of households.
- $86,025 for married individuals filing separate returns.

The deduction for personal exemptions is phased out by 2 percent for each $2,500—or fraction of $2,500—that your AGI exceeds the trigger point. The phase-out rate is 4 percent if you're married and file separately. Although this may at first seem a little confusing, the rule works this way:

To Calculate the Phase-out of Personal Exemptions:	
	Your adjusted gross income
Less:	Trigger level (above)
	Phase-out base
Divided by:	$2,500
	Result (rounded up to next whole number)
Times:	2 percent (4 percent if MFS*)
	Percentage of personal exemption lost
Times:	Your total personal exemptions
	Total phase-out of personal exemptions

* Married filing separately

◆ ℰXAMPLE

Your AGI for 1995 comes to $201,000. You're married, have two children, and file a joint return. That means you have four exemptions, which gives you a personal exemption deduction before the phase-out of $10,000 (4 times $2,500).

The difference between your AGI of $201,000 and the trigger level of $172,050 for married people filing a joint return is $28,950. Divide $28,950 by $2,500 to get 11.58 and round up to 12. Now, multiply 12 by 2 percent, which gives you 24 percent. The bottom line: Your deduction for personal exemptions is reduced by $2,400 ($10,000 times 24 percent). So you may deduct only $7,600 ($10,000 minus $2,400).

The phase-out is in effect for $122,501 of adjusted gross income over the trigger level ($61,251 if you're married and file separately). After this point you lose 100 percent of the benefit of your personal exemptions ($122,501 divided by $2,500, which equals 49.0004, rounded to 50 times 2 percent, which equals 100 percent).

What does this rule really mean? The maximum tax savings of one personal exemption—assuming you're in the 36 percent tax bracket—is $900 ($2,500 times the tax rate of 36 percent). In the above example, the phase-out of your personal exemptions costs you approximately an additional $864 in tax ($900 times four exemptions times 24 percent). If you are in the 39.6 percent tax bracket, the phase-out of personal exemptions will cost you even more.

If your AGI falls within the exemption phase-out range ($172,050 through $294,550 for a married couple filing a joint return), the phase-out has the effect of increasing your marginal tax rate up to approximately 0.7 percent for each exemption you claim. In our example, then, your marginal tax rate jumps from 36 percent to almost 39 percent. (In the next chapter we'll see how your marginal rate could be even higher if you itemize deductions.)

➢.𝒯P

If income is in the upper half of the phase-out range, consider failing the dependency tests for a child who's a full-time student, has income, and is between the ages of 18 and 24. That way, the child may claim an exemption for himself or herself and enjoy the full benefit of a personal exemption even though you can't.

QUESTIONS AND ANSWERS

Q.   My child was born in November of this year. May we claim him as a dependent for the year?

A.   Yes. You may claim a full dependency exemption for your child in the year he or she is born. This rule holds true even if your child was born on December 31.

Q.   In 1994 I claimed my mother as a dependent. She died in early 1995. Am I still entitled to a personal exemption for her for 1995?

A.   Yes, provided she qualified as a dependent for the portion of the year up to the date of death, even if that was January 1.

4

ADDING UP YOUR DEDUCTIONS

- What are the benefits of the standard deduction versus itemized deductions?
- Do taxpayers 65 or older or blind qualify for special tax breaks?
- Are itemized deductions subject to any limitations?

Deductions for many taxpayers are a significant tax-saving device. Nearly every taxpayer has *some* deductible expenses. It is worthwhile to know all the deductions you are entitled to claim.

The law gives you the option of claiming a *standard deduction* without requiring you to list the specifics. Should you claim the standard deduction? Or should you *itemize?* This chapter will help you to make that decision.

If you decide not to take the standard deduction and itemize your write-offs instead—that is, reduce your taxable income by claiming specific deductible expenses—you want to make sure that you can support the amounts you claim.

✪ CAUTION

In the event of an audit this is one part of your tax return that the IRS will very likely scrutinize carefully. And the auditor will ask for proof.

Don't be alarmed, however. This isn't meant to discourage you from claiming legitimate deductions. On the contrary, we encourage you to deduct every dollar you legally can from your taxable income. In this chapter we'll suggest several ways you can maximize the tax-saving value of your deductible expenses. We'll also explain a "wrinkle" in the law that may reduce the dollar amount of itemized deductions you may claim.

YOUR STANDARD DEDUCTION

As we noted, when it comes time to file your tax return, you have two options. You may claim the standard deduction or you may itemize your deductions.

Here, arranged by filing status, are the latest standard deductions. The law requires the IRS to adjust these figures each year to reflect inflation.

Your Standard Deduction	
Filing Status	1995
Married filing jointly	$6,550
Surviving spouse	6,550
Single	3,900
Head of household	5,750
Married filing separately	3,275

Your situation on the last day of the tax year determines your filing status, with this major exception: If your spouse died during the year, you're considered to have been married for the entire tax year, not just part of it.

What does this rule mean to you? If you would have qualified to file a joint return if your spouse had lived, you may still do so for the year he or she died.

The law also says you may use the standard deduction and rate tables for joint returns for the next two years as well if you qualify for surviving spouse status. You may not, however, claim an exemption for your spouse in the years following his or her death.

To qualify as a surviving spouse for the two years after the year of death, you must meet certain conditions:

- You were eligible to file a joint return in the year your spouse died;
- You don't remarry;
- You have a child, stepchild, adopted child, or foster child who qualifies as a dependent; *and*
- You paid more than half the cost of maintaining a home for the child.

By *single* the IRS means that you're unmarried or separated from your spouse either by divorce or by a court-approved separate maintenance decree and that you don't qualify as a head of household (defined below). If you and your spouse are living apart but are not legally separated, or if your divorce decree isn't yet final, the two of you may file jointly.

You may file a tax return jointly with your common-law spouse. The federal tax law recognizes common-law marriages as long as the state you live in, or the state in which the common-law marriage began, also recognizes its legality.

You qualify as "head of household" if, at the end of the year, you're unmarried and pay more than half the cost of keeping a home for yourself and at least one dependent.

There is a break for people who are 65 or older. If you're single, the law allows you to add $950 to your standard deduction in 1995. If you're married, you may add $750 in 1995 for each spouse who's aged 65 or older.

You may also claim these same amounts if you're blind regardless of your age. You are classified as blind if your vision is 20/200 or worse in the better of your two eyes while you're wearing glasses or contact lenses, or your field of vision is no more than 20 degrees.

◆ *Ｅ*XAMPLE

You're single and age 65 or older. Your standard deduction for 1995 adds up to $4,850; that is, you claim the 1995 standard deduction of $3,900, and you add $950 to that amount.

◆ *Ｅ*XAMPLE

You're married and file a joint return. You add $750 to your 1995 standard deduction, $6,550, if you or your spouse is 65 or older. If you're both in the 65-or-older category, you add $1,500.

◆ *Ｔ*IP

You may claim both the 65 or older and the blind deductions, if you qualify for both. In other words, a single taxpayer who's both blind and 65 or older may add $1,900 to the standard deduction. A married taxpayer may add $1,500 ($3,000 if you and your spouse are both blind, 65 or older, and file a joint return).

✿ *Ｃ*AUTION

Say you claim your father as a dependent and he's both blind and age 65 or older. May you claim a deduction for his blindness and advanced age?

Unfortunately, the rules say you may not claim a deduction for the blindness or old age of a dependent. This break is available only to people who file their own 1040s.

However, your father may claim his own standard deduction for blindness and old age on his own return, even if you claim him as a dependent on your return.

✿ *Ｃ*AUTION

Children and other dependents who file their own returns aren't always entitled to claim a full standard deduction. (For the details, see Chapter 24.)

FINE LINE

Before we go further, note two key definitions: *above the line* and *below the line*. The *line* refers to your adjusted gross income (AGI).

The tax law used to allow you to deduct *above the line*—that is, as part of your AGI calculation—such items as employee business expenses.

Now you must subtract these items *below the line*. That is, they're itemized deductions that no longer figure in your AGI calculation.

What difference does this change make?

◈ *E*XAMPLE

The year is 1985 and your only income is your salary of $100,000. From this amount you subtracted employee business expenses of $2,000.

The result—$98,000—was your AGI.

Once you calculated your AGI, you then deducted your itemized expenses or claimed the standard deduction, whichever was greater.

Now, say the year is 1995. Once again your only income is your salary of $100,000, and you report employee business expenses of $2,000. This time, though, you may not subtract your employee business expenses above the line—that is, to arrive at your AGI.

You must instead add your employee business expenses to all of your other itemized deductions—mortgage interest, property taxes, and so on—below the line. If these itemized write-offs top the standard deduction, you're entitled to itemize. If not, you take the standard deduction.

The bottom line? If you claim deductions above the line, you're guaranteed to receive a benefit. If you claim deductions below the line, you benefit only if you itemize.

TO ITEMIZE OR NOT?

If you may itemize, do so. You always come out ahead. How do you know if you may itemize? You add up your deductible expenses to see whether they're more or less than the standard deduction. If they're more, itemize; if not, take the standard deduction.

In the chapters that follow we'll take a look at those items that are deductible from your adjusted gross income. We'll also examine itemized deductions that don't kick in until they exceed a percentage of your adjusted gross income.

ITEMIZED DEDUCTION FLOOR

Here's a wrinkle in the tax code that may affect your return: a "floor" on itemized deductions. If your AGI exceeds the following threshold amounts, your itemized deductions are limited.

Threshold Amounts	
Filing Status	**1995**
Married filing jointly	$114,700
Single	114,700
Head of household	114,700
Married filing separately	57,350

This floor is imposed on all expenses that would otherwise be deductible—with the exception of medical expenses, casualty and theft losses, investment interest, and gambling losses.

The rules require you to reduce these otherwise allowable deductions by an amount equal to 3 percent of the excess of your AGI over the threshold. Your itemized deductions, however, will never be reduced by more than 80 percent. (You should know that only very high-income taxpayers will likely ever be affected by this 80 percent limit.)

To figure the reduction, you must make two calculations.

You must take the lesser of:

$$3\% \ \times \text{AGI minus the threshold amount} \ = \ A$$
or
$$80\% \ \times \text{Certain deductions*} \ = \ B$$

Next, reduce your itemized deductions:

All itemized deductions
<u>Less:</u>   Lesser of A or B
Allowed itemized deductions

◆ *E*XAMPLE

You're married, file jointly, and your AGI in 1995 adds up to $214,700. You add up your itemized deductions and come up with the following totals: $11,000 in state and local taxes, $7,000 in mortgage interest, $1,000 in investment interest, and $2,000 in charitable contributions—or a total of $21,000.

Now, since your AGI of $214,700 tops the threshold of $114,700, the rules require you to reduce the amount of itemized deductions you claim on your return by the lesser of:

- 3 percent of the excess of your AGI over the threshold.

or

- 80 percent of the applicable deductions.

First, you subtract the threshold amount—$114,700—from your AGI of $214,700 and multiply the difference—$100,000—times 3 percent. The result is $3,000.

---

*Certain deductions means all itemized deductions except for medical, casualty and theft losses, investment interest, and gambling loss deductions.

Now, 80 percent of the sum of your state and local taxes, mortgage interest, and charitable contributions—$20,000—equals $16,000. (Keep in mind that you can ignore the $1,000 investment interest expense—and any medical expenses, casualty and theft losses, or gambling losses if you'd deducted those items—when you calculate the 80 percent limitation.)

Since $3,000 is less than $16,000, your floor is $3,000. So you may deduct a total of $18,000 in itemized deductions—that is, the $1,000 in investment interest that's not subject to the floor, plus the $17,000 that remains once you subtract $3,000 from the rest of your deductions.

If you *are* subject to the 3 percent floor, your marginal tax rate effectively increases by 1.1 percent if you're in the 36 percent bracket. In other words, your marginal tax rate jumps from 36 percent to approximately 37 percent.

✪ 𝒞AUTION

When you compute the reduction, you must first apply any other limitations on itemized deductions. Your miscellaneous itemized deductions, for example, are first subject to a 2 percent floor, then subject to the 3 percent floor. (You will see how the 2 percent floor works in Chapter 9.)

QUESTIONS AND ANSWERS

Q.   I can't itemize this year because my deductible expenses are less than the standard deduction. Does that mean I totally lose the benefit of these deductions?

A.   You will, unless you take steps now.

Say you've run your numbers for 1995 and you know you can't itemize. What should you do? Put off paying some deductible expenses until 1996. That way, you increase the amount of your deductions for 1996, and with luck you can write off the costs in that year.

In short, you should always try to bunch your deductions in one year by either accelerating or deferring payments. In doing so you may exceed the standard deduction—and itemize—at least every other year.

For instance, say you normally receive your bill for real estate taxes on December 20, and you paid last year's bill when it was due: January 15, 1995.

By accelerating your payment of the current bill to December 31, you pay two years' worth of property taxes in 1995 and increase your deductions for that year.

Q.   I'm trying to maximize my deductions for the year. I know I'm going to owe my dentist more than $5,000 for the reconstruction work he will be doing. Can I pay him now, before he works on my mouth, and increase my medical expense deduction this year?

A.   Sorry, but the rules won't allow you to deduct payments for services not yet rendered. But say the dentist has already begun the reconstruction work, and you've agreed to pay him a flat fee when he's done. In this case you may claim the deduction this year if you pay the bill this year.

Q.   What about my mortgage interest payments and state income taxes? May I prepay and deduct these amounts?

A.   The IRS says you may not write off mortgage interest payments in advance. (See Chapter 5 for more information on interest deductions.)

But you may prepay—and deduct—your state income taxes for the current year as long as your payments are based on a reasonable estimate of your final tax bill at the time you make your payment. (For more information on prepaying state and local income taxes, see Chapter 8.)

5

$\mathcal{T}$HOSE LATE, GREAT INTEREST DEDUCTIONS

- How do the tax rules affect deductions for interest?
- When is investment interest deductible?
- How do you "trace" interest on a multipurpose loan?

Interest deductions aren't what they used to be. In the old days you could write off all of the interest you paid on personal loans and credit cards. But no more. After 1990 this write-off disappeared entirely.

The tax laws cover many types of interest, not just interest on consumer debt. But there are only five kinds of interest most individual taxpayers need to worry about:

- *Mortgage interest,*
- *Business interest,*
- *Personal interest,*
- *Investment interest, and*
- *Passive activity interest.*

Mortgage interest is, as the name suggests, the interest you pay on a loan secured by your residence.

Business interest is interest on money you borrow to pay salaries or other operational costs of your business or to purchase assets for it. You may write off business interest only if you are involved with operations on a regular, continuous, and substantial basis.

The IRS defines personal interest as interest on loans you take out to buy personal items—such as an automobile or furniture for your house.

Investment interest is interest you pay on a loan you have taken out to make an investment, such as buying stock.

Finally, the tax law defines passive activity interest as interest on money borrowed to invest in a business that you don't operate or manage.

In this chapter we tell you what you need to know about the tax rules governing each of these kinds of interest.

Understanding these rules isn't a job for accountants and lawyers alone. If you learn these rules—complicated as they are—you can alter your borrowing habits to make the most of the interest deductions available to you.

MORTGAGE INTEREST

Under the tax law owning a home can result in favorable tax treatment. The reason is the long-standing philosophy of the federal government that says people who buy homes deserve some sort of tax benefit.

One tax break homeowners receive is the right to deduct all or a portion of their mortgage interest on their tax returns. The interest on any *mortgage* loan signed on or before October 13, 1987, is fully deductible on your return. (You should know that special rules apply for alternative minimum tax purposes. See discussions later in this chapter and in Chapter 20 for the details.) The general rule of full deductibility holds true regardless of whether the debt is a first or *second mortgage,* a *home-equity loan,* or a refinanced mortgage.

But special rules apply to mortgage loans entered into after that date and to people who own three or more homes. We'll look at those rules one at a time.

You purchased a new home, refinanced an existing mortgage, or incurred additional mortgage debt after October 13, 1987. If you fall into this category, the tax law divides your deductible mortgage debt into two categories: *acquisition debt* and *home-equity debt.*

Acquisition debt is a loan secured by your primary or second home and is incurred when you buy, build, or substantially improve your home. Acquisition debt is limited to $1 million ($500,000 if you're married and file separate returns).

What if you refinance an existing mortgage? In that case acquisition debt includes only the debt that's outstanding at the time of the refinancing and only up to the ceiling of $1 million. You may still deduct interest on the amount of debt in excess of the old mortgage, however, as long as the additional debt is used to substantially improve your home or if the excess debt qualifies as home-equity debt.

Home-equity debt is a loan also secured by your primary or second home. But in contrast to acquisition debt you don't use the proceeds to buy, build, or substantially improve your primary or secondary residence. The maximum amount of home-equity debt you may have is limited to $100,000 ($50,000 if you're married and file separate returns), depending upon the fair market value of your home and the amount of acquisition debt you have outstanding.

➤.𝒯ᴘ

A mortgage loan can include both acquisition debt and home-equity debt.

Say you refinance your mortgage, using part of the proceeds to pay off your original mortgage and the rest to pay off some personal debts—a car loan, for example.

The interest on a home-equity loan, or on the home-equity portion of a mortgage loan, is fully deductible as long as the debt doesn't exceed the lesser of the following:

- The *fair market value* of your home minus the total acquisition debt, or
- $100,000 ($50,000 if you're married and file separate returns).

What if you own two homes? It makes no difference. The cap on your home-equity debt, whether on one or two residences, still may not exceed a total of $100,000.

➧.✐P

The best idea—for tax purposes, at least—is to lock in the largest possible amount of acquisition debt when you purchase or substantially improve your home. That way, if you need more money later on, you won't reduce your $100,000 home-equity debt ceiling.

✿ ✐AUTION

In the case of home-equity loans a caveat applies. Whether you're borrowing to buy a boat or a bond, putting your home up as collateral is serious business. You should think through all of the pros and cons before making that decision.

Your mortgage debts total more than $1 million. As noted earlier, you may deduct mortgage interest only on acquisition debt of up to $1 million—$500,000 if you are married and file separate returns.

However, the tax law provides a break to taxpayers who incurred their mortgage debt before October 14, 1987. This debt isn't subject to the $1 million ceiling.

✿ ✐AUTION

Any new debt assumed over $1 million is automatically home-equity debt.

Say your acquisition debt tops $1 million and you took out your mortgage loan before October 14, 1987. Say, too, you borrow money after that date—to improve your kitchen, for instance. This new debt is home-equity debt, not acquisition debt.

The reason? Your acquisition debt already tops $1 million.

✿ ✐AUTION

Here's another point homeowners should consider. Even if you may write off all of the interest on a refinanced mortgage loan for regular tax purposes, you may not be able to do so when you compute your alternative minimum tax (AMT).

The AMT was enacted in the belief that at least a minimum amount of tax should be paid by all taxpayers. Who pays it? Taxpayers whose legitimate deductions reduce the regular tax they owe substantially below the amount their incomes suggest they ought to be paying. (Chapter 20 explains the AMT rules in detail.)

Although home mortgage interest is allowed as a deduction for AMT purposes, refinanced home mortgage interest on any debt in excess of the outstanding mortgage before refinancing is not deductible for AMT purposes.

◆ ℰXAMPLE

Your house costs $80,000. The outstanding balance on your old mortgage is $70,000. Now you refinance, and the bank lends you $125,000.

What's the maximum amount of interest on this new loan that you may write off when computing your AMT? You subtract your old mortgage balance—$70,000—from the amount of the new loan—$125,000. The result is $55,000. And the interest on this amount isn't deductible for AMT purposes.

An easy way to calculate how much interest you may deduct is to divide your old mortgage balance ($70,000) by the amount of your new loan ($125,000). That's the amount (56 percent) of the interest on your refinanced mortgage loan you may write off when you figure your AMT.

Under the AMT rules you may also deduct interest on amounts you borrow to substantially improve your home, just as you take a regular tax deduction for mortgage interest. The big difference is that home-equity debt isn't deductible for AMT purposes.

You own three or more homes. The IRS classifies the mortgage interest on your third (or more) home(s) based on how you use the properties and the loan proceeds.

◆ ℰXAMPLE

You use your third house—a ski chalet in the Colorado mountains—solely as a weekend retreat for you and your family.

Since you use the chalet for personal purposes only, interest on the loan you take out to purchase the property is treated for tax purposes as personal interest. In other words it's not deductible at all.

◆ ℰXAMPLE

Say you borrow money on your chalet and use it to purchase stock in a high-technology company. The rules allow you to write off the interest on such a loan but only according to how you spent the money you received.

In this case you deduct the interest not as mortgage or personal interest but as investment interest, because that's how you used the cash.

BUSINESS INTEREST

The rules governing business interest are simple. The interest you pay on loans you take out to operate your business or buy assets for it is completely deductible.

PERSONAL INTEREST

Before Congress adopted the 1986 Tax Reform Act, interest you paid on personal loans—the money you borrowed to take a vacation, say, or the interest you paid on your charge cards—was fully deductible. Starting in 1991, after a brief phase-out period, the law says personal interest is not deductible at all. What are your options?

➲.𝒯ɪᴘ

You have three options. First, you can go on borrowing as in the past, knowing that you are gaining no tax benefit from the interest you pay. Or you might reduce your borrowing by delaying purchases, for example, until you accumulate all or even some of the cash required. A third alternative is to convert personal interest into another category—mortgage interest, for instance—that's still deductible.

What types of personal interest might you convert to deductible interest? The answer is any interest that you pay on personal loans for a car, a boat, or even a vacation.

Many people, in fact, are using their homes to finance some of their borrowing. You can too, but you should exercise caution if you go this route.

INVESTMENT INTEREST

Investment interest is the interest you pay on your *stock margin account* or on any other loan you take out to purchase an investment. Different rules apply to interest on so-called *passive activities,* a subject we get to shortly.

As a general rule, you may deduct investment interest only up to the amount of your investment income. If you earn $5,000 from various investments and pay your broker $1,000 interest on a margin account, you may deduct the entire $1,000.

But if your investment earnings had totaled a mere $50, that's also the maximum amount of investment interest you could deduct.

On the other hand, what you may *not* deduct in one year you may carry forward into future years. In our previous example you had $950 in unclaimed investment interest.

The law allows you to carry that amount forward indefinitely until you generate enough investment income to write it off. Investment income includes periodic earnings such as interest, dividends, royalties, and annuities, but does not include gain from the sale of investments.

⊚.𝒯P

> You may elect to include net capital gains as investment income for purposes of determining the investment interest limitation, but the net capital gain so included will be subject to ordinary income rates.

⊚.𝒯P

> As with personal interest, you may convert investment interest to deductible home-equity interest by borrowing against your first or second home. Doing so will make the interest totally deductible—as long as your borrowings do not top $100,000.

Again, consider all the pros and cons before using your home as collateral for an investment loan.

PASSIVE ACTIVITY INTEREST

In 1986 Congress created a new category of interest expense: interest relating to passive activities. We'll get to the definition of this term in a minute. First, though, you should know that the tax code treats this interest much like investment interest.

For instance, just as you may deduct investment interest only against investment income, you may write off passive activity interest only against passive activity income. If you report no passive activity income, you claim no deduction.

Also, like investment interest, you may carry passive activity interest expense forward indefinitely. That is, you may use the interest you carry forward—the interest you are unable to claim—to offset passive income in future years.

But there's one difference. In the year you dispose of a passive investment, the law lets you deduct any remaining undeducted passive activity interest related to the activity. This break does not apply to investment interest.

What is a passive activity?

The tax code says that it's any business in which you do not "materially participate." So you must be involved in the operation of a business on a "regular, continuous, and substantial basis." If you aren't, the business qualifies as a passive activity for you.

And if it's a passive activity, you may deduct any interest expense you incur only against income that you also derive from a passive activity. In other words, you may not deduct this interest from wages, investment, or business income.

➤.🖋P

Say you want to buy a new car and to invest in a passive activity. You've got the cash to do one or the other but not both.

Our advice is to pay cash for the car, then borrow to invest in the passive activity. That way, the interest is passive activity interest and is deductible against passive activity income, or can be carried forward to future years if you don't have enough passive income in the year the interest is incurred.

If you borrow to buy the car, the interest is personal interest, which is not deductible. Also, you can't carry forward any of the interest you are not able to deduct.

Limited partnerships are, in the eyes of the law, almost always passive activities. Most rental activities also fall into the category of passive activities. (See Chapter 19 for more information on passive activities.)

QUESTIONS AND ANSWERS

Q.   May I boost my mortgage interest deductions by making my mortgage payments in advance?

A.   The law won't allow you to claim a deduction for prepaid interest, no matter what category that interest falls into.

Most people actually pay their mortgage in arrears. That is, the interest portion of the payment you must make on January 1 is for interest that accrued in December. So if you make this January 1 payment on December 31, the amount isn't prepaid, and you may deduct it in the year paid.

You should check statements of interest paid reported to you by banks and other lending institutions on Form 1098. They often omit from these statements the interest on the payment you made in December. Check the statements to make sure the interest listed is the actual interest you paid during the year.

Also, when you buy a home or refinance your mortgage, make sure you pick up interest you paid from the date of closing to the end of the month in which you buy or refinance. This amount is seldom reported on statements issued by lending institutions.

Similarly, when you sell a house, the interest you paid at closing for the portion of the month up to the date of sale is usually not included in the Form 1098 you receive from the bank or other lending institution.

So make sure you account for all of the interest you paid, including amounts that appear only on the settlement papers.

Q.   Are points still deductible?

A.   *Points,* the additional amount of interest you pay when a loan is closed, are deductible in the year you buy your principal home and pay the points. (One point equals 1 percent of the amount of your loan.) Points paid on a loan to buy your second home are not immediately deductible.

But a word of warning: You may not be able to deduct points *currently* if you pay them with money you borrowed from the same bank that holds your mortgage.

Our advice is to write a separate check to your lender for points attributable to any borrowings secured by your home. Also, when it comes time to prepare your tax return, make sure you pick up the amount of points you paid from Form 1098 the bank sends you at the end of the year.

However, a word of caution: The IRS maintains—not without controversy— that you may not take a deduction in the current tax year for points that you pay as part of a refinancing.

Instead, it wants you to write off the points paid on a refinancing over the life of the loan—usually 15 years or more. What happens if you sell your home before you write off all of the points you paid? According to the tax rules, you may deduct any remaining points in the year of sale.

The Tax Court has ruled in favor of the IRS on this issue of refinancing a short-term loan, while side-stepping whether points paid on a bridge or construction loan fall under this rule. In fact, a circuit of the US Court of Appeals overturned this decision in at least one instance and allowed a current year deduction for points paid on refinancing a short-term loan. But the IRS announced it would not follow this decision.

The bottom line? If the loan you refinance falls into the category of a bridge, construction, or other short-term loan, or some other unusual category, check with your tax adviser.

The IRS has announced that you may deduct points even if they are paid by the seller. Under this new rule, you are allowed the deduction but you must reduce the purchase price of your home by the amount of seller-paid points.

Q.   How can a loan I make to my kids to purchase a home qualify as acquisition indebtedness?

A.   Make sure that the home secures the debt by filing the appropriate papers. Otherwise, the interest is personal interest and is not deductible by the kids.

Q.   We bought our house 10 years ago for $75,000. Its fair market value went up to more than $120,000. In January 1987, we refinanced our original mortgage and obtained a new loan. We used the money for personal purposes. Is the interest on our refinanced mortgage deductible?

A.   The interest is fully deductible because the mortgage is secured by your home and was incurred before October 14, 1987. In the eyes of the IRS your mortgage is acquisition debt, even though it exceeds the cost of your home.

Q.   I want to turn the equity in our house into cash. What's the best way?

A.   You have three ways to get at your accumulated *equity.*

- Refinance your house.
- Take out a second mortgage loan.
- Apply for a home-equity line of credit.

When you refinance, you apply for an entirely new mortgage loan. Doing so is usually costly. What is more, it takes time.

Second mortgages and home-equity loans are, in many respects, one and the same. Both allow you to borrow against a portion of the difference between the balance due on your existing mortgage and the current value of your home.

With a second mortgage loan, you usually get a single check for the full amount of the loan. Home-equity lines of credit, on the other hand, usually allow you to take the money as often as you need it by writing a check or using a credit card.

Although second mortgage loans usually run for 5 to 15 years, home-equity lines of credit can run years longer or can even be completely open-ended.

More and more people are using one of these three devices to tap the equity in their homes in order to finance other purchases. It can be smart, provided you understand the limitations and are aware of the pitfalls of borrowing.

The pitfalls, however, are sometimes subtle.

First, there's the expense. Banks frequently charge *loan origination fees,* or points, of 2 or 3 percent on second mortgages and home-equity credit lines. And there are closing costs that can add up to hundreds or even thousands of dollars.

You pay all of these fees up front—that is, the bank subtracts these amounts from the money you borrow before it gives you the rest of the cash.

Less obvious—and more significant—is the risk you assume when you use your house as collateral. Suddenly you have tens of thousands of dollars available to you.

Feeling flush, you succumb to buying the boat you've dreamed of for years. But the payments and maintenance costs turn out to be more than you can handle.

You fall way behind. With a standard loan you may lose only the boat, but with a home-equity loan it's your house the bank comes after.

Here is an example. Say you buy a new car. A standard auto loan requires you to pay off the principal over a specified period, typically three to five years. Now what if you buy the same car but pay for it with a home-equity line of credit?

Your home-equity line of credit requires you to pay interest only. Without self-discipline, at the end of five years you could easily have an old, unpaid-for automobile.

Another risk of the home-equity line of credit is rising interest rates. Because the rate on most home-equity lines of credit floats with the market, you may start out with an easy payment. But if interest rates rise, you could wind up with a monthly payment you can no longer afford.

We're not advising you to avoid tapping the equity in your home, but we're urging caution. Also, if you do opt to refinance or sign up for a home-equity line of credit, shop around. The rates and terms of these loans vary enormously from institution to institution.

Q. I'm in the process of purchasing a cooperative apartment. May I deduct my mortgage interest?

A.   As you probably know, you may deduct mortgage interest only as long as the loan is secured by your residence. But as the owner of a *co-op*, you do not actually own your apartment. Rather, you own stock in a cooperative that entitles you to occupy your residence.

But the IRS gives you a break. It considers indebtedness secured by stock you hold as a tenant-stockholder in a cooperative housing corporation as also secured by the house or apartment that you're entitled to occupy.

In other words, you are allowed to deduct the interest on debt secured by your stock, just as if the loan were secured by your residence.

Even if your co-op agreement won't allow you to use the stock or the apartment as security, the IRS still allows you to deduct the interest as mortgage interest.

Q.   Not all of my mortgage interest is deductible. What do I do with the rest?

A.   The rest of your interest is considered personal interest. You may not deduct it.

Q.   My son fell onto hard times and I made three mortgage payments for him. May I deduct the interest?

A.   Sorry, but you may write off interest only on debts for which you're legally liable. You aren't entitled to a write-off unless you are a signatory to your son's mortgage.

Q.   I ran up a big balance on my credit cards over the last few months, and I owe a bundle in interest. Unfortunately, I do not have the money to pay it. I know I won't get a deduction for the interest. Is there anything I can do?

A.   Yes. There's nothing preventing you from borrowing money at a lower rate—a personal loan from a bank, say—to pay the interest and principal on your credit cards. It's worthwhile to periodically shop around to see whether you're paying a competitive interest rate on your credit cards.

Some banks charge much lower rates than others. Also, some banks do not charge an annual fee for the privilege of having their credit card. (This annual fee, incidentally, doesn't qualify as interest, personal or otherwise, and isn't deductible.)

You should know, too, that some banks charge interest from the date you make your purchase, whereas others charge you no interest as long as you pay in full each month.

The bottom line: It may well be worth your while to take your credit card business elsewhere if you can get a better deal.

Q.   May I deduct interest I pay the IRS?

A.   It may not seem fair, but any interest that you pay as a result of your income taxes—both interest you pay to the IRS, say, and interest on loans you take out to pay your tax bill—is nondeductible personal interest. But any interest the IRS pays you is fully taxable. However, if any portion of the interest expense relates to your business, it may be possible to deduct the interest as an ordinary and necessary business expense. Consult your tax adviser.

Q.   How do I know whether interest is personal interest or investment interest?

A.   You need to trace how you use the money you borrowed. And you trace it from the day the money is in your hands until the day you repay the loan.

You take out a loan and you use the money to buy a new car for the family. The car is a personal asset, so the interest on the loan is personal interest.

This might sound simple, but that's not always the case. Let's suppose you borrow $25,000 and deposit the money in your checking account. Later in the year you use the money to purchase some stock, a car for your son, and a word processor for your business.

In the eyes of the IRS, this single loan generates three types of interest:

- Investment interest on the stock purchase,
- Personal interest on the car, *and*
- Business interest on the word processor.

And different rules govern the deductibility of these different types of interest.

Usually when you borrow money, you either use it immediately for a particular purpose or deposit it in your checking or savings account until you are ready to buy.

What happens if you deposit the money in an account that contains other funds? The IRS says the interest on the loan is investment interest. And it remains investment interest until you take the money out of your account and use it.

What's more, you must spend the money you borrow within 30 days before or after the debt proceeds are actually deposited into an account if you want interest on the loan classified according to how you use the money.

And if you wait longer than 30 days? The IRS bases the interest deduction on the first purchase you make from your account.

Here's an example of how the 30-day rule works. You borrow $1,000 on September 1 to purchase some stock. You put the money in your checking account, which already has a balance of $1,000.

On October 3 your washer goes on the blink, so you buy a new one for $600 and write a check for that amount. On October 9, 39 days after you took out the loan, you purchase the stock. You fork over $1,000 for 100 shares of ABC Co. What are the tax consequences?

The tax law treats the interest on the entire $1,000 as investment interest until October 3, when you purchased the washer.

Then it classifies the interest on $600—the amount you paid for the washer—as personal interest. Interest on the remaining $400 is investment interest.

Our advice is not to mingle borrowed funds with other monies and you can avoid a paperwork nightmare.

Also, maintain separate accounts for funds you borrow for personal, business, investment, and passive-investment purposes. That way, you will not be tripped up by the tracing rules. The tax benefits outweigh any additional bank fees for segregating accounts.

If you do not go this route—that is, if you put your borrowed funds and personal stash in one account—observe the 30-day rule.

Otherwise, you should be prepared to wade through the IRS debt allocation and tracing rules. And there are more than paperwork hassles involved. You could wind up with more nondeductible interest expense than you bargained for.

Also, make sure you can trace debts you incur for investments. For example, ask your lender to make the loan amount payable not to you but to a third party—your stockbroker, for example.

Q.   A friend tells me that there is a 90-day rule governing mortgage interest deductions. Is this true?

A.   Yes. You are given 90 days from the time you purchase your house to secure a mortgage. If you wait longer, you are entitled to write off your mortgage interest as acquisition debt only if you can prove, under the tracing rules, that you spent borrowed money to acquire or improve your home.

Q.   We are building a new home. Does our construction loan qualify as acquisition debt?

A.   The answer is a qualified yes. You may count as acquisition debt the amount of money you spent up to the time construction was completed and up to 24 months before you took out the loan.

Q.   I borrowed money to invest in tax-exempt bonds. Is the interest on my loan investment interest?

A.   This interest indeed falls into the category of investment interest, but you may not claim a write-off. The reason is simple.

The rules do not allow you to deduct interest on money you borrow to invest in instruments, such as municipal bonds, that do not produce taxable income.

Q.   I have $6,000 in my personal savings account, and I borrowed money to buy an interest-bearing bond. Six months later I sold the bond and used the sales proceeds to repay my credit cards. How does the IRS treat the interest on the money I borrowed?

A.   Your interest is treated as investment interest for six months because you used the loan to buy an investment. Then the interest is reallocated to the personal category because you used the money to pay off your credit cards.

If you had used your savings account money to pay off your credit cards instead, you could have kept the deduction as an investment deduction, and you would have been able to deduct the interest in full against your investment income.

Q.   I lent my daughter $15,000. I'm not charging her interest. What are the tax implications of the loan?

A.   Even though your daughter is paying you no interest, the law requires you to "impute," or assume, interest income. Unless the net investment income of the borrower is $1,000 or less (in which case the imputed income is zero), the interest equals the lesser of the following:

- The amount of the outstanding loan times the applicable federal rate (based on a rate the federal government pays on its borrowing).
- The net investment income of the borrower if it exceeds $1,000.

Say, for example, that your daughter reports $200 of investment income for the year. There's no imputed interest to you because her net investment income, $200, is $1,000 or less.

But say she reports $10,000 in net investment income. In this case you must impute interest income on the loan—that is, $15,000 times the applicable federal rate (say, 8 percent, or $1,200)—and declare this amount as income on your return. And this imputed interest, in addition to your being required to report it as income on your return, would also be treated as a gift from you to your daughter.

The law *does* make an exception to the imputed interest rules for so-called *de minimis loans* of $10,000 or less. If you make personal loans that total $10,000 or less, you don't have to impute interest income at all. But this exception doesn't apply if the loan is used to buy income-producing assets, such as rental property.

Another wrinkle: If the primary purpose of the loan was to avoid paying income tax—for example, you lent your daughter money to make an investment so that the investment income would be reported on her return instead of yours—the net investment income limitation does not apply. You must impute interest based on the applicable federal rate.

Depending on how your daughter used the money, she may be entitled to a deduction for the imputed interest even though she never actually paid that amount to you.

The rules governing imputed interest are lengthy and complex. If you've borrowed or lent money at no interest or at a rate below the applicable federal rate, see your tax adviser.

Q.   I own a business and a house, and I want to make the most of my interest deductions. Do you have any suggestions for me?

A.   If you must borrow, borrow for business purposes because business interest is 100 percent deductible. Alternatively, borrow on your home; mortgage interest is also deductible although certain limits do apply. But avoid using borrowed money for personal expenses, because personal interest is not deductible.

Q.   How can I tell what a partnership or S corporation in which I've invested is spending its borrowed money on?

A.   *Partnerships* and *S corporations* are supposed to provide you with this information on the Schedule K-1 that they're required to send you. If you don't get the information, you or your tax adviser will have to obtain it directly.

Q.   I'm a shareholder in an S corporation that operates a retail clothing store, and I don't participate in the management of the company. The corporation purchased some stock on margin. Is this interest passive interest or investment interest?

A.   Your S corporation owes interest on an investment that had nothing to do with selling clothing, its trade or business. So the interest is considered investment interest, not passive interest.

Your share of this interest passes through the S corporation to you, and you may deduct the expense if you have investment income. Otherwise, as we saw earlier in the chapter, you must carry the amount forward to future years.

Similarly, income from interest, dividends, annuities, or royalties earned by the S corporation are also passed through to you as investment income, which may be used to allow a deduction for investment interest expense.

Q.   I heard there are special rules for loans I take out against my life insurance policy. Is this true?

A.   Yes. Usually, the interest on loans against a life insurance policy follow the same rules as interest on other loans—that is, the interest categorization depends on how you use the loan proceeds.

For example, if you used your loan for an investment or for a passive activity, the interest is deductible under the rules that apply to these categories.

Though interest you pay on a loan against the cash surrender value of your life insurance policy may be deductible under the general rules, there are exceptions to these rules. For example, if the insurance company deducted the interest in advance from the amount of the loan, it is not deductible. Neither is the interest deductible if you used the loan to buy a single-premium life insurance policy, an endowment, or an annuity contract.

Finally, you may not deduct interest on your life insurance if you plan to systematically borrow part or all of the increases in the cash value of the policy to pay the premiums on the policy.

Q.   I took out a loan to purchase an interest in a partnership. How is the interest I pay on this loan treated under the tracing rules?

A.   The IRS has issued some temporary guidelines to address this question. (These rules also cover interest on a loan you take out to purchase shares in an S corporation.)

The rules generally require you to allocate debt among the partnership's assets. Or if your purchase was from the entity itself, you must trace the use of the money by the entity. You should consult your tax adviser to see how these rules apply to your own situation.

6

$\mathscr{W}$RITING OFF CHARITABLE CONTRIBUTIONS

- Are there strategies to help you maximize the tax benefits of charitable contributions?
- How do you determine the fair market value of contributed property?
- What do you need to do to substantiate charitable contributions?

We are not suggesting that the main reason most people donate to charity is to reduce their tax bills. But if you're going to make the contribution anyway, it's nice to be rewarded with a tax deduction.

Nonitemizers don't get to deduct *charitable contributions*. For them, the issue is simply whether they want to give and how much.

People who itemize deductions on Schedule A, however, have other questions they have to ask about their acts of charity. In this chapter we will tell you the questions and show you how to figure the answers. Let's start with a few general rules.

The IRS defines a charitable contribution as a contribution or gift "to or for the use of a *qualified organization.*" But do not let the jargon confuse you.

A qualified organization is simply a nonprofit charitable, religious, or educational group that meets government guidelines. In fact, an organization can (and undoubtedly will) tell you whether your contribution to it is tax-deductible.

Moreover, the tax law requires organizations to state clearly that donations are not deductible when that is the case.

$\mathscr{O}$ $\mathscr{C}$AUTION
You are still responsible for any additional tax if you are misled by an organization.

As a rule of thumb your contribution is probably deductible if an organization is operated solely for charitable, religious, scientific, literary, or educational purposes, and you have no power to earmark a specific individual as the recipient of your generosity. But if the organization you favor tries to influence legislation substantially or gets involved in political campaigns, it may lose its status as a qualified organization and your donation will not be deductible.

The law even permits you to write off contributions to federal, state, and local governments. The only requirement: The governmental body must use your gift solely for public purposes—to build a park or a playground, for example.

Furthermore, the law allows you to deduct 80 percent of your donation to a school if, in exchange for that donation, you receive the *right* to buy seating in its athletic stadium. Of course, you may not deduct the cost of any tickets you purchase in exercising this right.

However, if you purchase tickets and you can establish that your payment for the tickets exceeds the regular admission charges, you can deduct the portion of the payment in excess of the established admission charges. If instead of the right to buy tickets you receive the tickets themselves, the face value of the tickets (i.e., the admission charge) is not deductible.

VALUING CONTRIBUTIONS

The law allows you to contribute either money or property to a charity. If you donate money, you write off the amount of your gift. If you donate property, you deduct an amount equal to the *fair market value* of the property at the time you make the donation.

The government defines fair market value as "the price at which the property would change hands between a willing buyer and a willing seller, neither being under any compulsion to buy or to sell and both having reasonable knowledge of relevant facts," which means only the amount the property would bring if you sold it on the open market.

Fair market value is not always easy to determine, however. One acceptable indication: a sale or purchase of comparable property close to the date of your contribution.

So if you donate a Winslow Homer painting to your local museum and a comparable painting just sold at auction for $1 million, you may be fairly confident that you'll be able to write off $1 million. However, you must obtain a qualified appraisal (discussed below) to protect your deduction. Also, you may be subject to charitable deduction limitations.

The opinion of an appraiser is valid, too. In fact, appraisals are required if you donate property with a total value of more than $5,000. For example, if you donate two automobiles, valued at $3,000 each, to an area vocational school, you would be required to get an appraisal because the value of the two cars tops the $5,000 limit.

Additionally, the IRS requires you to attach to your income tax return a complete copy of a signed appraisal to support charitable donations of

Factors to Consider in Determining Fair Market Value*			
Cost or Selling Price	Sales of Comparable Properties	Replacement Cost	Opinions of Experts
• Terms of purchase or sale.	• Degree of similarity.	• Cost of buying, building, or manufacturing.	• Knowledge.
• Timeliness.	• Time of the sale.		• Facts.
• Rate of increase or decrease in value.	• Circumstances of the sale.	• Reasonable relationship between replacement cost and FMV.	• Experience.
• Arm's length offer.	• Conditions of the market.		• Thoroughness.
		• Supply and demand.	

* From IRS Pub. 561

works of art with a total value of $20,000 or more. A color photograph must also be provided upon request.

As far as appraisals go, the tax law does carve out an exception for publicly traded securities. No appraisals are required for them. Appraisals are required, however, if you donate nonpublicly traded securities with a value of more than $10,000.

If you make more than one gift, the values of your donations are added together to see if you exceeded the $5,000, $10,000, and $20,000 limits we just discussed.

✪ 𝒞AUTION

Make sure you get a qualified appraisal of property you donate and perform a good faith investigation of the value of the contributed property. You may be liable for a special penalty if you overstate your gift's value, even if the law does not require an appraisal of the property to secure the contribution deduction.

When does the penalty apply? Here are the two conditions: First, the value you claim on your personal return is 200 percent or more of the correct fair market value; second, you underpaid your tax by at least $5,000 because of the overstatement.

The penalty can be up to 20 percent of the underpaid tax the IRS attributes to the overvaluation. There's also a gross valuation overstatement penalty to pay if the value you claimed on your return is 400 percent or more of the correct fair market value. It amounts to 40 percent.

✪ 𝒞AUTION

The IRS wants to make sure an appraisal is not made by someone with a stake in overstating your gift's value. So appraisals may not be made by you, the organization receiving the gift, the party from whom you acquired it, or any *related entity*—that is, a member of your family or a corporation that is controlled by any of the above individuals or organizations. For the same reason, the appraiser must not base his or her fees on the gift's appraised value.

✪ *C*AUTION

The importance of obtaining a "qualified appraisal" from a "qualified appraiser" for donated items in excess of $5,000 cannot be overemphasized. Failure to meet these requirements could result in a loss of the contribution deduction even if the property is not overvalued.

➦ *T*IP

You may deduct the cost of an appraisal but only as a miscellaneous deduction, not as a charitable contribution. And miscellaneous deductions are subject to a 2 percent floor. (See Chapter 9 for more information on the 2 percent rule.)

➦ *T*IP

By using certain types of trusts you may donate a partial interest in property, such as stocks or bonds, to a charitable organization and still collect a tax deduction. Under this arrangement, you or another beneficiary continue to get the annual income from the trust. When you die, however, the property passes to the charity.

You get your deduction, which equals the present value of the gift, in the year you contribute property to the trust. If your gift consists of securities that have risen in value since you purchased them, you also avoid paying the capital gains tax on that appreciation.

Also, be aware that if you make noncash gifts of more than $500, you must file Form 8283, "Noncash Charitable Contributions," with your personal tax return. Form 8283 requires that you state when and how you acquired the property and the amount you paid for it.

✪ *C*AUTION

Note that a charitable deduction is not allowed for any contribution of $250 or more unless the donor obtains written acknowledgment from the donee of that contribution, including a good faith estimate of the value of any goods or services provided to the donor in exchange for the gift. Separate payments generally will be treated as separate contributions and will not be aggregated for the purpose of the $250 threshold.

Therefore, canceled checks are not sufficient to substantiate contributions of $250 or more.

➦ *T*IP

It makes no sense (from a tax perspective, that is) to make a donation of business or investment property that has dropped in value since you acquired it.

Although you may claim a deduction for the value of the property at the time you donate it, you may not claim a deductible loss on property when you make the gift.

So unless the charitable organization actually needs the property itself, you are better off selling it, then donating the proceeds to charity. That way, you may take a loss on the property and also claim the value of the charitable contribution.

◆ EXAMPLE

You own securities that cost $20,000 several years ago. Today those securities are worth $5,000. If you donate the securities, you may take a $5,000 charitable deduction. By first selling the securities, however, you may claim a $15,000 capital loss as well as the $5,000 donation.

✷ CAUTION

You may not use this strategy when you donate personal assets, such as clothing or an automobile, to a charity, since the law doesn't allow you to write off losses on personal assets.

The law also allows you to write off as charitable contributions expenses you run up when you provide volunteer services.

For example, say you work as a volunteer at a local nonprofit hospital. The hospital requires you to wear a bright yellow smock while you are on duty, and you purchase one from the hospital for $20. You can deduct the cost and cleaning of your garment. The reason? It is not suitable for everyday use, and you are required to wear it while you perform services for a charitable organization.

Or say every Tuesday you drive 24 miles from your home to a nonprofit child care center, where you donate three hours of your time. The law permits you to write off your actual out-of-pocket automobile expenses—that is, gas and oil—or claim a deduction at the standard rate of 12 cents a mile. You may also write off the cost of tolls and parking.

➘ TIP

As a practical matter you may find that it's more trouble than it's worth to keep track of your actual car costs. So opt for the standard rate of 12 cents a mile unless you log substantial mileage each year.

Finally, let's say you serve on the board of a nonprofit group. You are asked to attend a two-day training session in your state capital.

The law says you may deduct your travel expenses—in this case, the cost of your meals and lodging during these two days—under one condition. Your trip must not include any "significant element of personal pleasure, recreation, or vacation."

You should know that the rule about significant personal pleasure does not mean you must get no enjoyment out of your charitable activity. You will get the write-off as long as you are genuinely on duty throughout the trip.

✷ CAUTION

You may not write off the value of your time in connection with any charitable volunteer services you perform.

And you may not claim deductions for entertainment or for personal expenses, such as the cost of bringing your spouse or child along on the trip.

What if your charity pays you a per diem amount to cover the cost of meals and lodging while you are away from home?

If the per diem amount exceeds your actual costs, you must report the extra cash as income on your personal tax return. But if the amount adds up to less than your actual expenses, you may write off the deficit as a charitable contribution.

Charitable groups often hold or sponsor events in order to raise money. You may write off the cost of tickets to these charitable events. But the amount shown on the ticket is not necessarily the amount of your gift. You may deduct only the amount of your actual contribution.

◆ *E*XAMPLE

You pay $50 to attend a special showing of a movie for the benefit of a charitable organization.

Printed on the ticket is "Contribution—$50." If the regular price for the movie is $4, you made a contribution of $46. If the "regular price" is not indicated on the ticket or anywhere else, just note the normal price for similar events or activities in your area and reduce your donation by that amount.

✪ *C*AUTION

If you purchase a ticket for a charitable event and the amount of the deductible contribution is not specified, the IRS will assume the total amount paid is for your personal benefit. That means you could lose your entire write-off unless the charity shows the deductible portion of the ticket price or you can prove the amount you claim is a bona fide charitable donation.

However, the IRS has established "safe harbor" rules under which certain benefits received by donors will be considered insignificant or insubstantial (i.e., token items such as cups, mugs, calendars). If these rules apply to your contribution, the entire amount will be deductible. Check with your tax adviser to determine if these safe harbor rules may apply.

✪ *C*AUTION

Charitable organizations receiving payments exceeding $75 partly as a contribution and partly in consideration for goods or services generally must provide a written statement to the donor as to the portion of the payment that is deductible as a contribution, and the value of the goods or services provided to the donor.

◐.*T*IP

You may deduct the entire cost of a benefit ticket if you donate it back to the organization for resale or to another charitable group.

WHEN YOU MAY DEDUCT
YOUR CONTRIBUTION

You may deduct charitable contributions in the year you make them, which includes the year you mail them.

◆ *E*XAMPLE

On December 30, 1995, you mail a check for $200 to your church. The church receives your donation on January 2, 1996. Under the rules, you are entitled to write off the contribution on your 1995 return, because you mailed your check in 1995.

What if you charge your contribution to your bank credit card? You deduct these donations in the year you charge them.

If your gift is in the form of stock, you claim a deduction in the year in which a properly endorsed stock certificate is mailed or delivered to the charity.

But let's say you give a stock certificate to your agent or to the issuing corporation for transfer to your favorite charity. Your gift does not count for tax purposes until the date the stock is actually transferred on the books of the corporation.

CHARITABLE DEDUCTION LIMITS

Under a complicated set of rules the law limits your total yearly deductions for charitable contributions. If your contributions for the year total 20 percent or less of your adjusted gross income (AGI), you have little to worry about.

Say, for example, that your AGI is $50,000 in 1995. You should be able to deduct up to $10,000 in charitable donations.

But let's say you are exceptionally generous and you contribute 30 percent or even 50 percent of your AGI to charity. In this case the amount you may write off depends on what you contributed and to whom you contributed it.

Our advice: If your charitable contributions top 20 percent of your adjusted gross income, you should consult your tax adviser to make sure that all of your contributions are currently deductible.

QUESTIONS AND ANSWERS

Q.   My country club operates as a nonprofit organization. Are my annual dues deductible as a charitable contribution?

A.   Sorry, but the answer is a resounding no.

The law will not allow you to deduct as charitable contributions dues, fees, or bills you pay to country clubs, business or civic leagues, social clubs, or other similar groups—even if they are nonprofit organizations. Also, contributions to fraternal orders or lodges are not deductible unless the organization is using the contribution solely for charitable, religious, or educational purposes. Furthermore, contributions to tax-exempt organizations may not be deductible if the organization carries on lobbying activities. See Chapters 9 and 11 for further details.

Q.   I want to make a donation to a day care center. May I deduct this amount as a charitable contribution?

A.   Donations to nonprofit day care centers are deductible only if certain conditions are met. Specifically, the center must provide care primarily to children whose parents are gainfully employed. Also, the center must make its services available to the public, and the contribution cannot be a substitute for tuition or other enrollment fees.

Q.   Am I entitled to a deduction for the clothes I give to charity?

A.   Many people donate used clothing to charities, then forget to claim a deduction. So be sure to write off the fair market value of these items on your tax return.

The IRS says the fair market value of used clothes is the amount people would pay for these items in thrift shops and used clothing stores. So check with stores in your area to find out the value of articles you donate.

Q.   We donated our old couch to a local shelter for the homeless. Do we get a tax deduction?

A.   The same rules that apply to gifts of used clothes apply to donations of used furniture and other household goods. Claim a deduction on your return equal to the fair market value of these items. Keep a detailed list of every item, and write down the value of each item separately.

Q.   My spouse and I care for a foster child. Are any of our costs deductible?

A.   You are entitled to tax deductions if a foster child is placed in your home by a charitable organization, as long as you provide the child with food, clothing, and general care.

Also, you must not have a profit motive. For example, it does not count if you are paid for your time or services as a foster parent.

You may deduct the excess of your out-of-pocket expenses over the amount you are reimbursed by the charitable organization. Even the cost of the child's tickets to attend sporting events and movies qualifies for the deduction.

Q.   I buy a lottery ticket every week that benefits my state government. Can I deduct these costs?

A.   Lottery tickets you purchase are not deductible.

Also forbidden: The cost of raffle or bingo tickets, tuition expenses, the value of your time or services, the value of blood given to a blood bank, donations to homeowners' associations, and gifts to individuals.

Q.   An exchange student from Sweden is living with our family this school year. Are we entitled to any tax breaks?

A.   Part of the cost of housing an exchange student, whether from the United States or another country, is deductible as long as the student is not related to you and is not your dependent. The tax law allows you to write off up to $50 a month of these costs.

Here are the details: The student, enrolled in grade 12 or lower, must be a member of your household under a written agreement between you and a qualified nonprofit charitable organization. The purpose of the exchange must be to provide educational opportunities for the student.

You may take your $50 deduction for each full calendar month the student lives with you. But the youngster must attend a US school at least 15 days a month.

If, however, the organization reimburses you for your exchange student's costs, you may not take a deduction. In fact, the tax law says you may not take a write-off if you receive any reimbursement, in the form of either money or gifts, to help offset your expenses. This even includes, for instance, a series of food packages from your student's parents.

Reimbursement for extraordinary or one-time expenses, such as a hospital bill or vacation trip, however, will not deprive you of your deduction provided you paid the cost at the request of the student's parents or the sponsoring organization.

And keep this fact in mind: You may not deduct the costs of a foreign student living in your home if the arrangement is part of a mutual exchange program that also allows your child to live with a family in a foreign country.

Q.   Last year I donated a week's use of my family's vacation home to a charity auction. We used the home ourselves for 14 days during the year and rented it for 80 days. Am I entitled to a deduction for the week of use we donated?

A.   The answer is no. Furthermore, the IRS holds that your donation of a week's stay in your vacation home constitutes personal, not business, use of the house and is not deductible. (For more information, see Chapter 17.)

7

ℋOW TO WRITE OFF YOUR MEDICAL AND DENTAL EXPENSES

- What are deductible medical expenses?
- How do you determine the portion of medical expenses that are deductible?
- Can you deduct the costs of cosmetic surgery?

In theory you are allowed to write off almost any medical or dental expense. But in practice it is almost impossible for you to deduct medical and dental expenses on your tax return if you have health insurance.

Why? You may deduct only those nonreimbursed medical expenses that exceed 7.5 percent of your adjusted gross income (AGI). For example, a taxpayer whose AGI totals $50,000 would have to have medical expenses of $3,750 not covered by health insurance before he or she could claim a deduction.

➢.𝒯IP

Timing, therefore, is an important tactic when it comes to writing off medical and dental expenses. If the same taxpayer with AGI of $50,000 expected to incur $3,500 in additional medical expenses in each of the next two years, he or she should try to arrange to pay the entire amount during one year. In that way at least part of his or her medical expenses would be deductible.

This chapter provides a checklist of deductible medical and dental expenses.

WHAT QUALIFIES AS A MEDICAL EXPENSE?

The tax law defines *medical expenses* as amounts you pay for the diagnosis, treatment, or prevention of disease or for treatment affecting any part or function of the body.

Included in these expenses are the costs of medical and dental insurance and the costs of transportation for needed medical and dental care.

You may write off medical and dental expenses if you itemize your deductions on Schedule A of your Form 1040. However, you may deduct only those expenses that exceed 7.5 percent of your AGI. Furthermore, you must write off these expenses only in the year you pay them.

If you mail a check to your doctor on December 31, the law allows you to claim the expense in the year you mail the check. The same rule holds true for medical and dental expenses you charge to a credit card. You may claim the expense in the year you make the charge.

You may also claim a deduction for medical expenses you pay for your dependents. (See Chapter 3 for more information on who qualifies as a dependent.)

Also, you may ignore the gross income test for dependents when claiming medical expense deductions. If, in other words, your aging father would qualify as your dependent except for the fact that his income is too high, any medical payments you made on his behalf would still qualify.

➔.🎿P

If you are contributing toward your parents' living costs, pay for their medical and dental bills—rather than their other personal living expenses.

In addition to dependents, you may also claim medical and dental expenses you incur on your children's behalf—even if you are divorced and your ex-spouse is entitled to claim the kids as dependents.

➔.🎿P

Be sure to keep the canceled checks to substantiate your claim in such a situation.

WHAT IS DEDUCTIBLE?

Below is an alphabetical checklist of deductible medical and dental expenses.

ALCOHOL AND DRUG ABUSE TREATMENT

The law allows you to deduct the cost of treatment at a center for substance abusers. You may deduct charges for therapy and medical care. You may also deduct the amount you pay the center for lodging and meals provided during your treatment.

CARE FOR THE HANDICAPPED

The tax law allows you to deduct as a medical expense the cost of sending a mentally or physically handicapped person to a special school. There is just one requirement: The primary purpose of the special school must be to treat the student's medical problem.

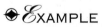

> You may deduct payments you make in advance for the lifetime care of a handicapped person as long as the prepayments are not refundable and are not for medical insurance premiums.

FEES FOR HOSPITAL SERVICES

You may deduct the cost of hospital services, including ambulances and fees for laboratory, surgical, obstetrical, and diagnostic services. You may also deduct the expense of private nurses, including the cost of meals you provide for them.

FEES FOR MEDICAL SERVICES

The tax law allows you to deduct fees you pay to any doctor, surgeon, or other qualified medical practitioner. Dentists, ophthalmologists, osteopaths, optometrists, acupuncturists, chiropractors, podiatrists, psychiatrists, and psychologists qualify.

HOME ALTERATIONS TO ACCOMMODATE A HANDICAP

If you install ramps or railings, widen hallways or doors, lower kitchen cabinets, or adjust electrical outlets and fixtures to accommodate a physical handicap, you may write off the full cost of these home alterations as medical expenses, because the tax law presumes that these alterations don't increase the value of your home.

HOME ALTERATIONS TO ACCOMMODATE A MEDICAL CONDITION

The amount you deduct depends on the cost of the equipment you install and on the amount by which the improvement you make increases the value of your home.

◆ EXAMPLE

> You suffer from heart disease and you are unable to climb the stairs in your home. Your doctor suggests you install an elevator. You do so at a cost of $2,000.
>
> An appraiser tells you the installation of the elevator increases the value of your home by $1,400.

You may deduct $600 as a medical expense—the difference between the cost of the improvement ($2,000) and the value it adds to your home ($1,400).

If the improvement does not increase the value of your home, you may deduct the entire amount you pay—in this case, $2,000.

➤.𝒯ıP

Under special circumstances you may deduct as a medical expense the cost of removing lead-based paints from your walls and woodwork.

For this to be deductible, you must perform the work to prevent a child who has or has had lead poisoning from eating the paint. Furthermore, the walls and woodwork from which you remove the lead-based paint must be in poor repair and within the child's reach.

✪ 𝒞AUTION

If the IRS audits your return, it may ask you to provide a written statement from the doctor who recommended you make your improvement. Our advice is to secure a statement from your physician before you undertake the work.

The IRS may also ask you to prove how much the value of your property was or was not increased by your improvement. So you should obtain a reliable written appraisal of the improvement from a qualified real estate appraiser or a valuation expert.

MEALS AND LODGING

The law provides that you may deduct as a medical expense the cost of meals while you are away from home for medical treatment under one condition: The meals must be provided as part of your stay at an inpatient hospital or similar facility—for example, an alcohol or drug treatment center.

For lodging outside a hospital the rules say you may deduct $50 per person per night for the cost of a room. Also, if you travel with your sick child for out-of-town medical care, you may deduct $100 per night for lodging expenses, but your meals are not deductible.

✪ 𝒞AUTION

The rules say lodging qualifies as a medical expense deduction only under these conditions: The lodging is essential for medical care provided by a doctor in a licensed hospital or equivalent medical care facility, it is not lavish or extravagant, and there is no significant element of personal pleasure, recreation, or vacation in the travel away from home.

➤.𝒯ıP

You may also deduct the cost of trips you take on doctor's orders—to a warmer or drier climate, for example. But the purpose of your trip must be to alleviate a specific ailment. You are not allowed a deduction if you travel for general health reasons.

◆ ℰXAMPLE

You suffer from a respiratory disease and each winter you travel from your home in northern Ohio to Arizona. You take the trip on the advice of your physician.

You may deduct as a medical expense your transportation costs between your home and your residence in Arizona. You may also deduct lodging expenses and meal costs that you incur when you travel from Ohio to Arizona. However, you may not deduct meals and lodging once you arrive at your destination.

MEDICAL AND HOSPITAL INSURANCE PREMIUMS

The cost of health and hospitalization insurance premiums are allowable deductions. This includes Medicare premiums and the premium cost for contracts to repair or replace lost or damaged glasses or contact lenses.

There is a break for sole proprietors, partners, and greater than 2 percent owners of S corporations who pay for their own and their family's health insurance. For 1995 and later years, they may deduct 30 percent of the cost of insurance coverage "above the line" (directly from their gross incomes).

If 30 percent was deducted above the line, the other 70 percent of the insurance bill is lumped together with other medical expenses and is deductible to the extent that it, when added to other medical costs, totals more than 7.5 percent of your adjusted gross income.

MEDICINES

You may deduct the cost of prescribed drugs and insulin.

You may also deduct the cost of birth control devices if they are prescribed by your doctor and are not available for purchase over the counter.

Drugs that you buy without a prescription—aspirin, for instance—are not deductible even if a physician recommends their use.

MENTAL HEALTH SERVICES

You may deduct as a medical expense amounts you pay for mental health services, including counseling and therapy.

NURSING HOME SERVICES

The tax law allows you to deduct the cost of nursing home services provided to you or one of your dependents—as long as the service is needed for medical reasons.

NURSING SERVICES

Amounts paid for nursing services are deductible. You may deduct these costs even if the services are not performed by a registered nurse.

The only requirement: The services must be similar to those provided by licensed nurses—for example, dispensing medicine, changing dressings, and bathing the patient.

You may claim as medical expenses the cost of nurses' salaries, any Social Security taxes paid on their wages, and the cost of any meals you provide them.

SPECIAL EQUIPMENT

The tax law allows you to deduct the cost of purchasing special medical equipment, including motorized wheelchairs.

In addition you may deduct the expense of installing special equipment, such as hand controls in your automobile. You may also deduct repairs or other operating costs of this equipment as long as the equipment helps you compensate for a specific disability.

However, you are not allowed to deduct operating costs that are ordinarily considered a personal expense. For instance, you may not deduct the cost of oil or gasoline for a specially equipped automobile.

SPECIAL ITEMS

Included in this catchall category: false teeth, artificial limbs, eye glasses, contact lenses, hearing aids, guide dogs, and crutches. The category also includes the cost of oxygen equipment and oxygen to relieve breathing problems caused by a medical condition.

✿ CAUTION

The costs of cosmetic surgery (for example, face lifts, liposuction, or hair transplants) are not deductible unless the surgery is necessary to alleviate a deformity arising from or directly related to a congenital abnormality, a personal injury, or a disfiguring disease. If health insurance provided by your employer reimburses you for any ineligible expenses, you must include the reimbursement in your income.

TRANSPORTATION

You may deduct the cost of transportation to and from needed medical care. Transportation expenses include automobile (including tolls and parking), taxi, train, and plane fares, as well as ambulance service fees.

TIP

Calculate your automobile expenses either by using nine cents a mile (the amount the IRS allows) or your actual out-of-pocket costs of operating the car, such as expenses for gas and oil (but not interest on a car loan, insurance, depreciation, and so forth). Parking fees and tolls are deductible in either case.

QUESTIONS AND ANSWERS

Q. What types of expenses are not deductible medical expenses?

A.
- Bottled water.
- Cosmetic surgery.
- Disability insurance.
- Funeral, burial, or cremation expenses.
- Health club dues.
- Household help, except nursing services.
- Illegal operations or treatment.
- Life insurance or insurance that pays ordinary living expenses if you are ill.
- Diaper services.
- Maternity clothes.
- Cosmetics and ordinary personal care items.
- Veterinarian fees for pets.

Q. What about the cost of stop-smoking and weight-loss programs? May I deduct these expenses?

A. You may deduct the cost of programs designed to help you lose weight or stop smoking only if the program is prescribed by a doctor to alleviate a specific ailment.

For instance, if you're told to stop smoking because of your emphysema, the cost is deductible. If you enroll in a program just to improve your general health, however, the cost is not deductible.

Q. I ran up $5,000 in medical bills in December of 1995, but my insurance carrier did not reimburse me until January of 1996. How do I handle these amounts on my tax return?

A. The tax law requires you to write off medical expenses in the year you pay them. Therefore, you must deduct your $5,000 medical bill on your 1995 return. Then you report the amount you received from your insurance carrier as income on your 1996 return to the extent attributable to the earlier deduction.

For example, you incur $5,000 in medical expenses, but you deduct only $3,000—that is, the amount of your medical expenses that exceed 7.5 percent of your AGI. The rules require you to report as income only the amounts you receive from your insurance carrier that are equal to or less than your medical expense deduction.

You received $5,000 from your insurance company but wrote off only $3,000. That means you do not have to claim $2,000 of your reimbursement as income on your 1996 return.

Q. I pay a nurse to look after my physically handicapped child so I can work. May I claim her salary as a medical deduction?

A. You may claim all or part of the nurse's wages as a credit for a dependent care expense (see Chapter 24 for details on this credit) or as a deduction for a medical expense.

The most beneficial treatment will depend on your marginal tax bracket. Your tax adviser can help you determine the best method.

If you claim the dependent care credit on these wages, and these wages add up to more than the maximum allowable for the credit, you may write off the remainder of the wages as a medical expense—subject to the 7.5 percent floor.

Additionally, any payroll taxes (i.e., Social Security, etc.) paid on these wages count toward the calculation of the credit or deduction.

Q.   My spouse and I are expecting our first child. May we claim a deduction for the cost of the childbirth classes we are attending?

A.   The tax law is strict when it comes to writing off the cost of childbirth classes. You may deduct only the cost of courses that prepare you for your "active role in the process of childbirth." What this means is that you may write off as a medical expense that portion of your program that consists of instruction in Lamaze breathing and relaxation techniques; stages and phases of labor, labor, and delivery processes; birthing positions; and cesarean delivery.

However, you may not deduct the cost of sessions that are not related to the labor process. For example, you may not deduct the cost of classes on fetal or child development.

Why? Attending classes or participating in programs on health-related topics are omitted from the definition of medical care if they merely benefit the general health of the individual and are not related to a specific condition.

In addition you may not deduct the cost of classes that your husband attends. For example, you pay $300 for you and him to attend Lamaze-type classes. Two-thirds of the course time is devoted to preparing you and your husband for actual childbirth. The other third is devoted to instruction on child care topics.

To calculate your deduction, multiply two-thirds times $300 and get $200. However, you may deduct only your portion—not your husband's—so your deduction is $100.

Q.   I have heard that people have successfully deducted the cost of a swimming pool. Is that true?

A.   It has been known to happen. It depends on the specific facts. In certain narrow circumstances the IRS has allowed a deduction for a swimming pool where it was considered a medical necessity but only to the extent the cost of the pool exceeded the amount by which the pool had increased the fair market value of the home. In addition the pool must be used primarily for the medical purpose.

For instance, a taxpayer's cost of constructing a special exercise or "lap" swimming pool to treat severe osteoarthritis, to the extent the expenditure exceeded any resulting increase in the value of the taxpayers's home, was deductible as a medical expense.

However, in another instance a taxpayer was not allowed a deduction for amounts spent to construct a pool at his home to aid in therapy for his broken leg. The installation of the personal pool was neither a medical necessity nor for the primary purpose of therapy, but rather was for personal convenience.

8

CLAIMING DEDUCTIONS FOR TAXES

- Which state and local taxes are deductible?
- How can timing the payment of state and local taxes yield tax savings?
- What is the impact of state and local tax refunds on your taxes?

When the income tax was first enacted back in 1913, taxpayers were allowed to deduct from income virtually every other tax paid. This practice was grounded in the belief that taxes are involuntary expenditures and that people should not be taxed on income used to pay taxes.

But in the past 80 years the practice—if not the belief—has changed. Today you may deduct only a few taxes from your federal taxable income.

Here are a few general rules: If you itemize deductions , you may write off some or all of the following:

- State and local income taxes.
- State and local *real property* taxes.
- State and local *personal property* taxes.

Writing off some or all of these taxes depends on certain qualifications and exceptions (covered later in this chapter). Generally, however, the deductibility of state and local income and property taxes is determined by a few basic rules.

The tax must be imposed on you, not on someone else. For instance, if you pay the property taxes on your mother's house, you may not deduct those taxes on your return. You must also actually pay the tax in the calendar year for which you are filing.

If you pay your taxes by check, the IRS considers the day you mail or deliver the check as the date of payment. If you use a pay-by-phone account, the date of payment is the payment date reported on the statement of the financial institution with which you have the account.

INCOME TAXES

Most states impose some kind of personal income tax. Some cities—New York, Cincinnati, and Philadelphia, for instance—impose their own income taxes as well. The law allows itemizers to deduct these state and local income taxes on Schedule A of Form 1040.

You can deduct the following income taxes in 1995:

- State and local income taxes withheld from your salary in 1995.
- State and local estimated tax payments made in 1995 for 1995.
- State and local estimated tax payments made in 1995 for 1994.
- State and local income taxes paid with your 1994 tax returns filed in 1995.
- Additional state and local income taxes paid in 1995 as a result of an amended or audited return for a prior year.

REAL ESTATE TAXES

If you itemize, you may also deduct nonbusiness state and local real estate taxes on Schedule A of your Form 1040 in the year you pay them. Again, you may deduct only those real estate taxes you actually pay.

For example, if you and your spouse own your home jointly but file separate returns, each of you may write off only the taxes you respectively pay. The one exception to this rule relates to taxpayers in community property states: Arizona, California, Idaho, Louisiana, Nevada, New Mexico, Texas, Washington, and Wisconsin. The IRS considers taxes paid from community funds as paid on a 50-50 basis.

In some cases you may want to transfer property to another family member who could make better use of the property tax deduction.

However, an obvious, serious drawback to this strategy is your loss of control of the property. Also, you may be liable for gift taxes on the transfer.

Furthermore, you may not deduct payments for real estate taxes that are placed in *escrow*—in the care of a third party—until the taxes are actually paid.

If your monthly mortgage payment includes an amount placed in escrow for real estate taxes, you may not write off the total of those escrow payments. You may deduct only the amount of the tax the lender actually paid to the taxing authority.

Most lenders pay taxes out of escrow accounts on the tax due date. If the due date is shortly after the end of the calendar year, you may want to ask your lender to accelerate the payment to just before the end of the calendar year so you can claim the deduction in the earlier year.

✪ 𝒞AUTION

Trash and garbage service fees listed separately on your real estate tax bill for your home aren't deductible.

However, if your municipality provides these services but does not break down their separate costs on your real estate tax bill, you may write off the entire amount.

You may also deduct taxes on properties that produce rent or royalty income on Schedule E of your Form 1040.

✪ 𝒞AUTION

If you buy or sell real estate during the tax year, whether it is your personal residence or income-producing property, you must divide real estate taxes between yourself and the buyer. The taxes should be split based on the number of days each of you owned the property.

If you're the seller, you pay and deduct the taxes up to the date of the sale. The buyer pays and deducts the taxes after the sale. (See Chapter 15 for more information on this topic.)

PERSONAL PROPERTY TAXES

Personal property taxes may be included as an itemized deduction on your return. To qualify for the deduction, the following three tests must be met.

The tax is imposed on personal property. The tax is considered to be imposed on personal property even if it is for the "exercise of a privilege."

What does this mean? Say, for example, your city imposes a yearly tax on your car based on its value, but describes it as a registration fee for the privilege of registering your car or driving it on the highways. As long as the fee is based on your car's value, it is considered to be a personal property tax.

The tax is based on the value of your property. Say your state imposes an annual motor vehicle registration tax of 1 percent of the value of your car plus 75 cents per hundred pounds of weight. You pay a tax of $124 based on your automobile's value ($10,000) and its weight (3,200 pounds).

You may deduct $100 (the part of the tax that is based on your car's value) as a personal property tax. The remaining $24 (based on the car's weight) is not deductible.

The tax is imposed annually. Your county mails you a personal property tax bill once a year. Even if you have the option of paying the tax quarterly, the tax qualifies as personal property tax because it is actually imposed annually.

OTHER TAXES

Taxes not otherwise deductible may be deducted if they are incurred in a trade or business or for the production of income. For example, if you are self-employed, you may deduct 50 percent of the self-employment tax as an adjustment to gross income. You may deduct on Schedule C other taxes you incurred as a cost of doing business. Examples include:

- Social Security taxes you pay on your employees' wages.
- Excise taxes you pay on merchandise sold in your business.
- 50 percent of the sales tax you pay on a deductible business meal.
- Sales taxes on nondepreciable business property. (If the property is depreciable, you add the tax to the cost of the property.)

However, there is an exception to this rule for state transfer taxes on sales of securities, such as stocks and bonds. Such taxes are treated as a reduction of the sales proceeds for purposes of computing your gain or loss.

Usually, foreign income and foreign real property taxes are deductible. However, you may not deduct the foreign tax if you paid it on income that was excluded from your federal tax return. Further, you may choose to take a *credit* for foreign income taxes instead of claiming an itemized deduction.

⮞.𝒯ɪᴘ

A *credit* generally reduces your tax dollar-for-dollar by the amount of the foreign tax paid. A deduction reduces only the amount of your income subject to tax. If you paid foreign taxes, consult with your tax adviser.

WHAT ISN'T DEDUCTIBLE?

Here's an alphabetical checklist of many *non*deductible federal, state, and local government taxes and fees:

- Car inspection fees.
- Cigarette, tobacco, liquor, beer, and wine taxes.
- Dog tags and hunting licenses.
- Driver's license fees.
- Estate taxes.
- Federal excise taxes on telephone service.
- Federal gasoline taxes.

- Federal income taxes.
- Fines—for parking or speeding, for example.
- Gift taxes.
- Homeowners' association charges.
- Inheritance, legacy, or succession taxes.
- Marriage licenses.
- Mortgage recording taxes.

- Occupancy taxes, such as taxes on hotel rooms.
- Parking meter fees.
- Passport fees.
- Penalties assessed as taxes.
- Sales taxes.
- Social Security or railroad retirement taxes.

- Stamp taxes.
- Trash and garbage pickup fees.
- Tolls for bridges and roads.
- Transfer taxes.
- Utility taxes.
- Water, sewer, and other service charges.

⊘.𝒯ɪᴘ

Some of the above taxes may be deductible if incurred in a trade or business or for the production of income. Consult with your tax adviser.

✿ 𝒞ᴀᴜᴛɪᴏɴ

You may not write off Social Security and other employment taxes you pay on the wages of a household worker. (For a discussion about household workers, see Chapter 31.)

However, any Social Security taxes you pay for baby-sitters can qualify for a tax credit as "child and dependent care" expenditures. (See Chapter 24 for details.)

QUESTIONS AND ANSWERS

Q.   I make estimated payments of my state income taxes. My last payment for 1995 is due in January 1996. Do I deduct this amount in 1995 or 1996?

A.   You write off a January 1996 payment of 1995 state income taxes on your 1996 return. But here is a way to claim the deduction in 1995.

By making your last quarterly estimated payment in December 1995 as opposed to January 1996, you accelerate your deduction by a full year.

However, we have seen IRS auditors deny deductions to taxpayers who wrote off state estimated payments that substantially exceeded their actual state tax liability for the year.

To ensure a deduction, you must be able to prove that your payments were based on a reasonable estimate of your actual tax liability at the time payment was made. (If circumstances change later on, your deduction should still be safe.)

Say that you paid $3,000 in estimated state income taxes last year. But the payment you made was far beyond what you estimated you would actually owe. In fact, at tax time you discover you are entitled to a refund of the full amount you paid.

The IRS—on audit—may disallow the $3,000 in estimated payments you deducted from your income because you were not required to pay this amount.

In any case the amount the IRS may disallow is the difference between what a reasonable estimate would have been—based on facts at the time the payment was calculated—and the estimate claimed.

Q.   I made a mistake on my 1994 state tax return and as a result I owe an extra $210 in state taxes and a $40 penalty. How much is deductible?

A.   If you owe additional state taxes because you filed an *amended return* or the state audited or otherwise adjusted your return, you may deduct these additional tax payments in the year paid. However, penalties and fines are not deductible.

If you file an amended 1994 state return in 1995 and pay an additional $210 in state income taxes plus a $40 penalty, $210 may be deducted in 1995.

You may *not* write off the $40 penalty.

Q.   I overpaid my state taxes by $400 in 1994. I received a refund for that amount in 1995. Must I report the $400 as income?

A.   The answer depends on whether you obtained a benefit by taking itemized deductions in the year you overpaid.

If you itemized deductions in 1994, you must report the full $400 refund as taxable income on your 1995 return—but only if your itemized deductions in 1994, minus the amount of your state income tax refund, exceeded the standard deduction.

To figure out if you must report a tax refund as income on your tax return, add up your itemized deductions for the year in which you paid the state income taxes that resulted in the refund and subtract the standard deduction for that year. Compare this result with the amount of your state tax refund; the smaller of the two amounts is the amount of your refund that's taxable.

There are some complications to the computations. Although refunds are generally fully includable in gross income, under the tax benefit rule, if you were subject to the itemized deduction limitation in 1994 (see Chapter 4), some exceptions can apply. The rules can also be complex if you are subject to the alternative minimum tax. In these cases you should consult with your tax adviser.

What if you claimed the standard deduction in 1994? You may pocket the $400 refund tax free.

Q.   I am self-employed and pay personal property taxes on the business equipment I own. Where do I write off these local taxes?

A.   Taxes you pay in connection with operating your business should be deducted on Schedule C (Form 1040). Farmers should use Schedule F (Form 1040).

Q.   The county where I live won't be sending out its real estate bill for 1995 until March 1996. Can I estimate the bill and pay it during 1995 to obtain a tax deduction in 1995?

A.   If you make a reasonable estimate of your real estate tax liability for the current year and pay that estimate before the end of year, you should have a proper deduction. You may want to call your county tax office to learn the actual amount of your real estate tax liability.

It is also worth noting that if you make estimated state tax payments related to a current year liability (for example, on a state personal property tax return), you are allowed to take a deduction whether or not your state requires estimated tax payments. However, this will apply only if you have a reasonable basis for believing you owe the tax.

In both of these cases, make sure your payment is accepted by the taxing authority before year-end.

9

$\mathcal{M}$AKING THE MOST OF YOUR MISCELLANEOUS DEDUCTIONS

- What are miscellaneous deductions, and how do you write them off?
- How do you deduct casualty losses?
- Are job-related moving expenses miscellaneous deductions?

Deductions for tax accountants' services, financial advice, professional journals, and a host of other items are known in the tax code as miscellaneous deductions. They are only partially deductible from your adjusted gross income (AGI). You may write off only that portion of these costs that exceeds 2 percent of your AGI.

Here's an example. Let's say that in 1995 your AGI totals $50,000. And you report miscellaneous itemized deductions of $1,200. That means you may deduct only $200—the amount of these expenditures that tops $1,000 ($50,000 times 2 percent).

Remember, too, that this 2 percent limitation is independent of the 3 percent overall limitation on itemized deductions we discussed in Chapter 4. You must first calculate how much in miscellaneous itemized deductions you may write off—that is, the amount that tops 2 percent of your AGI. Then add this figure to those other itemized deductions that may be limited further by the 3 percent floor.

So what are these partially deductible expenses? You will find out in this chapter.

BASIC RULES

You may write off your miscellaneous deductions only if you itemize. You claim these deductions on Schedule A of your Form 1040.

The IRS says you may consider as a miscellaneous deduction any expense that is related to your job, to your investments, or to your taxes.

It makes sense to bunch your miscellaneous deductions in one year. By doing so, you may top the 2 percent limitation and be able to claim a write-off.

For example, you might want to accelerate these deductions into 1995. This tactic makes sense only if these total expenses are going to top the 2 percent limit in 1995.

If you fall below the limit, another strategy is to defer miscellaneous deductions until 1996, when you may be able to take a write-off.

If you're self-employed, claim any expenses that relate to your work on Schedule C—not Schedule A—and avoid the 2 percent limitation. These expenses include the cost of summarizing the information and other accounting and record keeping for the business portion of your tax return. You may also write off on your Schedule C any fees you paid to have your Schedule C prepared. (Deduct the remainder of your tax preparation fees as miscellaneous itemized deductions.)

JOB-RELATED EXPENSES

You may deduct expenses that are related to your job only if you pay them out of your own pocket. If your employer reimburses you—or would reimburse if you asked—you are not entitled to write-offs.

Here's our alphabetical checklist of some of the more common costs you may deduct.

CAREER COUNSELING

The law allows you to deduct the cost of career counseling as long as you incur the expense as part of your efforts to find a new job.

Moreover, you must look for the same kind of work you are now doing. Otherwise, the tax law does not require the government to help shoulder the cost.

◆ *Example*

Say you are a history teacher by training but are tired of teaching. With the help of a career counselor, you find a position as a speech writer for a local politician.

You cannot write off the cost of your counseling because you landed a job in an entirely different profession.

You may write off career counseling expenses even if you don't ultimately change jobs. But you may not claim a deduction if you are looking for your very first job or a job in a new profession.

⊘.𝒯p

You may deduct career counseling expenses even if you're currently unemployed. The only catches: You must be seeking the same kind of work, and it's only been a relatively short time since your last job.

CLUB DUES

Club dues paid to a country club or any other social, athletic, or sporting club are not deductible. For the details see Chapter 11.

COMPUTERS

Under the law you may deduct a personal computer only if it:

- Is a condition of your employment,
- Is for the convenience of your employer, *and*
- Enables you to perform your duties as an employee.

Say you sign on with a wire service as a reporter, and you are stationed in an outlying area. You work out of a spare bedroom in your house. As a condition of your employment the wire service requires that you purchase a personal computer and modem so that you can transmit the stories you write.

You meet all three of these tests, so you are entitled to a deduction through depreciation or by use of a limited expensing election—on Schedule A of your Form 1040. (See Chapter 18 for more on how to write off computers.)

DUES

You may write off dues you pay to professional organizations. You may also deduct union dues and expenses, such as initiation fees.

EDUCATION

You are allowed to deduct the cost of *employment-related education* as long as it meets one of two requirements:

- Your courses must help you maintain or improve your present work skills, *or*
- Your education must be required either by your employer or by law to keep your salary, status, or job.

For example, a nurse may write off the cost of continuing education courses that the state requires to maintain a nursing license.

Among the costs that you may deduct: tuition, books, supplies, lab fees, and the cost of travel to and from your courses.

✿ CAUTION

You are not permitted to deduct education expenses that enable you to meet the minimum education requirements of your profession. The key word here is *minimum.*

Suppose you are hired as a lab technician by a large corporation. You never graduated from college, and the company requires you to complete your education.

You may not deduct the cost of attending school. Why? Your education simply allows you to meet the minimum requirements of your profession. You may, however, write off the cost of continuing education classes—but only after you secure your degree.

Also, you may not deduct professional accreditation fees, such as bar exam fees or medical and dental licensing fees, that you pay when you begin your career.

Finally, you may not deduct education expenses that qualify you for a new trade or business. For example, even if earning a law degree would meet the requirement of improving your present work skills, you may not deduct the cost of obtaining the degree. Why? Because it will permit you to practice law, a new trade or business.

EMPLOYMENT AGENCY FEES

You may deduct employment agency and headhunter fees. But as with career counseling, you must satisfy this condition: The agency must help you in seeking a new job in the same occupation.

You may write off these fees even if the agency fails in its mission. Again, you may not claim a deduction if you are seeking a job for the first time.

ENTERTAINMENT

You may write off some or all of the cost of business entertainment. (See Chapters 10 and 11 for the rules on deducting entertainment expenses.)

GIFTS

You may deduct the cost of business gifts, but the deduction is limited to only $25 to any one person in any single year.

◈ EXAMPLE

Helen makes her living as a literary agent. Every Christmas she purchases a copy of a favorite hardcover book for each of the 50 authors she represents.

She may write off the cost of these books—up to $25 each—as long as she made no other gifts to these clients during the year. If she made other prior gifts, which, say, added up to $15 each, she may deduct only up to $10 per book per client for her Christmas gift.

HOME OFFICE EXPENSES

Turn to Chapter 16 for information on how to write off an office in your home.

JOB SEARCH EXPENSES

Keep track of all the expenses associated with changing jobs—everything from telephone calls to the cost of postage.

These expenses are deductible as long as you are looking for a position in your same profession or not seeking employment for the first time.

◆ *E*XAMPLE

You are set to graduate from a Boston-area college with a degree in computer science. You travel to San Francisco for an interview with a computer manufacturer. Because you are looking for your first job, you may not write off your travel expenses.

You land the job with the computer manufacturer in San Francisco. A few years pass and you are still employed there. In fact, you are doing so well that a Boston computer company contacts you about an exciting new position, so you travel to Boston for an interview.

This time you may deduct your travel expenses because you are seeking a new position in your current profession.

JURY DUTY

You may claim an above-the-line deduction—not subject to the 2 percent floor—for jury pay you received and paid to your employer while you're on jury duty. Deduct this amount by including it in your "total adjustments to income" on page 1 of your Form 1040. Label this amount "Jury Pay" on the dotted line next to the total.

You're entitled to this write-off only if your employer requires you to surrender that amount in exchange for your continuing to receive your regular salary while on jury duty. Remember, you must also include your pay for jury duty in your income.

MEDICAL EXAMINATIONS

The cost of a physical examination required—but not paid for—by your employer is deductible as a miscellaneous itemized deduction.

✿ *C*AUTION

Health club expenses are not deductible, even if your job—as in the case of a police officer—requires that you stay in top physical condition.

Military Uniforms

If you're on active duty in the armed services, the law will not allow you to write off the cost of your uniforms. But it does permit people in the reserves to claim this deduction.

If you are in the reserves, you may write off the unreimbursed cost and maintenance of your uniform as long as military regulations prohibit you from wearing it off duty.

✪ Caution

The law will not allow you to deduct the cost of uniforms that replace regular clothing—uniforms worn by students at military academies, for example. But you may write off the cost of insignia, shoulder boards, and related items.

Resumé Preparation

Keep tabs on how much you spend typing, printing, and mailing copies of your resumé to prospective employers. These costs are deductible—as long as you are looking for a new job in your present occupation.

Rewards

Most people are not aware of it, but you may also deduct a reward you pay for the return of lost business property.

✦ Example

You leave your briefcase on the train. You advertise in your local paper that you will pay $100 for its return.

Your luck is good and a fellow commuter returns your briefcase to you. You may write off both the reward and the cost of your advertisement.

Subscriptions

The law allows you to deduct subscriptions to professional and trade journals as long as these publications relate to your work.

✪ Caution

Do not make the mistake some taxpayers do and write off the cost of a three-year subscription all in one year. The IRS may disallow a portion of your deduction. The rule says that you may write off magazine subscriptions only one year at a time. Here is how it works.

Say you pay $300 in December 1995 for a three-year subscription to a technical business journal. The subscription begins in January 1996.

You may deduct only $100 of the subscription price in 1995—subject, of course, to the 2 percent AGI limitation. You may deduct $100 in 1996 and $100 in 1997.

The news is not all bad, though. Since you paid in December, you get to deduct the portion representing your 1996 subscription a whole year in advance.

TELEPHONE

You may deduct the cost of the unreimbursed business portion of your telephone expenses and long-distance telephone calls. These costs may even include answering services and beeper expenses, as long as they are required for your job.

You may also write off the cost of your cellular phone—but only that portion of the expenses that is attributable to business.

✪ CAUTION

You cannot deduct any portion of your standard monthly base charge for the first telephone line into your home. But you may write off the cost of additional work-related lines and work-related long-distance calls.

Also, you may not deduct cellular phone expenses unless your employer requires you to maintain the phone as a condition of employment and the phone is for the employer's convenience only. Furthermore, if your cellular phone is used less than 50 percent of the time for business, you may only write off its cost using the less favorable straight-line depreciation. In other words, the same restrictions that apply to computers apply to cellular phones. (See Chapter 18 for details.)

TOOLS AND SUPPLIES

Say you purchase a $20 mechanical pencil for use in your work. This may be deducted in the year of your purchase.

You are also permitted to write off the cost of larger items—a desk and couch for your office, say—but you must depreciate these items, meaning you write off their cost over several years. (See Chapter 18 for more on depreciation.)

TRANSPORTATION AND TRAVEL

You may write off the cost of business transportation and travel if your employer does not reimburse you for the full cost. (See Chapters 10 and 12 for more on deducting transportation and travel expenses.)

➤ TIP

Generally, the cost of commuting is not deductible, although the IRS allows you to write off the cost of traveling between your home and a *temporary* place of work. (See Chapter 13 for information on writing off the cost of your automobile.)

WORK CLOTHES AND UNIFORMS

The rules allow you to deduct the cost and upkeep of work clothes and uniforms as long as you meet two conditions. Your employer must require you to wear special clothes on the job, and the clothing must not be suitable for ordinary or everyday wear.

So write off the cost of your uniforms if you are employed as a:

- Civilian faculty member of a military school.
- Firefighter.
- Jockey.
- Letter carrier.
- Nurse.
- Police officer.
- Professional ballplayer.
- Transportation worker, such as an airline pilot or bus driver.

⊘.𝒯ıP

You may also deduct the cost of protective clothing required in your work, for instance, safety shoes and glasses, hard hats, or work gloves.

INVESTMENT-RELATED EXPENSES

The law allows you to deduct expenses associated with those investments that produce taxable income. Expenses associated with investments that produce tax-free income are not deductible. Before we get to our alphabetical checklist of what you may write off, here are a few general rules.

You may not write off commissions and other expenses you pay when you purchase investments. These expenses are "capital costs." That is, they are considered part of the cost of your investment and contribute to its basis—the cost of your property for tax purposes.

Sales commissions and other expenses you pay when you sell investments are treated as a reduction of the sales proceeds. However, if your broker has already subtracted them from the sales proceeds and has reported *net* proceeds to you, then obviously no further reduction is required. It is important that the proceeds you report on your tax return are reconciled to the amount reported to you and the IRS on a *Form 1099-B*, *"Proceeds From Broker and Barter Exchange Transactions."*

◆𝓔XAMPLE

You purchase 100 shares of stock at $20 a share, or $2,000, and pay your broker a sales commission of $150, for a total cost of your investment of $2,150.

A year later you sell the stock for $25 a share, or $2,500. You pay your broker a sales commission of $100. To calculate your gain, you subtract the broker's commission of $100 from the sales proceeds of $2,500 for net proceeds of $2,400.

Next, you subtract the cost of your investment, $2,150, from the net amount you received when you sold the stock, $2,400. The result, $250, is your taxable gain. (Sales of stock are reported on Schedule D.)

Now, on to the checklist.

ACCOUNTING FEES

If you pay an accountant to keep track of your taxable investments or help you with planning, you may write off these fees.

COMPUTERS

If you use a computer to keep track of your investments, you may be entitled to a deduction for its cost either through depreciation or a limited expensing election. (See Chapter 18 for more information on writing off computers.)

CUSTODIAL FEES FOR DIVIDEND REINVESTMENT PLANS

You may have heard of dividend reinvestment plans. These programs allow you to use your dividends to purchase additional shares of stock. Some companies offering these plans charge participants a custodial or service fee. And you are entitled to deduct these charges on your return.

ENTERTAINMENT

The law says you may claim a deduction equal to 50 percent of those meal and entertainment expenses that are associated with your taxable investments. So if you take your stockbroker to lunch to discuss her recommendations, you may write off a portion of the cost of the meal. (See Chapters 10 and 11 for more information on entertainment deductions.)

HOME OFFICE EXPENSES

The law won't allow you to deduct office expenses—such as rent—that are related to managing your investments and collecting taxable income from them. (See Chapter 16 for the details on home offices.)

✍ CAUTION

The IRS says you may not write off the cost of hiring someone to guard your personal residence against burglary attempts—even if your home is loaded with evidence of your favorite investment, your valuable art collection, for example. Nor may you write off a security system to protect coin or other collections.

Investment Adviser Fees

If you pay someone to manage your investments, you may deduct any amounts you pay that person. The only requirement: Your investments must produce *taxable* income.

Say you decide to put all of your money in tax-free municipal bonds, and you pay someone to manage these investments. Under the rules you may not deduct the fee you pay your money manager. The reason: Your investments don't produce taxable income.

Mutual funds usually charge you for investment advisory fees they pay by reducing the amount of dividend income you receive. As a result any fees paid by the mutual fund for investment advice are effectively fully deductible since you report only the net dividends you receive from the mutual fund—that is, your share of the income the fund receives minus its expenses including the investment advisory fees. If you paid these fees directly, they would be subject to the 2 percent floor.

IRA Administration Fees

The law allows you to write off trustees' administration fees that you pay to maintain your Individual Retirement Accounts (IRAs).

➲.𝒯ip

Pay this fee separately if your miscellaneous deductions for the year top the 2 percent floor. But if such deductions fall below the floor, save yourself the trouble of writing a separate check. Let the administration fee be paid from your IRA. (However, you will have that much less in your IRA to generate tax-deferred earnings.)

Legal Fees

The same rule that applies to fees for investment advisers applies to fees for legal services. You may deduct the amounts you pay as long as the lawyer's advice was related to the determination of your tax liability, tax planning, or keeping track of investments.

✺ 𝒞aution

You may not write off those legal fees that are part of the cost of acquiring an investment or defending title to it.

If you purchase an apartment building, and you hire an attorney to handle the closing, the lawyer's fee is a capital cost. It is related to acquiring the property, so it is not deductible.

The fee is added to your cost in the land and the building, and the portion allocable to the building increases the amount eligible for depreciation.

POSTAGE AND SUPPLIES

Again, as long as your investments produce taxable income, you may write off the cost of postage and supplies associated with these investments.

SAFE DEPOSIT BOX RENTAL

You may deduct the cost of renting a safe deposit box if you use the box to store investments—or papers related to investments—that generate taxable income. But you may not write off the cost if you use the box only for personal items or tax-exempt securities.

SERVICE FEES

You may write off fees you pay to a broker, a bank, a trustee, or other agent to collect your taxable interest or dividends on shares of stock.

But you may not deduct a fee you pay to a broker to buy investment property, such as stocks or bonds. You must add this fee to the cost of your property.

✿ CAUTION

The IRS won't allow you to write off bank check-writing fees on an interest-bearing personal checking account.

SUBSCRIPTIONS

You're allowed to claim a deduction for subscriptions to investment-related publications. But remember, you may not write off in one year the cost of a multiple-year subscription. You may deduct subscriptions one year at a time.

TELEPHONE

You may deduct the cost of investment-related telephone charges, including the cost of cellular and long-distance calls. However, as we discussed earlier, the law imposes limits on the deductibility of cellular phones (similar to those for computers).

Also, you may not deduct any portion of your standard monthly basic charge for the first telephone line into your house. But you may still write off the cost of other investment-related phone expenses.

TRANSPORTATION AND TRAVEL

The rules let you write off the cost of transportation and travel associated with investments that produce taxable income. For example, you may claim a deduction for your mileage and parking fees when you visit your stockbroker, so long as you do not invest solely in tax-exempt instruments.

✷ *C*AUTION

You are not allowed to write off the cost of travel to an investment seminar or convention. Nor may you deduct the cost of the seminar or convention itself.

Transportation and other expenses you pay to attend stockholders' meetings of companies in which you own stock but have no other interest are not deductible. This is the case even if you are attending the meeting to get information that would be useful in making future investments. (See Chapter 12 for more on transportation and travel expenses.)

TAX-RELATED EXPENSES

Here is our checklist of deductions related to tax planning and preparation.

APPRAISAL FEES

You may deduct these fees if you pay them to determine the fair market value of property you donate to charity. The reason? The fees go to determine the amount of your deduction.

LEGAL FEES

If you pay for tax advice, the cost is deductible. You may even deduct legal expenses for tax advice related to a divorce, as long as your attorney's bill specifies how much is for tax advice.

TAX PLANNING AND PREPARATION FEES

Usually you may write off, in the year you pay them, tax counsel and assistance fees, such as fees you pay to have your tax return prepared. You may also deduct the cost of computer tax preparation programs you use to prepare your return.

So you may deduct on your 1995 return those fees you pay in 1995 for preparing your 1994 return, as well as fees for an early start on your 1995 return.

You also may write off expenses you pay for determining, collecting, or refunding any tax—including income tax, estate tax, gift tax, sales tax, or property tax.

And you may deduct fees you pay to a consultant to advise you on the tax consequences of a transaction.

If you contest a tax assessment, any fees you pay are deductible, even if your defense is unsuccessful. Finally, you may also write off the cost of defending yourself if you are audited.

&.$\mathcal{T}$P

> You are allowed to claim a deduction for tax preparation and planning books—including *The Price Waterhouse Personal Tax Adviser.*

CASUALTY LOSSES

If you itemize, you are allowed to deduct your casualty losses, but the amount of the deduction will be less than the loss you suffer. Casualty losses are not subject to the 2 percent limit discussed earlier, but are subject to other limitations, discussed below.

If you incur a loss that is sudden, unexpected, or unusual—such as an earthquake, hurricane, flood, or fire—you may have the start of a casualty loss deduction. If the loss occurs over time, say, a period of several years, such as termite damage, you're not entitled to a deduction.

Theft losses are also considered casualty losses (but no deduction is allowed for merely lost or misplaced items).

If you have a loss that qualifies, you must make a few calculations before you find out how much you may write off. First you must determine the decrease in the property's fair market value and your *basis* in the property. The lesser of these amounts is the loss incurred.

Fair market value is the price you could sell the property for, not what it costs to replace it. You can support the fair market value decrease by using pictures, appraisals, or published listings, such as automobile "blue-books." The cost of making repairs to bring the property to its condition before the casualty may indicate its decrease in fair market value.

&.$\mathcal{T}$P

> The cost of pictures, appraisals, and the like are deductible as miscellaneous itemized deductions, since you need this information for your tax return.

Once you figure out the amount of the loss incurred, reduce it for any insurance reimbursements you receive or expect to get. Then subtract $100.

Do this calculation separately for each of the casualty losses you incur during the year. Then add up the amounts calculated for all your losses. Once you total your casualty losses, you subtract 10 percent of your AGI and the remainder is the write-off.

$\mathcal{O}$ $\mathcal{C}$AUTION

> You must file an insurance claim if you have insurance that may cover the loss. If you don't, the IRS won't allow you to deduct any part of the loss as a casualty loss. However, any portion of the loss not covered by insurance is not subject to this rule.

✪ 𝒞AUTION

The $100 reduction applies to each loss during the year. However, if several losses are incurred as a result of the same event, only one $100 reduction applies, no matter how many pieces of property are involved.

A single event may be two closely related causes—like wind and flood damage from the same storm. Also, a hailstorm could damage both your house in the suburbs and your car downtown—again, a single event, and only one $100 reduction applies.

➤ 𝒯IP

Casualty losses are generally only deductible in the year in which the casualty occurs. But before you claim your casualty loss deduction, consider the special rule for designated disaster losses—that is, losses incurred in areas declared by the president of the United States as disaster areas—such as the floods in California in 1995. The IRS allows you to elect to deduct these losses in the year the disaster occurred, or the immediately preceding year (in which case you can file an amended tax return to obtain a tax refund). The limits discussed above apply to the year you take the deduction.

➤ 𝒯IP

If the property is used for business, such as a rental condo, the casualty loss is not personal in nature (since it is a rental property). Such a loss will not be subject to the 10 percent of AGI floor. It is deductible above the line rather than as an itemized deduction. Furthermore, the loss will not be subject to the passive loss rules that may otherwise limit the deductible loss. (See Chapter 19 for more information on passive losses.)

GAMBLING LOSSES

The rules allow you to deduct gambling losses up to the amount of your winnings. You must include your winnings on page 1 of Form 1040, and your losses are deductible as a miscellaneous itemized deduction not subject to the 2 percent floor. However, if you have no winnings during the year, you may not write off any of your gambling losses.

QUESTIONS AND ANSWERS

Q. In addition to my regular work, I operate a small kennel. This year my little business was awash in red ink. How much may I deduct?

A. It depends. You are generally allowed to deduct the loss from a bona fide business. But the IRS doesn't want to help foot the bill for what is essentially a personal activity—hence, the so-called *hobby loss* limitation rules.

Under these rules, you must first determine whether your operation is a hobby or a for-profit business. If it is a hobby, you may deduct hobby expenses that aren't otherwise deductible only up to the amount of your hobby income. What does "not otherwise deductible" mean? Well, let's say that you breed and sell show dogs. Dog food isn't ordinarily a deductible cost—unlike, say, real estate taxes—so it falls into the category of expenses that are "not otherwise deductible."

You aren't allowed to create a tax loss from your hobby to slash your overall tax bill. One other point: You must claim your hobby expenses as miscellaneous itemized deductions (subject to the 2 percent floor) on Schedule A, not on Schedule C.

This rule—the requirement that you claim your hobby expenses as miscellaneous itemized deductions—may restrict your hobby write-offs to an amount less than your hobby income.

So although you must include the full amount of your hobby earnings in taxable income, your hobby write-offs will offset this income only to the extent your total miscellaneous itemized deductions top the 2 percent floor. If your total miscellaneous itemized deductions are less than 2 percent of AGI, you get no tax deduction for your hobby expenses.

How does the IRS determine if your enterprise is a hobby or a for-profit business?

First, the IRS provides an objective test. If you meet this test, the government presumes—at least for the current tax year—that you are engaged in a for-profit business.

Under the objective test you must realize a profit from an activity in three out of the most recent five consecutive years. If horse breeding and racing are your passions, you need to make a profit from these activities in two out of seven consecutive years.

And second, there is a subjective *facts-and-circumstances test.* Under this test, the IRS considers whether you operate your business in a businesslike way. It also examines your expertise in your chosen activity, the time and effort you devote to it, and the amount of personal pleasure you derive from it.

Q.   I now know what I may write off as a miscellaneous deduction. But what may I not deduct?

A.   Here's an alphabetical checklist of some items you may not deduct:

- Burial or funeral expenses. (Note: The executor or administrator of the estate may deduct such expenses on a federal estate tax return.)
- Campaign expenses.
- Commuting expenses.
- Fees and licenses, such as driver's licenses, marriage licenses, and dog tags.
- Fines and penalties, such as parking tickets.
- Home repairs, insurance, and rent.
- Life insurance premiums.
- Losses from the sale of your home, furniture, personal car, and so forth.
- Lost or misplaced cash or property.
- Lunches and meals you eat while working late.
- Personal legal expenses.

- Personal living or family expenses.
- Political contributions.
- Self-improvement expenses, such as the cost of attending a self-enrichment workshop.
- Voluntary unemployment benefit fund contributions.

Q.   I started a new job this year that required me to move to another city. May I write off my moving expenses?

A.   The law allows you to deduct moving expenses that are due to a change in your employment. So if you accept a job in a new city, you may deduct the expenses of moving to that city—as long as you meet IRS guidelines.

The IRS guidelines require that you must stay in your new full-time job at least 39 weeks. Also, you must relocate within one year of the date you assume your new post, and your new job must be at least 50 miles farther away from your existing home than your old job. You should be aware that more stringent requirements apply to self-employed individuals.

You deduct moving expenses in arriving at adjusted gross income (i.e., above the line), and they are not subject to itemized deduction limitations.

Q.   What may I deduct as moving expenses?

A.   You may write off, without limitation, the cost of moving your household goods and personal belongings, including your car and pets, from your former residence to a new location. There is no ceiling on this write-off as long as the amount you claim is reasonable in light of the circumstances of your move.

In addition you may deduct travel expenses and lodging costs for you and your family en route to your new home. However, you may not deduct the cost of meals in transit, house-hunting trips, temporary lodging, and expenses to sell and buy a home or settle or acquire a new lease.

10

$\mathcal{S}$AFEGUARDING YOUR TRAVEL AND ENTERTAINMENT DEDUCTIONS

- What records do you need to substantiate your travel and entertainment deductions?
- When should you document this information?
- What are the requirements if your employer maintains an "accountable plan" for expense reimbursements?

Expenses incurred for business-related travel, entertainment, and meals *may* be legitimate deductions from taxable income. We stress *may* for two reasons.

First, to qualify as deductions, these expenses must conform to a stringent set of rules. The IRS does not want to subsidize a taxpayer's personal travel and entertainment expenses.

Second, you must prove you actually incurred the expense. That means you must maintain adequate records of such expenses.

In this first of three chapters covering business-related travel and entertainment expenses, we explain the record-keeping requirements. The next two chapters cover the specific rules that apply to deductions, first for meals and entertainment, then for business-related travel.

Before we begin, though, keep in mind this important point: You can claim on your return only those deductions for business expenses that are *not* reimbursed by an employer.

WHAT RECORDS YOU NEED

Suppose the IRS decides to audit you and asks you to provide support for your deduction for business travel, meal, and entertainment expenses.

You will be required to provide written and other corroborative evidence, such as detailed oral testimony from you or your client. However, the latter type is of less value, since it is not as convincing to the IRS. Therefore, practically speaking, it is critical to maintain written evidence.

There are basically two types of written evidence. The first is ***documentary evidence,*** which the IRS defines as any kind of receipt issued by a third party. Paid bills meet this requirement, and so do credit card slips.

The second is a *log* or diary. The government, however, doesn't require you to keep a log as long as you note all the required information on your documentary evidence—for example, on the back of credit card slips. Here's the information you're required to record.

BUSINESS PURPOSE

For each expense you must record the business reason or nature of the business benefit you have realized—or expect to realize—from the trip or entertainment.

◆ *E*XAMPLE

You purchase drinks for a customer and yourself and the drinks follow a lengthy sales presentation during which you describe your company's new computer.

If the business purpose of the drinks is to try to close the sale, you must document the topic of business conversation that took place before, during, or after the entertainment, such as "Discussed possible purchase by XYZ Corporation of 10 computers."

BUSINESS RELATIONSHIP

You must identify each person you entertain by name and your business relationship—for example, Joe Jones, President, XYZ Corporation. Also, write down the names and business relationships of any people you visit on a business trip.

COST

Record the amount you spend for each item—dinner and theater tickets, followed by a round of drinks at your favorite nightspot, for example. Remember not to overlook tips and incidental items, such as taxi fares and telephone calls.

TIME

If you conduct a business discussion during a meal or while you entertain, there's no need to record the length of your business conversation, but you must note the date.

If you don't discuss business during the meal or entertainment, the rules require you to jot down both the date and the length of the business discussion that took place before or after the meal or entertainment.

In the case of travel expenses write down the dates you leave and return from your trip and the number of days you spend away from home.

PLACE

You must record where you incur the expense—the name of a restaurant, for example. If you don't discuss business during the meal or entertainment, note where the business conversation took place before or after the meal or entertainment.

When it comes to travel, jot down your destination—the name of the city will do.

WHEN TO RECORD

You should document your expenses as closely as possible to the time you take a business trip or entertain business colleagues. Why? The IRS places greater value on records you keep currently.

◆ XAMPLE

You dine out on business three times a week. The morning after each business meal, you record on the back of your charge slip all the data required—the time, date, and place of your meal, the nature of your business discussion, and so on.

Now let's assume your office mate also wines and dines customers several nights a week but doesn't write down anything until the end of the month.

The IRS is far more likely to challenge your office mate's evidence. The reason: The information isn't timely, but rather is based on memory.

Of course, a log where you record all your business engagements and a file of your receipts are the best evidence.

◆ *T*IP

Stationery stores offer a variety of easy-to-maintain log books that are no bigger than a checkbook. You may find one of these logs useful.

✪ *C*AUTION

Never underestimate the importance of writing down the required information. Without this documentation the IRS may disallow your otherwise perfectly legitimate deductions.

RECORDS YOU DON'T HAVE TO KEEP

You are not required to keep receipts for certain expenses.

Documentary evidence is not required if:

- Your expense, other than lodging, is less than $75.
- You have a transportation expense for which a receipt is not readily available.

- You used the per diem allowance method to account for your meals and/or lodging while away on a business trip.
- You are reimbursed under a mileage method for car expenses.

ACCOUNTING TO YOUR EMPLOYER

When you account to your employer for your business expenses, you generally don't have to account for the same expenses in your tax return. However, to receive this relief, your employer's arrangement for advances, allowances, or expense reimbursements must be an "accountable plan" by meeting three requirements.

The following are the three requirements of an "accountable plan":

- The reimbursements you receive must be for business expenses you incur as an employee.
- You must provide your employer with substantiation. The substantiation required depends on the type of expense you've incurred.
- If you received more from your employer than you actually spent, you must return the excess.

If your employer has these requirements and you comply with them, you don't need to report either the expenses or the reimbursements received from your employer on your tax return.

If your employer's arrangement lacks any or all these requirements or you just fail to comply, the IRS requires all the advances, allowances, or expense reimbursements you receive to be reported as income on your W-2.

The income is subject to both income tax withholding and FICA. Moreover, you will only be able to deduct your business expenses as itemized deductions subject to the 2 percent of adjusted gross income floor (see Chapter 9).

◈ ℰXAMPLE

You receive an advance of $300 for a business trip and your actual business expenses are $300. Your employer's expense reimbursement arrangement has all three requirements of an accountable plan and you comply. You show neither the business expenses nor the advance on your return.

Now, assume the actual business expenses you incur are $400. You just haven't received enough in reimbursement. The amount received still isn't income, but you may be able to deduct the "excess" expenses as miscellaneous itemized deductions subject to the 2 percent floor.

One more twist: Assume you receive an allowance from your employer for business expenses you expect to incur. Your employer stipulates that amounts spent must be for its business and you must provide substantiation. You account to your employer for how you spent the money, but your employer does not require you to return any amounts over your expenses.

In this case your employer does not have an "accountable plan," and the entire allowance is considered taxable income to you because the excess is not required to be returned. You may, however, deduct all of the business expenses as miscellaneous itemized deductions, subject to the 2 percent floor.

♻ *C*AUTION

This situation, or situations where you fail to account to your employer whose arrangement contains the proper requirements, can cost you real dollars. You may think your business expenses will offset the income paid to you by your employer. But don't forget that the income may be subject to FICA. Further, the benefit of the expenses may be limited by the 2 percent floor on miscellaneous itemized deductions.

The IRS makes one exception to these rules. Assume your employer imposes all three requirements. You receive an advance of $300, which your employer does not reasonably believe will exceed your actual expenses and which is paid to you just before you incur them. However, you actually only spend $250 on legitimate business expenses. You provide substantiation, but contrary to the arrangement, fail to return the excess. You expect to use it for business expenses sometime in the future.

You don't have to report the expenses on your return, but now you'll have an additional $50 of income to report. That $50 shows up on your W-2 and is subject to payroll tax withholding.

QUESTIONS AND ANSWERS

Q.   My employer reimburses me for my travel, meal, and entertainment expenses. I don't have to keep records for the IRS, too, do I?

A.   If you make an adequate accounting of your expenses to your employer and your employer maintains an "accountable plan," you don't have to substantiate them again for your personal tax return.

But if you claim any deductions on your personal return—say, for expenses beyond those reimbursed by your employer—you must keep records to back up these claims.

The IRS also requires you to document your expenses if you're related to your employer or if your employer doesn't require you to account for your expenses.

Q.   When it comes to the $75 rule, do I add up what I spent the entire evening or only at each spot?

A.   The IRS looks at each expenditure separately.

For example, if you take a client to dinner and a play, the cost of dinner is treated as one expenditure, the play as another. If you spend less than $75 for dinner and less than $75 for theater tickets, receipts aren't required for either expense.

However, if you purchase several rounds of drinks at your favorite bar, the amount you spend is treated as one item for purposes of the $75 rule.

11

DEDUCTING BUSINESS MEALS AND ENTERTAINMENT

- Which business meal and entertainment expenditures are deductible?
- What are the limits on the deductibility of business meal and entertainment expenditures?
- How should business meal and entertainment deductions be reported on your tax return?

You and a business client attend a professional football game, and you want to know whether the cost of the tickets is deductible as a business-related expense.

The answer depends on what the two of you did before or after the game, why you went to the game with that particular client, and—not least of all—where you sat.

The rules governing business-related entertainment and meals are at least as complex as those governing football, and like the football rules the tax law sometimes involves difficult judgment calls upon which two reasonable people might disagree.

Nonetheless, if you do any business-related entertaining or dining, the deductions available are certainly worth taking.

In this chapter we tell you what you need to know to claim these deductions.

WHICH MEALS AND ENTERTAINMENT QUALIFY?

The law allows a 50 percent deduction for meal and entertainment expenses that are *directly* related to the active conduct of your business. A 50 percent deduction is also allowed for meal and entertainment costs *associated* with the conduct of your business.

The IRS defines *directly related meals and entertainment* as any meal or entertainment during which you actively discuss or conduct your business. Also, your primary purpose must be to transact business. That is, you must expect to gain some benefit from your meals and entertainment—other than goodwill.

Consider this tax case. A company invited a number of people to attend the Super Bowl as its guests. Customers, employees, and friends came with their families.

When the company invited its guests, it made no mention of a sales seminar. Nor did it reserve space in the hotel for any sales meetings. A dinner meeting that the company claimed was for business was held in a hotel dining room with other patrons present.

The trip was for pleasure, not business.

The court noted that no preweekend correspondence referred to business meetings. No bona fide business purpose was served by the presence of wives and children, and only random conversations with some guests involved business.

Also, there was no evidence that the weekend promoted business or that other companies used similar programs to do so. The court concluded the weekend was little more than a group social excursion to the Super Bowl and disallowed the deduction.

➲ 𝒯IP

No amount of Monday morning quarterbacking can convert a Super Bowl weekend into a business-related sales seminar once the game is over. With careful planning, though, you can deduct these expenses as long as the business purpose of the gathering is clear.

For example, you can refer to the get-together as a sales seminar from the start. You can also distribute an agenda prior to the meeting and schedule and hold business discussions in surroundings that are conducive to business, such as a private meeting room in a hotel.

◆ ℰXAMPLE

You're an accountant at a client's office going over her business plan. Your meeting starts at 10 AM and continues through 4 PM.

But the two of you don't break for lunch. Instead, you order out and have a working lunch while sitting at her conference room table. Under the rules the meal is directly related because you continue your business discussion through lunch.

But the IRS assumes the meal or entertainment isn't directly related if it takes place in a setting that makes doing business difficult—if not impossible. For example, the IRS presumes you can't conduct business in a noisy nightclub or a theater.

Associated meals and entertainment are far more common among businesspeople than directly related meals and entertainment—and far harder to pin down.

The IRS rule for associated meals and entertainment is that they must precede or follow a bona fide business discussion. Also, you must prove that your expense was for a specific business purpose—to obtain a new client, say, or keep an old one.

Simply taking your attorney to a baseball game to cultivate good feelings doesn't qualify as associated entertainment, for example. But if you met before the game to discuss the status of pending litigation, you could write off the cost subject to the applicable limitation (i.e., 50 percent).

It isn't enough, in other words, that the person you take to the baseball game has a business relationship with you, as an important potential sales account, for instance. You must actually conduct business before, during, or after the game.

➤.🖉P

When the IRS says you must conduct business, it doesn't mean that you must close on a sale. Assume that you are a distributor of a new product and you are scrambling to secure retail shelf space for that product.

You take a retailer to lunch but, despite your best efforts, he does not agree to give you the shelf space you desire. The meal is still 50 percent deductible.

BUSINESS MEALS

When is a meal a *business meal?* It qualifies if it's directly related to or associated with the active conduct of your trade or business. If it's not, its cost is not deductible at all.

◆ 🖉XAMPLE

You sell paper products and one of your best customers is the XYZ Corporation. You take the president of XYZ out for a fancy dinner.

You don't discuss business before, during, or after the meal. You didn't expect to talk shop because all sales to XYZ are negotiated by the company purchasing agent.

The cost of the meal isn't deductible because it doesn't meet the requirements of either directly related or associated entertainment—that is, you and your guest didn't actually discuss business before, after, or during the meal.

When we refer to the cost of the meal, we mean the cost of the food and drink you consume, plus the cost of tips and taxes. Also included in the cost are cover charges, room rental fees, and other entertainment expenses.

OTHER RULES GOVERNING DEDUCTIBLE BUSINESS MEALS

You or someone else acting for your employer or company must be present at the business meal, or your deduction will not be sustained. You may not, in other words, treat visiting clients to a deductible dinner and night on the town unless someone from the company is willing to share the meal.

But you may deduct 50 percent of the cost if your attorney, accountant, or other professional adviser attends the business meal as your representative.

The cost of including spouses—yours and your business associate's—at a meal may be 50 percent deductible. The meal must qualify as business related. Your own expenses and those of your associate must meet all of the qualifications for deduction.

The percentage limit on deductibility applies to all business meals—whether you're dining with someone in your own city or dining solo at some out-of-town motel during a business trip. But the costs of getting to and from a restaurant—by taxi, say—are still fully deductible.

The limitation also applies to so-called *single-sum expenditures.* What's a single-sum expenditure? Here's an example to illustrate.

◆ *Example*

A hotel includes one or more meals in its room charge. In this case the IRS says you must allocate part of the room charge for food and part for lodging. The part for lodging is fully deductible, but you may write off only 50 percent of the food costs.

The single-sum rule also applies to *per diem arrangements.*

The cost of food and beverages served at conventions, seminars, or meetings is also subject to the limitation.

But the limitation doesn't affect employer reimbursement policies at all. Your employer may still reimburse you 100 percent for the cost of your business meals as long as you account to it for the money you spend. Note, however, that your employer's deduction is subject to the meals limitation.

Nor does the limitation generally apply to most food-related employee fringe benefits. The holiday ham, the employee cafeteria that qualifies as a *de minimis fringe benefit* (one too small to really matter), and the food and refreshments served at the company picnic are still fully deductible expenses to your employer and nontaxable to you.

✪ *Caution*

Also not subject to the meals and entertainment limitation are taxable employee benefits, such as the vacation packages awarded to salespeople for meeting quotas. (The value of these benefits, however, must be reported on employees' W-2 forms and is subject to withholding.)

◆ *Tip*

Under the rules you may deduct 50 percent of the cost of business meals you prepare and serve in your own home—as long as you can prove the meals were for business, not pleasure.

BUSINESS ENTERTAINMENT

The rules for deducting business entertainment expenses parallel those for business meals—they must be directly related or associated with the active conduct of your trade or business. Also, 50 percent of the cost of legitimate entertainment expenses is deductible.

Parking costs at a sporting event, unlike the cab fare to a restaurant, aren't considered transportation expenses. Rather, your parking tab is part of the entertainment expense—and subject to the same 50 percent limitation.

Furthermore, with one exception, the price printed on the entertainment ticket is deductible, although it too is limited. If you pay a premium to an agent or a scalper, you alone bear that part of the cost; that is, the premium is not deductible.

The only exception to this rule is the *charitable sporting event*—one in which all of the proceeds go to charity and practically all of the labor is voluntary. You may deduct as a business entertainment expense the full cost of these tickets plus the agent's fee, if any.

Moreover, any food and beverage costs that are part of the ticket package are also 100 percent deductible. Note that high school, college, and professional sports league games don't qualify as charity events.

✪ *C*AUTION

The costs of skyboxes are not deductible business entertainment expenses. If you lease a skybox for more than one event per season, the rules say you may deduct only the face value of the number of nonluxury box-seat tickets that equals the number of seats in the skybox—and that's *before* you apply the limitation. You may not deduct any additional cost incurred to lease the skybox.

➔ *T*IP

You may write off—subject to the applicable limitation—your spouse's share of entertainment costs if he or she accompanied you during entertainment that the IRS considers "directly related."

The IRS also recognizes it can be difficult to entertain an out-of-town client or customer without his or her spouse. Accordingly, you may deduct the cost of the spouse's entertainment, subject to the limitation, as long as the expense of entertaining the customer or client was deductible.

Furthermore, if your spouse joined the party because your client's spouse came along, you may also deduct your spouse's expenses subject to the limitation.

LAVISH OR EXTRAVAGANT

The IRS allows you to write off business meal and entertainment expenses as long as they aren't *lavish or extravagant*. Having said that, there is no guidance in the law, and little elsewhere, as to what the IRS considers lavish or extravagant.

However, we have never seen IRS auditors disallow a deduction simply because it exceeded a certain dollar amount.

⮞.𝒯IP

Dine and entertain in any style, so long as you think it would be perceived as being reasonable.

◆ ℰXAMPLE

You're a plumbing contractor and you do business in Texas. You take your favorite customer to lunch in Paris—not Paris, Texas, but Paris, France.

You may write off the cost of the meal, but chances are, the IRS will consider the cost of your two round-trip airline tickets as lavish and extravagant. The reason is simple: The trip to France is neither ordinary nor necessary to your business.

QUESTIONS AND ANSWERS

Q. I belong to a luncheon club. May I write off the dues I pay?

A.   No deduction is allowed for any club dues paid or incurred after 1993. Specific business expenses such as meals incurred at a club will continue to be deductible to the extent such expenses satisfy the applicable rules (i.e., the 50 percent limitation and the substantiation requirements).

Q. I belong to a professional society. Once a month we hold a breakfast meeting. The cost of these breakfasts is not broken out but is included with my dues. How do I write off the breakfasts?

A.   You must deduct these meals as meals, subject to the limitations.

It's up to you to calculate how much of the amount you pay is for dues and how much is for breakfasts.

Q. Are meals I eat while I'm out of town on a business trip subject to the meals limitation?

A.   The law says you may write off only 50 percent of the cost of business meals. It makes no difference that they occur during out-of-town business trips. (See Chapter 12 for more information on travel expenses.)

Q. I own my own company. I pay a per diem amount to my employees when they travel to cover meals, laundry expenses, tips for baggage handlers, and so on. Do I write off the whole amount?

A.   The answer depends on how your per diem rate compares to the federal per diem rate for meals and incidental expenses. The federal rate is an amount set by the IRS as allowed for each day of travel. You may deduct your per diem as expenses for meals, subject to the 50 percent limitation, as long as it is not greater than the federal rate. If your per diem is greater than the federal rate, then the excess must be included in your employees' income on their W-2s and you can deduct 100 percent of the excess as compensation expense.

Q.   My employer reimbursed me for my moving expenses, including the cost of meals while traveling from our old home to our new home. What are the tax consequences relating to meals?

A.   Meals are not deductible as moving expenses; thus, the reimbursement of the meals will be considered taxable income (compensation) to you.

Q.   My employer pays me a flat $100 a month for entertainment, and I do not have to account for how I spend this money. How do I treat this amount on my tax return?

A.   Since you are not required to account for how you spent this money, the IRS does not consider these amounts to be reimbursements, but rather considers them taxable income.

Accordingly, your employer must report your monthly entertainment allowance as income on your Form W-2, and the amount is subject to all payroll tax withholdings.

If you want to claim deductions for business meal or entertainment expenses actually incurred, these deductions are subject to the meals and entertainment limitation and to the 2 percent floor on miscellaneous itemized deductions (see Chapter 9).

Q.   I'm self-employed and run up about $2,000 a year in business meal and entertainment expenses. May I still write off a portion of this amount from my self-employment income?

A.   Self-employed people may deduct the expense of business meals and entertainment before they determine their self-employment income—so long as they abide by the meals and entertainment limitations.

12

How to Write Off Travel Expenses

- How do you write off travel expenses when combining business and personal travel?
- Do special rules apply to deducting foreign travel costs?
- Are there limitations on deducting luxury cruise expenses?

Y ou may not know it, but there is still ample opportunity to collect generous write-offs for business travel. And combining business with pleasure may still pay off as well. Just be sure that you know—and follow—the IRS regulations.

In this chapter we analyze the rules governing write-offs for business travel, and we let you know what is deductible—and what is not.

TRAVEL AWAY FROM HOME

When you travel strictly on business, your expenses are deductible. The amount you spend for lodging and transportation—hotel bills, taxi fares, and so on—is deductible. So is the cost of tips, baggage handling, business calls, faxes, laundry, and dry cleaning.

You are also allowed to write off the cost of meals you consume while you are away from home—although these expenses are deductible only up to 50 percent. (See Chapter 11 for more on deducting business meals.)

✪ CAUTION

If you are working for more than one year away from home at a single location, your travel expenses are likely not deductible. Consult your tax adviser.

✪ CAUTION

You are not allowed to write off the cost of travel expenses that are "lavish or extravagant."

For example, say you own and operate a chain of dry cleaning stores, and you charter the Concorde to take you and a customer to a business meeting in London. You can be certain that upon audit the IRS will disallow your deduction for the trip.

However, you do not have to suffer to avoid raising IRS eyebrows. You can travel in a comfortable fashion as long as it is not "lavish or extravagant." First class is acceptable, and you do not have to shop around for super-saver fares.

COMBINING BUSINESS AND PLEASURE

Your travel deductions become less clear-cut when you combine business with pleasure—sightseeing, or visiting old friends, for example.

If you take a vacation or other trip primarily for personal reasons, you may not deduct any of your transportation costs, even if you do some business once you arrive at your destination. You may, however, write off any expenses that are related to your business activities once you arrive at your destination.

◆ EXAMPLE

Suppose you take your family to New York for a holiday. While you are there, you take time out from your vacation to see a customer.

You may deduct the cost of the cab fare between your customer's office and your hotel. And you may also write off 50 percent of the meal you buy.

What if your primary reason for the trip was business?

You are entitled to a deduction for all your transportation as well as 50 percent of the cost of business meals and entertainment. It makes no difference if you add a few days to a business trip to see the sights—although any extra transportation, meal, and entertainment costs incurred in seeing these sights are not deductible.

◆ EXAMPLE

Your company requires you to attend its annual sales conference, so you fly from New York to Palm Springs, where the conference is being held. You spend a week at the conference, then five days vacationing.

You could deduct your hotel bill and other expenses for attending the one-week meeting. You could also write off all your airfare to and from Palm Springs because—in the eyes of the IRS—you took the trip for bona fide business reasons.

To determine if your trip is primarily for business or pleasure, you should consider the amount of time you spend on both activities.

❖ CAUTION

The IRS scrutinizes borderline "business" trips, meaning trips that are part personal and part business. But as long as you can document the main reason for your trip was business, you may deduct the entire transportation cost—even if your trip includes some personal R&R.

FOREIGN TRAVEL

When you travel overseas, the law requires you to allocate all costs—including transportation to and from a foreign location—between the business and personal portions of your trip. It makes absolutely no difference that the reason you took the trip was for business. It only matters how you spend your time on the trip.

Say, for example, your trip consisted of 70 percent business and 30 percent vacation. You could deduct only 70 percent of your transportation and lodging costs. But there are exceptions to this rule.

The IRS will allow all your transportation costs if one of the following applies:

- You spend less than a quarter of your travel days on personal matters.
- You are overseas for less than seven days.
- You are not in "substantial control over arranging the trip"—that is, as far as the IRS is concerned, you are not self-employed, a managing executive, or you are not related to your employer.
- Your major reason for taking the trip was not a holiday or vacation.

The IRS may disallow a deduction for a trip to a convention outside North America if it concludes holding the convention in, say, Beijing or Hong Kong was less reasonable than holding it here.

Also, the rules require you to show that the convention you attend is related to the active conduct of your trade or business.

Obviously, if you belong to the International Association of Criminal Attorneys, you may write off the cost of your participation in an association meeting held in London.

But if you belong to the Green County Pipefitter's Association, the cost of attending your annual convention in Amsterdam wouldn't be deductible.

LIMITS ON CRUISES

The law limits the amount you may write off for luxury cruise expenses, even if the ship takes you from one place to another on business.

The limit is twice the highest federal government allowance for US travel by executive branch employees. Currently, the allowance is $180 per day. So you may deduct no more than $360 per day for luxury cruise travel expenses.

Unless the cruise company lists food and beverage expenses separately, these costs are fully deductible—up to the $360 per day limit, of course. If the company does itemize your meal and beverage expenses, they are only 50 percent deductible.

What happens if you attend a convention or seminar aboard a cruise ship? You are not subject to the rules we just described for general travel.

First, the IRS says you get no deduction unless you can show the convention is directly related to the active conduct of your trade or business.

Also, the cruise ship must be registered in the United States—and there are few that are—and you must sail to ports of call in the United States or its possessions.

Finally, to claim your deduction, the IRS requires you to attach a statement to your tax return specifying, among other items, the length of your trip, the schedule of business activities, and the number of hours you attended these sessions. The statement must be signed by an officer of the sponsoring organization.

✿ 𝒞AUTION

The rules cap deductions for conventions or seminars aboard cruise ships to $2,000 per year per person.

QUESTIONS AND ANSWERS

Q. May I deduct the cost of taking my spouse along with me on a business trip?

A.   The IRS generally will not allow you to write off the expenses of bringing along your spouse—or any other relative, for that matter—on a business trip.

But the government provides an exception to this rule in cases where (1) a spouse is a bona fide employee of the person paying or reimbursing the expenses, (2) the accompanying spouse's travel is for a bona fide business purpose, and (3) the expenses otherwise would be deductible by the accompanying spouse.

Taking notes at meetings does not fit the definition of a bona fide business purpose. But entertaining clients may. The courts have upheld deductions for a spouse's traveling expenses in cases where entertaining constituted a reason for his or her presence.

If your employer sends you on a business trip and allows your spouse to accompany you, employer reimbursements for his or her expenses will be reported as taxable income to you. These expenses include transportation for your spouse and the difference between the cost of a single room versus a double room.

Q. I took my spouse with me on a business trip not paid for by my employer. I do not intend to claim a deduction for my spouse's expenses. But how do I write off my own expenses?

A.   If you traveled by automobile, the law allows you to deduct the full expense—even though your companion was riding in the car with you.

But if you traveled by any other mode of transportation—an airline or train, say—you may write off only the price of your ticket.

In the case of lodging, claim a deduction for the single room rate—$100 a night, say—rather than the double room rate you paid—$120 a night, for example.

Q.   Are there any IRS restrictions about where meetings can be held in order to claim a travel expense deduction?

A.   No, the IRS does not require you to hold meetings close to home in order to claim a deduction for your travel expenses.

For instance, say your company is in the midst of reorganizing, and you and other key executives need to discuss this new structure in a place with few interruptions.

You can hold these meetings anyplace you choose—a meeting room in a hotel a few blocks away or in a hotel at an oceanside resort.

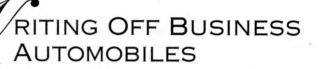

13

WRITING OFF BUSINESS AUTOMOBILES

- How does the use of a business car affect your taxes?
- Which is the best method to write off business use of a personal car?
- What do you need to do if you lease your car?

U nfortunately, the rules governing write-offs for business cars are not as clear-cut or as easy to understand as we'd like them to be.

In this chapter we'll make it easier for you to understand the complicated rules for writing off business automobiles. However, first a few words about record keeping.

KEEPING THE RECORDS

The law requires you to substantiate the business use of your car, and that means maintaining adequate records. You are not relieved of this responsibility if you use a car owned by your employer, either. These record-keeping rules apply whether you own the car or your company provides it to you.

The best way to keep track of the necessary information is to keep a log handy to record your business miles, your destination, and the business purpose of your trip. (See the Appendix for a copy of a sample log.)

These records are not just for show. When you or your employer files annual tax returns, the IRS wants proof of your automobile expenses and usage.

The IRS reviews the number of miles you logged for business and the total number of miles you drove. Also, if you are driving a company car, the IRS wants to know if your employer allows you to use the automobile to commute.

In short, the IRS wants to know if you have support for your deduction. If the answer is yes, you are much better off if your evidence is written.

BUSINESS DRIVING DEFINED

The first question in writing off automobile expenses is to determine what percentage of your car's use you may attribute to business.

The IRS defines *business use* as the miles you drive your car between two business locations (i.e., between your office and the office of a customer).

Commuting is never business use, no matter what type of work you do, how far you travel to your office, or what crisis you are about to face.

A trip to work is personal and not deductible. Making a business phone call or holding a business meeting in your car while you drive will not change that fact.

The IRS has taken the position for years that, for an employee, *commuting* is the first trip in the morning and the last trip home. In the past, if you drove from your home to a customer's office, you were—in the eyes of the IRS—commuting, so you weren't entitled to classify the trip as business.

However, you were able to avoid this rule if you were temporarily assigned to work at a client's place of business that was located some distance from your normal place of business. In this instance, you could claim as business miles the distance from your home to your client's office.

◆ *E*XAMPLE

Say you're a salesperson for ABC Furniture Co., which is located five miles from your home. You're due at a client's office at 9 AM on a Monday morning, and you decide to drive directly from your house to your client's place of business.

Your client is based in a city 80 miles from your home and 75 miles from your office. The IRS lets you classify 80 miles as business use because your client is located outside your geographic work area and much farther from your home than your normal place of business.

In addition, if you have one or more regular places of business, daily transportation expenses you pay or incur in going between your residence and temporary work locations are deductible business expenses *whether or not* these temporary locations are outside your metropolitan area. However, employees may claim these expenses only as miscellaneous itemized deductions, which are subject to a 2 percent floor.

For example, daily transportation expenses incurred by an accountant (who is an employee with a regular work location) between his residence and a temporary work location are now deductible business expenses.

◆.*T*IP

There is an exception to the commuting rule for people who are self-employed and do business from a bona fide home office. These taxpayers may claim—as business mileage—trips to and from home.

◆ *Ꮛ*XAMPLE

You are a salesperson and maintain a home office that is used regularly and exclusively to set up appointments, store product samples, and write up customer orders. Most of your work is done from the home office, but you spend a few hours a week visting customers. You may claim as business mileage trips to your customer locations—and the mileage back—even though you are driving to and from your home. This is because your home is your principal place of business.

✪ *Ꮯ*AUTION

A 1993 U.S. Supreme Court ruling established two primary considerations to determine whether a home office is a principal place of business. (See Chapter 16 for more information.) Since these rules are very restrictive, consult a tax adviser if you're considering writing off home office and related transportation expenses.

DRIVING THE COMPANY CAR

If your employer provides you with a company car, the law requires your employer to report the value of your personal use of the car on your W-2 form.

Your employer must also withhold income and Social Security taxes (FICA) on the value of this benefit. However, with the exception of FICA, your employer may choose not to withhold income taxes as long as you are informed of such fact by the later of January 31 of each year or 30 days after the day you are given the vehicle.

✪ *Ꮯ*AUTION

If your employer does not withhold income taxes, you may need to pay estimated taxes to cover what you will owe on the value of this fringe benefit.

When it comes time to report the value of your personal use of the company car on your W-2, your employer has two options. It can report only the value of your personal use as income, or it can report the total value of your use of the car as income.

If your employer reports only personal use, you must provide your employer with evidence documenting how you used the car.

◆ *Ꮛ*XAMPLE

Say you log 23,176 miles—based on odometer readings at the beginning and end of the year—in your company car in 1995. You drive 15,677 miles on business, 3,466 miles commuting to and from work, and 4,033 miles on personal trips.

At the end of 1995, your employer asks you to submit a form detailing how you used your car. So you report 15,677 business miles and 7,499 personal miles (your mileage for commuting and personal trips).

Your employer determines, based on these numbers, that your personal use amounted to 32 percent of your total miles.

Your employer will report the value of your personal use on your W-2 form by multiplying this personal use percentage by the total value of the use of the car.

Your employer may determine the value of your use of the company car in a number of ways. The most popular way is to use the annual lease value table issued by the IRS based on fair market value. (The Appendix contains the IRS lease table. The IRS table includes the cost of maintenance and insurance. You cannot subtract these amounts from the table even if your employer makes you pay for insurance or maintenance.)

Another method to measure the value of personal use is to use standard car lease rates in your area.

One other option available to your employer to report the value of the personal use of your company car is the cents-per-mile method. This method applies to cars that are valued at less than a threshold amount—$15,500 for cars placed in service in 1995—that log at least 10,000 miles a year, and that are used regularly for business.

What is regular business use? If at least 50 percent of the car's total mileage is for business, or if the car is generally used each workday to transport at least three employees in an employer-sponsored car pool, then the regular business test is met.

The rules say that your employer may report your personal usage of the company car at a flat rate of 30 cents a mile in 1995.

✪ CAUTION

The IRS will announce a new, inflation-adjusted threshold amount for cars placed in service in 1996. In addition, the mileage rate is subject to change, so check with your tax adviser for the new amounts.

Your company may also report the *total* value of your use of the car (both business and personal) on your Form W-2. In this case you may deduct the value of the business use on your personal return subject, of course, to the 2 percent floor on miscellaneous itemized deductions.

◆ EXAMPLE

In 1995, the value of your total use of the company car, based on the annual lease value method, is $5,100. This amount is added to your Form W-2 by your employer.

When it comes time to file your 1995 tax return, you provide your tax preparer with a copy of your W-2 and a statement summarizing how you used your company car. For illustration purposes, assume that you used it 12,433 miles for business and 5,321 miles for personal purposes.

You or your tax preparer multiplies the percentage of business use (70 percent) by your car's value, as recorded on your W-2 ($5,100). The result—$3,570—is the amount you may deduct on your return as a business expense.

However, your ability to claim this deduction as a direct offset against the imputed income may be severely restricted. Where employers simply impute 100 percent of the lease value on employees' W-2s—as in this example—the business use deduction will be subject to the 2 percent floor on miscellaneous itemized deductions.

You may also write off as miscellaneous itemized deductions certain other expenses you paid—such as parking fees and tolls—that represent business use. Again, these are subject to the 2 percent floor.

✿ 𝒞AUTION

If your company reports the total value of your car use on your W-2, you and your employer must pay Social Security taxes on that amount. This may mean money out of your pocket.

◆ 𝓔XAMPLE

Assume your employer reports the total value of your company car use—$5,100. You and your employer must pay Social Security taxes on the entire amount. However, if you have already paid the maximum OASDI portion of Social Security tax, the amount you will owe on the imputed value of the car will be at a lower rate. In 1995, 7.65 percent is the rate that applies on income up to $61,200 (the OASDI limit) and 1.45 percent is the rate that applies on income beyond this amount.

If your employer changes its method, your company reports the value of only your personal usage of the company car, or $1,530. You are clearly better off paying Social Security taxes on $1,530 than on $5,100.

OTHER POINTS WORTH REMEMBERING

The rules will not allow you to depreciate your car using the accelerated method (which allows you larger deductions in the early years of ownership) unless you use the vehicle more than 50 percent of the time for business. Therefore, you must calculate your deductions using the straight-line method—that is, 10 percent in year one, 20 percent in years two through five, and 10 percent in year six. (For more on depreciation, see Chapter 18.)

If the only personal use of your company car allowed by your employer is commuting, your employer may use a commuting valuation method (valued at $1.50 per one-way commute or $3 per day) to calculate the value of your personal use "fringe benefit." This method may be used only if you aren't an officer whose compensation equals or exceeds $66,000 (for 1995), a director, an employee with compensation of $132,000 or more (for 1995), or at least a 1 percent shareholder of your company.

The compensation amounts are indexed for inflation, so be sure to check with your tax adviser for the 1996 amounts.

BUSINESS USE OF PERSONAL CAR

If you use your personal automobile for work, there are three requirements you must meet before deducting business-related automobile expenses on your personal tax return.

First, you must use your automobile "for the convenience of your employer." In other words your employer must require you to have a car to properly perform your duties as an employee. Second, your employer must require the automobile as a condition of employment. In other words, no car would mean no job.

An example of an employee who would meet these two tests: A messenger service's representative who must deliver packages to customers.

Last, but most important, you need to substantiate business use and maintain adequate records.

When you deduct car expenses, you have two choices: You may claim a flat amount for each business mile you drive (the *standard rate*), or you may write off the *actual costs* of operating your automobile. Here is how the two methods work.

USING THE STANDARD RATE

The standard mileage rate for 1995 stands at a flat 30 cents a mile.

✪ CAUTION

The standard mileage rate has historically been reviewed by the IRS each year. When the rate is modified, it generally is effective retroactively to January 1—so check with your tax adviser for the rate in effect for 1996.

✪ CAUTION

Sometimes you are not allowed to use the standard mileage rate and must write off actual expenses. The two instances: when you lease your car and when you have claimed accelerated depreciation on your car in a previous year.

ACTUAL EXPENSES

In most cases, your actual expenses will exceed the standard mileage deduction. So you should opt to write off actual costs.

A portion of all of the following expenses is deductible (the percentage you write off equals the percentage of your car's mileage that you attribute to business):

- Automobile club memberships.
- Batteries.
- Driver's license.
- Garage rent.
- Gasoline and oil.

- Insurance.
- Lubrication and repairs.
- Registration and other licensing fees.

- Supplies, such as antifreeze.
- Temporary rentals.
- Washing and waxing.

You also may write off tires with a life of less than one year. (You should depreciate tires that last longer and are purchased separately from the car.) Again, your deduction for tires should not exceed the business percentage of your mileage.

You may not, however, deduct on your personal return the cost of parking your car at or near your office. However, if your company provides you with parking, the value of this fringe benefit isn't taxable to you as long as it does not exceed certain levels ($160 a month for 1995). Your employer will not report it as income on your Form W-2.

Nor may you deduct interest on a car loan if you are an employee—even if you buy the car strictly for business. This interest is considered personal interest, which is not deductible. If you're self-employed, a portion of the interest may be deductible to the extent attributable to your business use of the car.

You also may depreciate your car in the same way you depreciate other personal property you use for business. If you are buying a car that will be used for business, you calculate your depreciation deduction based on the total purchase price of your car.

If you are converting your family car into a business automobile, you base depreciation deductions on the lower of the fair market value at the date you convert or its purchase price. In either case, you must multiply the depreciation amount by the percentage of your actual business use.

✪ CAUTION

Special limitations apply to cars placed in service after 1986. Cars with a purchase price in 1995 over $15,300 (smaller amounts applied to cars purchased during the period 1987–1994) will be subject to these depreciation limitations.

Depreciation Limits			
	Year of Depreciation Deduction		
Year Placed in Service	Year 1	Year 2	Year 3	Thereafter
---	---	---	---	---
1987/1988	$2,560	$4,100	$2,450	$1,475
1989/1990	2,660	4,200	2,550	1,475
1991	2,660	4,300	2,550	1,575
1992	2,760	4,400	2,650	1,575
1993	2,860	4,600	2,750	1,675
1994	2,960	4,700	2,850	1,675
1995	3,060	4,900	2,950	1,775

◈ *Example*

On January 15, 1995, you purchased an automobile for $19,000 and began driving it immediately. The IRS considers that day as the date you "placed it in service."

In 1995 and 1996 you use the car for business 70 percent of the time. So your depreciation deductions for 1995 and 1996 are $2,142 (the $3,060 limitation times your 70 percent business use) and $3,430 (the $4,900 limitation times 70 percent).

✪ *Caution*

If business use of your car is 50 percent or less, you are not permitted to use the more favorable accelerated depreciation. You must go back to the first year you depreciated the car and recompute your depreciation using the straight-line method. The difference between the deductions under the accelerated and straight-line methods must be "recaptured" into income in your current year return.

However, the above limits on these depreciation deductions apply regardless of which depreciation method you use.

Also, the sales tax you pay upon purchasing the car isn't deductible on your return. You may, however, add this cost to the purchase price of your car when it comes time to calculate your depreciation deduction, thereby increasing the write-off.

✪ *Caution*

If you take the standard mileage deduction in year one, then write off actual costs in year two, you must depreciate the car using the straight-line method.

But if you deduct your actual costs from the start, you may depreciate your car using the accelerated method.

◈ *Tip*

If you use the actual cost method, you must report as taxable income reimbursements that exceed your expenses. But if your reimbursement is based on your use of the standard mileage rate, the excess over your actual costs is tax-free income.

◈ *Tip*

Whether you write off your actual automobile expenses or claim the standard mileage rate, you are still entitled to deduct as miscellaneous itemized deductions (subject to the 2 percent floor) parking fees and tolls you pay when you travel for business. You may not, however, write off fines for violating traffic and parking laws.

SPECIAL RULES FOR LEASING

The IRS also imposes tough restrictions on cars that you *lease*. These rules apply whether you are an employer or employee.

The law still allows you to deduct that portion of your lease payment that is attributable to business. For example, if you use your leased car 90 percent for business, you may write off 90 percent of your lease payments during the year.

However, the IRS has set forth rules to put people who lease business automobiles on an equal footing, tax-wise, with those who purchase their business autos outright.

If you lease, the law requires that you calculate a certain amount to be added to your taxable income or subtracted from your deduction. The effect of including this amount is to limit your deduction for lease payments so that it takes into account only the depreciation deduction you would have had on the car if you owned it. You determine this amount each year by using tables and formulas provided by the IRS. The lower a car's business use, the smaller the adjustment.

◆ *E*XAMPLE

On January 17, 1995, you leased a car for three years and placed it in service for use in your business. The car had a fair market value of $24,250 on the first day of the lease term. You use the car 75 percent for business and 25 percent for personal purposes during each year of the lease.

To arrive at the amount to include in your gross income, you must refer to an IRS published table for the inclusion amount. The dollar amount provided by the table must also be prorated for business use and the number of days of the lease term during the tax year.

The amounts to be included are as follows:

	Inclusion Amount			
	Dollar Amount (IRS Table)	Prorated Days of Lease Term	Business Use	Inclusion Amount
1995	$96	349/365	75%	$69
1996	$210	366/366	75%	$158
1997	$311	365/365	75%	$233
1998	$373	16/365	75%	$12

In our example, for a car with a fair market value of $24,250, you must include $69 in income in the first year of the lease, $158 in the second, $233 in the third, and $12 in the last year.

QUESTIONS AND ANSWERS

Q.   My employer reimburses me at 30 cents a mile for every business mile I travel in 1995. Is that amount reported as income on my Form W-2?

A.   No. Since your employer reimburses you at the standard mileage rate, the amount isn't reported as income to you on your Form W-2 as long as your employer requires you to substantiate the miles traveled.

Q.   **My employer reimburses me at 30 cents a mile for every business mile I travel in 1995. But my actual costs are greater than the amount I receive. May I write off the difference?**

A.   If your actual expenses exceed the amount you are reimbursed, you deduct the difference as a miscellaneous expense—subject to the 2 percent floor. When you file your tax return, you should file Form 2106, "Employee Business Expenses." On that form you report your actual expenses. You also record any reimbursements you receive from your employer.

Q.   **My company reimburses me at a flat $100 a month for automobile expenses. I do not have to account to my employer how I spend this money or how I use my automobile. How do I treat this $100 a month for tax purposes?**

A.   Since your employer has no way of knowing whether you spent the $100 on "ordinary and necessary" business expenses, it must report this amount as income on your Form W-2. The law also requires your employer to withhold taxes—including FICA taxes—on your automobile stipend.

However, you may claim a deduction for your business-related expenses as a miscellaneous itemized deduction, subject to the 2 percent floor.

Q.   **Business use of my car added up to 70 percent last year. But this year my business use will fall to about 45 percent. Are there any tax consequences?**

A.   When business use falls below 50 percent, you may have to "recapture" in the current year some of the depreciation deductions you claimed in the previous year.

Say you purchased a car in 1994 for $13,000, and depreciated the car using the accelerated method (providing larger write-offs in the early years of ownership).

In 1995, however, your business use falls to 45 percent. The law says you must recalculate the depreciation on the car using the straight-line method.

This change in depreciation methods results in a lowering of your depreciation deduction for 1994. The difference between your 1994 deduction under the accelerated and straight-line methods must be reported as income in 1995. Furthermore, you must use the straight-line method for 1995 and future years even if your business use in future years is more than 50 percent.

Q.   **If I use the actual-cost method, what is the best way to keep the data in one place?**

A.   Many people jot down mileage in a small pocket notebook, then attach expense receipts to the pages with paper clips.

You may also purchase a mileage log. Most mileage logs include a place to list these expenses so that you can find them easily when you summarize your tax data.

Q.   I keep a log to document my automobile expenses, and I find it a real headache. Is there any way to reduce my record-keeping?

A.   You could try a method known as sampling. However, this method may only be used if your percentage of business use remains consistent from month to month.

Say you have your own interior decorating business and operate out of an office in your home.

You use your automobile for local business travel: to visit the homes or offices of clients, to meet with suppliers and other subcontractors, and to pick up and deliver materials to your customers. You log no other business miles on your car.

You maintain a diary for the first three months of 1995, and it indicates that 75 percent of your use of your automobile was for your interior decorating business. Based on invoices from subcontractors and other paid bills, you can prove that your business continued at approximately the same pace for the rest of 1995.

If there are no other significant changes in your business operations in the last nine months of 1995, you may use the log that you maintained for the first three months to document your business use of 75 percent.

Or you could maintain a log for the first week of every month during 1995. If your invoices indicate that you did about the same volume of business during the other weeks of each month, your records—in the eyes of the IRS—would support your claim of using your car 75 percent for business each month.

Q.   My company will not allow me to use the company car during off hours. Do I still need to maintain records, since I do not use the car personally?

A.   If you have a company car but company rules do not allow you to use the car for personal reasons, or if you use it only to commute, then you are off the hook when it comes to record keeping. You do not have to keep a log.

Q.   My employer has just started a plan that is intended to reimburse me for both the fixed and variable costs of using my personal car on the job. The plan is called FAVR and is based on certain standards for the area where I live. How does this plan work, and what does it mean to me?

A.   Employers have usually relied on one of the traditional methods allowed for determining the amount to reimburse employees for their automobile usage—the actual cost method or the standard mileage method. Under these methods, as long as you record your actual costs and/or mileage, provide support for your costs or mileage to your employer, and keep no more of the reimbursement from your employer than the amount to which these methods entitle you, you report no income for the reimbursement you receive. Your reimbursements are considered to offset the expenses you incurred.

The IRS allows another method—the FAVR method. FAVR stands for fixed and variable rates. Your reimbursement under a FAVR plan is determined from a formula developed from certain fixed costs—such as depreciation, insurance, registration and license fees, and personal property taxes—of owning an auto where you live, combined with variable expenses (including gasoline, applicable taxes, oil, tires, and routine maintenance and repair) associated with driving a car where you work. In developing a FAVR plan, your employer totals all these costs and, using guidelines established by IRS, determines the amount of the reimbursement allowance. Parking and tolls are not included in the FAVR formula, so you need to claim reimbursement for these separately from the plan.

There are limitations to the FAVR method. If you are a board member, a 1 percent or greater shareholder-employee, or an elected officer whose annual compensation equals or exceeds $66,000 (in 1995), you can't participate. Also, if the original cost and age of your auto don't fit within predetermined guidelines of your employer's plan, or you have previously taken depreciation on your car using an accelerated method, you are not eligible for the FAVR method.

The FAVR method requires you to keep appropriate records. You don't need to maintain all the records required under the actual cost method, but you must still substantiate the number of miles you drive, the time and place of travel, and the business purpose.

Q.   I use my car for work a lot—probably more than the average. Will I be able to get any benefit for this extra mileage under my employer's FAVR plan rules?

A.   Under most FAVR programs, employers may provide employees with a "high mileage payment" to cover additional depreciation attributable to business miles driven over certain predetermined thresholds. This payment is viewed differently than your regular FAVR allowance. Although you can prove the legitimate business purpose of your excess mileage, your employer must include the high mileage payment in your income. The high mileage payment is also subject to the reporting and employment tax withholding rules.

Of course, you may deduct the expenses of operating your car for these excess miles, using either the actual cost or standard mileage methods. You take the deduction as a miscellaneous itemized deduction subject to the 2 percent floor.

14

*M*AKING THE MOST OF YOUR CAPITAL GAIN

- How can you lock in a lower tax rate on capital gains?
- What are some of the ways you can utilize your capital losses?
- Are there investments that result in the deferral of capital gains?

T he tax law provides a break on the tax rate for *long-term capital gains*—that is, profits from capital assets you sell that you held for more than one year. The top statutory tax rate on ordinary income is currently 39.6 percent, but the statutory tax rate on long-term capital gains is limited to 28 percent.

Of course, the break applies only when your taxable income puts you in a tax bracket where you will be taxed at a rate greater than 28 percent. (If you're in the 15 percent tax bracket, your long-term capital gains would still be taxed at 15 percent.)

Filing Status	Tax Benefit for Capital Gains When Taxable Income Is Above:
Married filing jointly	$94,250
Single	56,550
Head of household	80,750
Married filing separately	47,125

Since the law gives a tax-rate break to long-term capital gains, you must remember to distinguish them from ordinary income. In order to do this you must maintain accurate and complete records.

This chapter explains the best way to handle this record-keeping chore. We also tell you how to time your sale to maximize the capital gains advantage and how to report your profit or loss from the sale of assets.

LOCKING IN LOWER RATES

What can you do to reduce your capital gains tax rate? The answer depends on your personal tax situation. As you may know, in 1995, the 28 percent tax bracket kicks in at $23,350 for single filers and at $39,000 for joint filers.

If you are below the 28 percent bracket in 1995 but you will be in the maximum 28 percent long-term capital gain tax bracket in 1996 and possibly future years, consider selling a stock or other security now to benefit from the lower 15 percent rate on your gain to date. Then, if you believe it will continue to appreciate in the future, immediately repurchase the security.

CAUTION

The best tax strategy is not always the best financial strategy. The additional brokerage charges you will incur in the repurchase may reduce or wipe out the tax savings. Also, it may make sense, when you consider the time value of money, to pay taxes later rather than sooner.

WRITING OFF YOUR CAPITAL LOSSES

The tax law allows a deduction of up to $3,000 in capital losses from your ordinary income in any one year, and it makes no difference whether these are long-term or short-term losses.

In addition you may carry forward any losses that you are unable to write off in the current year to future tax years.

You may carry a capital loss forward indefinitely.

EXAMPLE

You have accumulated net long-term capital losses of $10,000 from prior years. This year you had $5,000 in short-term gains.

You may use $5,000 of your $10,000 in long-term losses to offset your gain this year, and you still have $5,000 in long-term losses remaining. You may deduct $3,000 of these losses in the current year and carry the remaining $2,000 forward to future years.

If you had zero or negative taxable income before you deducted your capital losses, you may be able to carry forward all or a portion of your losses to next year.

◆ ℰXAMPLE

You're single and your taxable income—before you subtract your capital losses but after you claim your personal exemption—adds up to a $200 loss.

How do you calculate how much of your capital losses may be carried forward to next year? Add back to your taxable income (in your case, a $200 loss) your 1995 personal exemption of $2,500. The result is taxable income of $2,300.

Your capital losses for the year add up to $4,000. You subtract $2,300 from $4,000 and the result—$1,700—is the amount you may carry forward to next year.

QUESTIONS AND ANSWERS

Q.   Do states tax long-term capital gains at the same rate as ordinary income?

A.   A few states tax long-term capital gains at a lower rate than short-term capital gains. Consult your tax adviser.

Q.   What is a wash-sale, and what is its significance for me?

A.   You could be in for a large and unexpected tax bite if you plan to offset your capital gains with losses the IRS considers to have resulted from a *wash-sale*.

A wash-sale occurs when you sell a stock at a loss and then immediately buy the stock back. The wash-sale rules prevent you from deducting that loss on your tax return.

These rules say that you may not take a loss if, within a period beginning 30 days before you sell your security and ending 30 days after that date (a period covering 61 days), you have acquired or entered into a contract or option to acquire "substantially identical stock or securities."

Moreover, the Supreme Court has ruled that you may not take a loss if your spouse purchases the substantially identical securities.

The rules do not apply if you received your replacement stock or security through a gift, bequest, inheritance, or tax-free exchange.

For an example of how the wash-sale rule works, assume on September 15, 1994, you bought 100 shares of XYZ Company stock for $1,000, and on March 22, 1995, you bought an additional 100 shares for $975. On April 6, 1995, you sold the 100 shares you purchased on September 15 for $900. Since you bought 100 shares of the same stock within the period beginning 30 days before the date of the sale and ending 30 days after that date, you may not claim a loss on your return from the April 6 sale of stock.

Q.   I hear there is a way to postpone paying taxes on my stock market investments until next year. How do I do it?

A.   It's possible to nail down a 1995 paper profit on your stocks and have it taxed in 1996. In effect you freeze a profit (or loss) and postpone the tax result by using a technique known as a "short sale against the box."

For example, you inform your broker you want to arrange a short sale. You own 100 shares of XYZ Corp. The stockbroker allows you to borrow another 100 shares, using your existing shares as collateral. You then sell the borrowed shares in December 1995, thus fixing your profit.

You do not owe the stockbroker money. You owe the broker shares. You deliver your original shares to the broker in repayment in January 1996.

The result: The profit on the 1995 short sale is 1996's taxable income.

Although the technique of selling short against the box can yield tax savings, you also need to evaluate the economics of such sales. If the stock appreciates in value after the short sale, you effectively will not enjoy that added appreciation. (Of course, you will also effectively be protected against any decline in value after the short sale.) Further, you must factor in the costs of borrowing as well as the additional broker's commissions to see if this strategy makes sense for you.

Q.   I have bought several tax-exempt bonds over the years at their par, or face, value. Because interest rates have fallen, these bonds are currently selling at a premium. If I sell my tax-exempts now, is my gain taxable?

A.   Yes. The interest paid on the bond is tax-exempt, but any capital gain you realize is taxed just like the gain on the sale of a taxable security.

A word of caution, however. If you sell a bond, tax-exempt or not, for which you paid either more or less than face value, the price you paid may not be your basis in the bond for figuring gains or losses.

Rather, the price you paid for the bond may have to be adjusted mathematically so that by the time the bond matures, your basis in the bond is equal to the bond's face value. The rules here are complicated, so you should see your tax adviser to help you make these computations and determine which rules apply.

Q.   I have purchased stock in the same company on three different occasions at three different prices. Now I want to sell just some of the stock. When I am calculating my gain (or loss) for tax purposes, which of the three stock prices do I use in computing my basis?

A.   Use the price of the shares actually delivered. If you can't identify the specific shares you're selling by, say, certificate number or by virtue of having held them in different accounts, you must abide by the "ordering rule." It says that you're considered to be selling the stock in the order in which you bought it.

Q.   I own stock in a company and the stock recently split. How long do I have to hold the new stock before it qualifies as a long-term capital gain?

A.   For capital gain purposes you calculate your holding period from the day after you originally bought the stock, not from the time the stock split.

This same rule holds true for companies that pay dividends in the form of additional shares. The holding period for the new shares is the same as for the old shares.

Another rule applies to dividend reinvestment plans that allow you to use your cash dividends to purchase additional shares of stock, sometimes at a discount. The holding period for stock purchased through these plans begins on the day after you purchase the new shares.

Q.   I recently sold some stock of a publicly traded company. Is there any way to defer paying capital gains taxes?

A.   You are in luck! There is a provision that allows an individual to elect to roll over an otherwise currently taxable capital gain from the sale of publicly traded securities where the sales proceeds are used to purchase common stock or a partnership interest in a Specialized Small Business Investment Company (SSBIC) within 60 days of the sale of the securities.

An SSBIC is a partnership or a corporation licensed by the Small Business Administration under the Small Business Act of 1958 as in effect on May 13, 1993. The amount of gain eligible for rollover is limited to $50,000 each year for individuals, with a lifetime cap of $500,000.

Q.   I lent money to a friend of mine to start a business. She has filed for bankruptcy, and I am not going to get my money back. May I write off this bad debt?

A.   The tax law says that you may deduct this amount as a *short-term capital loss* on your tax return—as long as it is truly uncollectible. For a debt to be treated as worthless, a true creditor-debtor relationship must be established and the inability to collect must be demonstrated.

Q.   I lent money to my brother and he failed to pay me back. May I write off this amount as a bad debt?

A.   You may claim a short-term capital loss deduction—but again, only if the money is truly uncollectible. Also, if the IRS audits you, be prepared to prove that the money you gave your brother was a loan and not a gift. The IRS likes to see a signed note, plus evidence that you charged the going interest rate.

Q.   I invested in a small company that went out of business. The company's stock qualifies as small business stock under Section 1244 of the Internal Revenue Code. How is my loss treated for tax purposes?

A.   To encourage investment in small companies, Congress is willing to share the risk with you. You may deduct from your ordinary income losses of up to $50,000 ($100,000 if you are married and file a joint return) on *small business stock*. This amount has no bearing on your other capital losses. Make sure you verify with your tax adviser that your stock qualifies for this advantageous treatment.

Q.   A few years ago the law allowed taxpayers to exclude from their in- come dividends they received from public utility stocks, as long as they reinvested these dividends in additional shares. I did just that. Now I want to sell the stock I acquired through this reinvestment plan. What are the tax consequences?

A.   The entire amount you receive from the sale of stock bought with dollars that were exempt from tax is now taxable. The reason is that your basis in the shares acquired is zero.

Q.   I'm considering an investment in a start-up furniture store run by my brother. Are there any special rules I should know?

A.   The 1993 Tax Act established a capital gains exclusion from qualified small business stock acquired at its original issuance after August 10, 1993. If you hold stock in a qualified small business for more than 5 years, 50 percent of any capital gain resulting from the sale of the stock is excluded from taxable income.

One-half of excluded gains under this provision is treated as a tax preference for AMT purposes. (See Chapter 20 for a further discussion of AMT.) However, since the earliest year taxpayers will be able to take advantage of the exclusion will be 1998, the AMT preference will not arise until then. There are certain restrictions on the types of small businesses that qualify for the exception, so contact your tax adviser for details.

Q.   On December 27, 1995, I sold stock listed on a public exchange at a gain, but the settlement date on the slip my brokerage firm mailed to me was January 2, 1996. In what year do I report the sale?

A.   The law requires you to report your sale, whether at a gain or a loss, in the year you initiated the sale (your trade date)—in your case, 1995.

15

*T*AX RULES YOU NEED TO KNOW WHEN SELLING YOUR HOME

- How do you calculate the gain when you sell your house?
- Are there any strategies to reduce the gain on a house sale?
- What are the special rules for taxpayers age 55 or older?

Selling your home—and selling it at the best possible price—is never an easy job. Even when the sale is over, the transaction is not yet complete. If you sell your home at a profit, the IRS wants to know how much you made on the sale and if any taxes are due.

The good news is that you are allowed to defer paying taxes on that profit as long as you reinvest the proceeds from the sale of your home in the purchase of another home of equal or greater value.

If you recently sold your home or are contemplating a sale, this chapter tells you what you need to know about a rather complicated transaction—the sale of your home.

To begin, though, we'll provide a few key definitions of terms used in this chapter and elsewhere.

A *residence* is a place that contains basic living accommodations. In other words, houses, apartments, condominiums, mobile homes, and even houseboats count as residences.

A *principal residence,* on the other hand, is your primary home, meaning the one that you live in most of the time. The fact that you own a house does not make that house your principal residence. You must actually live in the house for it to qualify as your primary residence.

The tax law does not set limits on the amount of time you must spend in your home for it to qualify as your primary residence. But we suggest you use common sense.

WHEN ARE YOU TAXED?

The IRS allows you to defer paying taxes on gain from the sale of your home as long as you meet these two conditions:

- You must buy or build and occupy a new principal residence within 24 months before or after the date you complete the sale of your old home, *and*
- That new principal residence must cost an amount that equals at least the *adjusted selling price* of your old home.

The tax law defines the adjusted selling price as the amount you pocket from the sale—that is, the sales price minus any *selling costs*—less any *fixing-up expenses.* (Fixing-up expenses are the expenses you incur in fixing up your home and getting it ready to sell.)

Ordinarily, you gain no tax benefit from fixing up your personal residence. Painting and wallpapering, for example, are not currently deductible and do not directly reduce your gain when you sell, either. But when you sell your home, these expenses reduce your adjusted selling price, meaning the amount you must reinvest in a new home to defer tax on your gain from the sale of your old home.

The rules say that the work must be for repair and maintenance, not for improvements—a distinction explained shortly.

Finally, you must do the fixing up during the 90 days before you sign the contract to sell your house, and you must pay for your repairs within 30 days after the sale.

But what about direct selling expenses, such as real estate commissions? Unlike fixing-up costs, these expenses actually reduce the gain on your home, whether you get to defer the gain or not. (More on selling costs and how you should compute your gain later.)

✪ 𝒞AUTION

Postponement of the gain applies only to the sale of your principal residence, whether that is a house, a condominium, a co-op, or even a houseboat. However, a vacation cottage—or any second home—does not qualify.

So far, rolling over the gain from your old home to a new one sounds simple. It can be, but often there are complicating factors.

◆ 𝒞XAMPLE

You are transferred to another division of your corporation in another city. You put your home up for sale. You sign a contract to purchase a house for a slightly higher price in a suburb of the new city, figuring you will sell your old house at about the same time you move into your new home.

But it does not work out that way. The housing market in your old neighborhood is depressed, and although several buyers are interested in your property, you have no firm offers.

You decide to rent your house until you find a buyer. The rental agreement includes an option to buy, but your tenant never exercises the option. It takes you a year to locate a buyer.

Here is how the situation gets sticky. The rules say that you may defer the gain on the sale of a house only if it is your principal residence *at the time of the sale.* So does that mean your old home is no longer considered your principal residence, since it is occupied by a tenant at the time you sell it?

Well, not really. The courts have ruled that temporarily renting out your old house because of a depressed real estate market will not prevent you from deferring your gain. So in this case you do not have to actually occupy the house at the time of the sale.

➤. 𝒯IP

In this situation, not only may you consider your old house as a principal residence for the purpose of deferring your gain, but you may also treat the property as rental real estate. This means you may claim operating expenses and even depreciation deductions on your individual tax return for the period you rent it, subject to the rules related to passive losses and rental real estate discussed in Chapters 17 and 19.

What if the new house you buy costs less than the adjusted selling price of your old one?

◆ 𝒠XAMPLE

You are 52 years old and your spouse is 50. You commute every day from your home in Connecticut to your job in New York. Weary of your 90-minute trek into Manhattan, you suggest selling your 10-room house and purchasing a small condominium near your midtown office.

Your spouse agrees and you put your home on the market. A buyer offers $610,000. You are delighted since you purchased the house 20 years earlier for $150,000.

You sign a contract and pay the real estate agent a 6 percent commission, or $36,600. Since you have no remaining mortgage and no other selling expenses, you collect $573,400 from the sale.

All told, your gain amounts to $423,400—$573,400 less the $150,000 cost of your home. You begin looking for a condominium but find nothing you like.

So you decide to temporarily rent an apartment in midtown Manhattan. A year later you locate the perfect condo. Its price: $550,000, or $23,400 less than the $573,400 you pocketed from the sale of your home in Connecticut. You move into the condo immediately.

Since you did not reinvest all of the proceeds from the sale of your previous house, you must report on your federal tax return the difference between what you sold your old house for and what you paid for your new one—in this case, $23,400, to be taxed as a capital gain. But you still get to defer $400,000 of the gain from the sale of your old house ($423,400 less the $23,400 you do have to report).

If you had paid for your condo an amount equal to or greater than the adjusted selling price of your previous home, you would defer paying tax on all of your $423,400 profit.

➤. 𝒯IP

If you plan on making improvements to your new home, do so within 24 months before or after the sale of the old one. Then you may add the cost of the improvements to the cost of the home. Acting fast is important if, as in this case, the cost of your new home is less than the selling price of your old one.

Still another complication in the law involves taxpayers who are building new homes. Suppose you hire an architect or a contractor to build a house or you contract the work yourself. Ready or not, you must move into your new home within 24 months after the sale of your old home. Otherwise, you pay taxes on your gain.

What is more, the house must be substantially complete when you move in. You cannot pitch a tent on the foundation and claim you occupy your new home. The IRS is strict on this point—despite the house-building delays people suffer—and the courts have backed up the IRS.

Include a clause in your construction contract that calls for your contractor to pay any taxes you owe if construction is delayed beyond the 24-month limit.

HOW DO YOU CALCULATE YOUR GAIN?

What happens if your new home does cost less than the amount you collect from the sale of your old house or you do not buy a new residence at all but choose to rent?

In these cases some or all of any gain is taxed. So, clearly, you should consider strategies to keep your taxable gain as low as possible.

To begin with, however, you need to know how to determine the actual profit and the taxable gain or loss on the sale of your home. The calculation is simple:

	Selling price
Less:	Selling expenses (Sales commissions, advertising, legal, etc.)
	Amount realized
Less:	Basis of home sold (Including improvements but not fixing-up expenses)
	Gain on sale

You may use some of the costs you ran up when you bought your home—and while you owned it—to slash your taxable profit when you later sell.

Some expenses you may include in your basis are:

- Purchasing Costs.

Add to your house's original cost any of the following fees paid when you bought your home: appraisal fees, attorneys' fees, cost of removing any cloud on the title, costs for title search and insurance, fees for the recording of the deed and mortgage, late closing charge, and survey expenses.

- Improvements.

Also add to your cost all amounts you paid for improvements, that is, anything that adds to your home's value or appreciably prolongs its life. (You will find a checklist of these items at the end of this chapter.)

✷ CAUTION

You may not increase the basis by the cost of ordinary repairs and maintenance designed to keep up the building and grounds.

What counts as a repair? Common examples include repainting inside or out, fixing the gutters or floors, mending leaks, replastering, or replacing broken window panes.

➤ TIP

In certain circumstances, such as the restoration of an old house, some of these items may be considered improvements. Check with your tax adviser on how to treat these items.

◆ EXAMPLE

The original cost of your home was $200,000 and you had purchasing expenses of $9,000. Over the years, you added a new room for $30,000 and installed central air conditioning and heating for $15,000.

Finally, you sell the old homestead for $300,000. But your broker's commission and other selling expenses total $25,000.

Is your gain $100,000 (your $300,000 sale price less your $200,000 cost)? Definitely not. As we have seen, to determine your gain, you add your purchasing expenses and the cost of improvements to your basis, and you subtract your selling expenses from the sales proceeds.

	Selling price	$300,000
Less:	Selling expenses	(25,000)
	Amount realized	275,000
Less:	Basis of home sold (original cost basis of $200,000 plus $54,000 in improvements and purchasing expenses)	(254,000)
	Gain on sale	$21,000

✷ CAUTION

You must be prepared to substantiate your expenses and improvements. And doing so requires accurate and careful record keeping. So keep detailed records of all of your home-related expenses.

DEFERRING TAX ON YOUR GAIN

Returning to the above example:

You pay no tax on your $21,000 profit as long as you buy a new residence costing $275,000 or more—or at least you do not pay any tax now.

Say you buy a new house for $280,000. Your purchasing costs add up to $14,000. Your basis in your new home is $294,000 ($280,000 plus $14,000). Right? No, as you must reduce your basis in your new house by the amount of gain from your old house that you rolled over, or deferred.

Your basis in your new home then comes to $273,000—that is, $280,000 plus $14,000 minus the $21,000 gain you rolled over.

Now suppose it is a year later and you decide to sell the second house for $300,000, but you do not buy a new one.

The law says you must report on your tax return the difference between the selling price ($300,000) and your basis in that home ($273,000). And your gain—$27,000 (which consists of the $21,000 gain you rolled over plus the additional $6,000 difference between the selling price of $300,000 and the second home's original cost of $294,000)—is taxable now because you did not buy a new home.

If you had purchased another house, you still will owe taxes on the $6,000 gain. This is because under the rules you may roll over your gain from the sale of a house only *once every two years*—unless you take a new job in another location or are transferred as part of your old job.

❖ *E*XAMPLE

You sell your old house on January 15, 1995, at a $10,000 profit. Then you buy a new one on February 15. The cost of your new home tops the amount you received for your old house.

Then you discover an oil deposit in the backyard of your new home. So on March 15 you sell the second house at a hefty profit. And finally, on April 15 you move into yet another, even more expensive home. Under the rules, you may defer only the $10,000 gain from your original home.

Why? Because the tax law says that only the last principal residence purchased in the two years following the sale of your old residence qualifies as the replacement residence for the rollover break. So the rollover break does not apply to the sale of your second home. Instead, you must report and pay taxes on the gain from the March 15 sale of the house with the gusher in the backyard. And you reduce the basis of your last home—the one you bought on April 15—by the $10,000 gain you deferred on the sale of your first one.

❖ *C*AUTION

As mentioned above, there is an exception to the once-every-two-years rule for taxpayers who take a new job in another location or are transferred as part of their old job. In such cases the rollover break applies sequentially to each sale and purchase within the two-year period. Although this exception was generally designed to benefit taxpayers, and it does just that in the majority of cases, it may lead to unexpected and undesirable tax consequences.

❖ *E*XAMPLE

In 1994 an individual sold his home for $200,000 and moved to another state, where he purchased a new home for $220,000. His basis in the first home was $150,000.

Accordingly, he had a gain of $50,000, which he was able to defer, since the cost of the new home exceeded the sales price of the old. The deferred gain reduced the basis of the new home to $170,000 ($220,000 minus $50,000).

A year later, in 1995, the individual was transferred to a new location where he bought a new home for $190,000. Shortly thereafter, he sold the second home for $215,000. His gain, of course, was $45,000 ($215,000 minus $170,000). But since the purchase price of the third home was less than the sales price of the second home, he could defer only $20,000 of the $45,000 gain. And, unfortunately, he had to pay tax on $25,000 of gain.

On the other hand, if the general rule—which permits the rollover of gain on the sale of a principal residence only once every two years—had applied, the individual would have paid tax on only $10,000 of gain because the third residence would have been the one relevant for gain deferral on the first. Thus, since the purchase price of the third home ($190,000) was less than the sales price of the first home ($200,000), he would have reported $10,000 of the $50,000 gain and deferred the remaining $40,000. The purchase and sale of the middle residence would have no effect on the deferral of gain rules. Accordingly, the individual would have incurred a nondeductible loss of $5,000 on the sale of the second home ($215,000 selling price minus $220,000 cost basis.)

In a similar case, a taxpayer asked the IRS if he could apply the general rule instead of the exception for work-related moves, since the general rule resulted in less current tax liability. The IRS declined the request and held that the exception for work-related moves requires that each sale and purchase be considered in sequence. The bottom line: The exception for work-related moves, designed to help the taxpayer, may actually result in greater current tax in certain cases.

✪ 𝒞AUTION

The IRS has a special rule for married taxpayers when the title to the house they sell differs from the title to their new house. For example, the husband might have had sole title to the old house, but the new house is jointly owned.

As far as the IRS is concerned, a husband and wife can be considered one taxpayer in this situation. This means it does not matter, for purposes of the tax law, which spouse owned the old house or which buys the new house.

There are only two catches: Both houses must be principal residences of both spouses, and both spouses must sign a consent statement (on Form 2119, "Sale of Your Home") that says they agree to divide any gain and cost basis of the new house. (This rule applies whether the couple files jointly or separately.)

◆ 𝓔XAMPLE

You hold title to a house, your and your husband's principal residence, that you sell for $300,000. The cost basis of the house was $280,000, so you realize a $20,000 gain. Within a year you and your husband each contribute $150,000 to buy a new house in your joint names.

You pay no tax on your gain as long as you and your spouse file consent statements agreeing to allocate between yourselves the deferred gain and the basis of your new house. You file the consent on Form 2119 in the year you realize your gain. So the basis of the new house is $140,000 to you and $140,000 to your husband.

What if you fail to file the consent form? The IRS requires you to pay tax on the $20,000 gain because the amount you contributed toward the purchase of your new house—$150,000—is less than the adjusted selling price of your old house.

REPORTING THE SALE

Use Form 2119, "Sale of Your Home," to report the sale of your residence, even if the sale resulted in a loss. If you replaced your home within the replacement period, also use Form 2119 to postpone paying tax on all or part of the gain. If you postpone tax on any gain, keep a copy of Form 2119, and any documents used to complete it, with your records for the basis of your new home. Any gain you calculate on Form 2119 that you do not rollover is reported on separate Schedule D, Form 1040.

TIMING YOUR SALE

If you plan to sell your home in the near future for a profit—and you *don't* plan to purchase a replacement residence—figure out your tax rate for 1995. Then figure out your tax rate for 1996. See Chapter 2 to determine your tax rate.

If your tax rate is lower in 1995, sell in 1995, and if it is lower in 1996, sell in 1996. What if your tax rate is the same? Then it makes no difference— tax-wise, at least—when you sell your home. (Of course, you must also factor into your decision other economic considerations.) But if it is close to the end of 1995, you may want to wait until 1996 so that your reporting of the gain and payment of tax will be delayed a year.

⮞.𝒯P

Currently, the top tax rate for ordinary income is 39.6 percent, but the top tax rate for capital gains (which include the gain from the sale of your home) is 28 percent. So remember to take into account this tax break; it could affect your strategy when it comes to timing the sale of your home.

Make sure also to review Chapter 14 if you have a potential capital gain to report on the sale of your home—there may be other important considerations, such as using capital losses, that you don't want to miss.

✪ CAUTION

If you sell your home at a loss, it is *not* a deductible capital loss.

TAX BREAK IF YOU'RE 55 OR OLDER

Say you are a 64-year-old widow. You owe no money on your eight-room house because you paid off the entire purchase price of $50,000 years ago.

Tired of property taxes and the expense of maintaining your large home, you decide to sell the house and move into an apartment building near your daughter. You contact a real estate agent and learn that the property, which you bought 30 years ago, is now worth $170,000. You sell it at that price.

What is the tax consequence for you? Under the law, you may owe no tax as a result of selling your home—even though your gain is $120,000.

It does not matter whether you use the proceeds from the sale to buy another house or place the entire amount in the bank.

The law allows older taxpayers who sell their principal residence to pocket the profit tax-free—*if* they meet the following four conditions (discussed in detail below):

- The tax-free profit on the sale of your house may not top $125,000,
- You must be 55 years of age or older on the date of sale,
- You own and live in the same house and maintain it as your principal residence for at least three of the five years immediately before the sale, *and*
- You tell the IRS that you are making use of the exclusion by filing Form 2119 with your Form 1040.

The tax-free profit on the sale of your house may not top $125,000. This ceiling applies to a single person or a married couple filing jointly. In the case of a married couple filing separately, the limit is $62,500 per spouse. Any profit on your house above $125,000 (or $62,500) is taxed as a capital gain.

You must be 55 years of age or older on the date of sale. The rules treat a married couple filing a joint return as one person. So a couple qualifies for the tax break if only one spouse is age 55 or older on the date of the sale.

You may exclude a profit on the sale of a house from your taxable income only if you did not previously take advantage of this break.

✪ CAUTION

The $125,000 exclusion is a once-in-a-lifetime offer. What happens if you remarry? Neither you nor your new spouse may claim the exclusion if either of you took it previously.

➤.🖉ip

If you both plan to sell your homes and buy another after remarrying, consider selling your homes before the wedding. That way you each may use the exclusion.

⚡ 𝒞aution

Don't allow your buyer to take possession of your house before you turn age 55. Sometimes, simply taking possession constitutes a sale for tax purposes, even though title has not actually changed hands.

You own and live in the same house and maintain it as your principal residence for at least three of the five years immediately before the sale. The house does not have to be your principal residence at the time of the sale. Under the rules up to two years may elapse between the time you move out and the sale takes place as long as you occupied it for the previous three years.

➤.🖉ip

When it comes to meeting the three-out-of-five-years rule, a special rule applies to individuals who become physically or mentally incapable of caring for themselves at least five years before the sale.

These taxpayers must use their house as their principal residence for periods that total at least one year during the five-year period. In addition, they must live in a state-licensed facility, such as a nursing home, to have that time count toward the three-year requirement.

You tell the IRS that you are making use of the exclusion by filing Form 2119 with your Form 1040. You must inform the IRS of the sale of your principal residence and your decision to make use of this part of the law. The IRS calls filing this form "making a formal election," and it is the government's way of making sure you do not capture the break more than once. The required "formal election" actually is made on a government-printed, government-provided form telling the IRS when you sold your home and how much profit you made.

If you want to complete the form yourself, just stop by or telephone your local IRS office for a copy. (Ask for Form 2119, "Sale of Your Home.") The IRS will also provide instructions on how to prepare the form and will offer assistance if you need it.

➤.🖉ip

Plan carefully to use this tax break. It is far too valuable to waste and, if you are not careful, you may lose part of your benefits.

◆ 𝒠xample

You bought a house in early 1984; your basis in the house is now $200,000. By 1995 you're over age 55, and you and your spouse decide to sell your house. You plan to invest the tax-free profit in securities, then move to the Florida vacation cottage you purchased some years earlier.

A willing buyer pays $300,000 for the house. Taking into account a 6 percent real estate agent's commission, the gain on the sale of your house is as follows:

	Selling price	$300,000
Less:	Commissions	(18,000)
	Amount realized	282,000
Less:	Basis of home	(200,000)
	Gain on sale	$ 82,000

You notify the IRS that you intend to make use of the one-time, age-55, home-sale exclusion. You invest your $82,000 and move south.

So far so good—until you think about your situation a little more carefully. You used only $82,000 of the amount of gain you are allowed to exclude—$125,000—on the sale. And the difference between the amount you use and the amount allowed—$43,000—is gone forever. The reason: The law lets you make use of this exclusion only once.

This provision is fine if you can exclude the maximum amount you are allowed or close to it. But you cannot exclude the difference later on.

If you could have waited a year or two before you sold your house, you might have been better off. By then the housing market might have become stronger, and you could have gotten a better price and been able to take better advantage of this once-in-a-lifetime tax break.

➲.𝒯ɪᴘ

If you own more than one home, it usually does not make sense to cash in on the $125,000 exclusion if you can make better use of it later.

Say you just sold your home and are retiring to your vacation house in the mountains of North Carolina. Your vacation home has appreciated more in value than the house you just sold.

Why not wait to claim the $125,000 exclusion until you sell your North Carolina home, which has become your principal residence? That way you can take better advantage of the exclusion.

✿ 𝒞ᴀᴜᴛɪᴏɴ

Don't make the mistake that some taxpayers do and decide to claim the $125,000 exclusion without taking into account estate planning. Timing the exclusion is important. Our advice is to seek the help of your tax adviser *before* you opt for the $125,000 exclusion.

➲.𝒯ɪᴘ

You can cash in on a really impressive tax-free parlay. How? Combine the $125,000 exclusion and the sale-and-replacement break.

And doing so is a big break for the home seller who is "buying down"—for example, a retiree who is selling his or her big home and buying a smaller one.

By combining the exclusion and the rollover, you may collect more than $125,000 in profit and buy a much less expensive home without paying one dime in taxes.

◆ ✐XAMPLE

You paid $165,000 for your house in 1985, then 10 years later you sold it for $380,000. You pocketed a hefty $215,000 profit, and you opted for the one-time exclusion. So $125,000 of your $215,000 gain is tax free to you—forever.

Now you want to purchase a house of equal value to your old one, so you will qualify for the sale-and-replacement break.

But wait: When it comes time to calculate how much you must spend on a new home, the law allows you to subtract the amount of your exclusion ($125,000) from the selling price of your old home ($380,000). So you need to spend only $255,000 for a new house—not $380,000.

As long as your new house costs $255,000 or more, you defer paying taxes on your remaining gain of $90,000. You reduce the basis of your new house by only the $90,000 gain that you do not pay taxes on now.

QUESTIONS AND ANSWERS

Q. We sold our old house, which we bought for $100,000, for $125,000. We bought a new one for $100,000, then six months later, spent $50,000 making improvements (we remodeled the kitchen and both bathrooms). How much of the $25,000 gain do we include in our tax return?

A. You might think that you have to include the entire $25,000 on your return because the amount you paid for your new house is less than the selling price of your old home. Not so.

The law gives you a break. You may add to the cost of your new house the amount you spend on improvements within 24 months before or after the sale of your old home.

So your taxable gain equals zero. The $100,000 you paid for your new house plus the $50,000 you spent on improvements is greater than the $125,000 you collected for your old house.

Q. The real estate market in our area is really depressed. We had to sell our house at a loss. May I claim this loss on my tax return?

A. You may not deduct a loss from selling a personal residence. But you do get a write-off for a loss upon sale when you have converted a home to rental property. The reason: Your home is no longer considered your personal residence; it now qualifies as business property. The deduction is limited, however, and taking advantage of it is complicated. So check with your tax adviser.

Converting a personal residence into rental property has another advantage. You may also deduct operating expenses and depreciation during the rental period.

If you have to sell a home in a depressed market and it looks as if you are going to take a loss, consider renting out your house until conditions improve.

Q.   We sold our old home, but we will not buy a new one before we file our next tax return. Do we have to notify the IRS of the sale?

A.   Yes. Attach Form 2119 to your return, showing how you figured your gain. Form 2119 asks for the date you sold your old residence, the sale price, and your basis in the house. Also check the box that you intend to acquire a new residence within the replacement period. Once you replace your home, let the IRS know in writing on another Form 2119.

But what if you decide later not to buy another house, or the 24-month period has passed? In these cases you report your taxable gain for the year of your sale on Form 1040X (an amended 1040) to which you attach a Schedule D (to report capital gains and losses) and a new Form 2119.

Q.   Before we got married, my spouse and I each owned homes, which we have since sold. Now we have bought a new house together. Can we both defer the gains on our old home?

A.   Yes. Under a special rule the IRS will let you both defer all your gains under two conditions: One-half of the cost of the new home must add up to more than the adjusted sales price of each of your old homes (if it does not, some or all of the gains may be taxable), and you must have taken joint title to your new home. Moreover, you do not have to file the special consent statement we discussed in this chapter.

Q.   How does the IRS know that I sold my house?

A.   The law requires that all real estate sales be reported to the IRS on *Form 1099-S, "Proceeds From Real Estate Transactions"*—including sales of any permanent structure, condominium unit, stock in a cooperative housing corporation or co-op, land (improved or unimproved, including airspace), and commercial real estate.

Who does the reporting? Usually the person listed as the settlement agent on a settlement statement or the person who prepares the settlement or closing statement.

If there is no statement, responsibility passes in descending order to the buyer's attorney, the seller's attorney, the title company, the mortgage lender, the seller's broker, the buyer's broker, and finally the buyer. Or both the buyer and seller may designate someone to file Form 1099-S with the IRS.

Whoever the person is, he or she must report the total amount—with no reduction for selling expenses—received by the seller. And he or she must list the seller's name, address, and Social Security number, as well as the closing date of the sale and the address of the property sold.

The information must be submitted to the IRS by February 28 following the year of the closing, and a copy must also be sent to the seller by January 31 following the year of closing.

Q.   I do not own a house. I own a condo. Do the same rules apply?

A.   First a critical distinction: A condominium owner owns his or her residence outright, whereas a cooperative apartment is owned by a corporation in which the resident owns stock. Stock ownership entitles the co-op "owner" to the exclusive right to lease his or her apartment. But whether you own a condo or a co-op, you get the same tax treatment as owners of single-family homes.

You may deduct mortgage interest and taxes. Of course, if you are a condo owner, you, like the owner of a house, pay your interest and taxes directly. If you are a co-op shareholder, you pay a portion of the corporation's interest and taxes, based on the number of shares you own.

And you may deduct the portion of your co-op payment that is allocated to the corporation's interest and taxes. (Of course, your co-op or condo interest must meet the tests for deductibility. See Chapter 5 for more on interest deductions.)

When it comes time to sell, your basis is increased by the amount you spend for improvements—again, just as if you owned a house. Remember to include your share of maintenance charges or special assessments that your association spends on improvements for the benefit of all of the condos or co-ops in your building.

Q.   I bought a hot tub five years ago and added its cost ($2,000) to my basis in the house. Now the hot tub has to be replaced. I have bought a new one for $3,500. Do I also add its cost to my basis?

A.   Sorry, the tax law does not allow you to increase your basis by the purchase price of both tubs. It says you must subtract the amount you paid for the first hot tub ($2,000) from your basis. Then you may add the price of the new tub ($3,500).

So your basis in your home increases by $1,500—the difference between the price of the first and second tubs—at the time you purchase the second tub.

Q.   What counts as improvements?

A.   An improvement is anything that adds to the value of your home or appreciably prolongs its life. Here is a checklist of some items that count as improvements.

Additional acreage	Bathroom addition
Additional rooms	Bathtub
Air cleaner	Bathtub enclosure
Air conditioning	Bathtub sliding doors
Alarm system	Beams (decorative)
Aluminum siding	Birdbath
Attic fan	Boiler
Attic improvement (converting it into living space)	Bookcases
Awnings	Breezeway
Barbecue grill	Built-in furniture
Baseboard heating	Burglar alarm system
Basement improvement (converting it into living space)	Cabana
	Cabinets
Basketball goalpost	Carpeting
	Caulking

Ceilings (acoustical)
Chimes (door)
Chimney
Circuit breakers
Circulating system
Closets and closet organizers
Clothes dryers
Cold water pipes
Concrete walks
Cooling equipment
Copper tubing
Cornice
Countertops
Cupboards
Curtains
Deck
Dehumidifier
Dishwasher (built-in)
Doors
Doorbells
Dormers
Drainboards
Drain pipes
Drainage system
Drapes
Driveway (paving or blacktopping)
Dryer
Dry wells
Ducts
Electric heat
Electrical outlets
Electrical wiring
Electronic air filter
Exhaust fans
Fences
Fire alarm system
Fireplace
Fireplace mantel
Fixtures (lighting and plumbing)
Flagstone walks
Flooring (wood, tile, etc.)
Food freezer
Furnace (replacement)
Furnace filter system

Fuse boxes
Garage
Garage door
Garage door opener
Garbage disposal systems
Garden and grounds
Gates
Glass enclosure
Grading
Grease traps
Greenhouse
Grills, air ducts
Gutters
Hamper
Hardware (fixtures and locks)
Heat ducts
Heat pumps
Heating system
Hedges
Hot tub
Hot water heater
Hot water pipe
House numbers
Humidifier (furnace)
Humidistat
Inside walls (altering)
Insulation
Intercommunication system
Kitchen
Lamppost
Landscaping
Laundry equipment
Lawn sprinkling system
Lighting fixtures
Lightning rods
Linen chute
Linoleum
Locks (door)
Mailbox
Medicine cabinet
Mirrors
Outdoor lighting
Ovens
Paneling

Partitions
Pathways
Patio
Play yard
Plumbing
Porch
Pumps
Racks (garage)
Radiator covers
Radiators and valves
Railings
Range (gas or electric)
Range hood
Refrigerator
Retaining walls
Roofing
Room dividers
Screen doors
Screens
Security system
Septic system
Sewer assessment
Sewers
Shades
Shed
Shelves (built-in)
Shower controls
Shower doors
Showers
Shrubs
Shutters
Sidewalks
Siding
Sinks

Skylights
Smoke detector
Softwater system
Solar heating unit
Solar room
Space heater
Stairs
Steam room
Steps
Storm doors
Sump pump
Supply cabinets
Survey (property)
Swimming pool
Switch plates
Telephone outlets
Television antenna
Termite-proofing
Terraces
Thermostat
Tiles
Toilets
Topsoil
Towel racks
Trees
Trellis
Vacuuming system
Vanity
Venetian blinds
Vent pipe
Walks
Wall coverings
Washer
Weather stripping

16

HOME OFFICE DEDUCTIONS

- Who is entitled to a deduction for home office expenses?
- How is the home office deduction calculated?
- Why is it so important that the home office is a principal place of business?

You may not know it, but some 39 million Americans now work at home, at least part-time. One reason is technology. Inexpensive computers and communications devices, such as modems, now make it easy for people to go to work without ever leaving home.

Working at home, at least as far as taxes are concerned, is both a blessing and a curse. The blessing? The IRS allows you to deduct part of the cost of owning or renting and of maintaining your home. The curse? The IRS believes many people who maintain *home offices* and claim *home office expenses* on their tax returns are abusing the law. So the IRS tends to look carefully at tax returns containing home office deductions.

Our advice? Take the deductions to which you are genuinely entitled. Just be sure you are prepared to defend them on audit.

In this chapter we show you which home office deductions you may legitimately claim and how to be sure you can back them up if the IRS should inquire.

WHO QUALIFIES FOR A HOME OFFICE DEDUCTION?

If you work at home—and your office qualifies—you may deduct the costs of operating and maintaining that portion of your home you use for business.

If you own your home, you may deduct a portion of your operating expenses (i.e., utilities, repairs, and insurance) and you may depreciate that part of your home you use as an office.

If you rent your house, you may deduct part of your rent, in addition to your operating expenses for the office portion of your home.

But the qualifying rules are stringent. You must use whatever space you designate as your home office regularly and exclusively as your *principal* place of business. Or you must use it regularly and exclusively as a place where you meet with customers, patients, or clients, if meeting with clients is a normal part of your business.

A Supreme Court decision found that a "principal place of business" means the most important or significant place for business as compared to all others. The result of the Supreme Court's decision is that the IRS takes a very strict position on the deductibility of home office expenses.

The two primary considerations in determining the deductibility of expenses associated with a home office are:

- The relative importance of the activities performed *and*
- The time spent at the home office relative to any other business location.

To illustrate how the Supreme Court's two tests will be applied, the IRS has provided some examples.

Example 1—the Plumber. A self-employed plumber spends 40 hours per week installing and repairing plumbing in customers' homes and offices. The plumber also spends 20 hours per week at home talking with customers on the phone, and has hired a full-time employee to perform administrative services in the home office. Since the most important aspect of the plumber's business requires that services be performed at the customer's location, the home office is not considered to be the principal place of business and does not qualify for the home office deduction, even though the tasks performed there are considered to be essential.

Example 2—the Teacher. A teacher spends 25 hours per week at school, and 30–35 hours per week at home preparing for classes and grading papers. The teacher did have a small shared office at the school. Although more time was spent there, the office at home was not the teacher's principal place of business since the more important activities were conducted at the school. The teacher was not eligible for the home office deduction.

Example 3—the Writer. An author spends 30–35 hours per week writing in a home office and 10–15 hours at other locations (meeting with publishers, conducting research, etc.). Since the writer's business is writing (the other activities are less important and take less time), the writer is eligible for the home office deduction.

Example 4—the Retailer. A self-employed retailer of jewelry sells merchandise at craft shows, on consignment, and through mail order, spending 25 hours per week at home filling orders, ordering supplies, keeping the books of the business, plus 15 hours at the shows and consignment locations. Since several locations were important to the retailer's trade of selling jewelry, the IRS allowed the retailer's home office to qualify for the home office deduction.

➲.𝒯IP

A home office you use for a *second* business may qualify for a deduction. For example, assume you teach in the public schools but also work as a consultant in the evenings and on weekends. You use your den regularly and exclusively to run your business, that is, manage various activities, maintain the books, make phone calls, and so on. You may be able to take the home office deduction.

✪ 𝒞AUTION

The IRS may disallow your home office deduction, claiming your business is not carried on with the intention of making a profit. Make sure you can demonstrate there is a profit motive behind your business, and that it is not carried on for tax-avoidance purposes or as a hobby.

A home office you use exclusively to manage your own investment portfolio does not qualify for a home office deduction. Managing your personal investments may be how you make your money, but it is usually not your trade or profession.

You do not need to maintain an office in a separate room to qualify for a deduction. You need only use some separately identifiable space exclusively and regularly for business.

Additionally, an area need not be exclusively used in the trade or business if it is used for storing inventory of a business of selling retail or wholesale products (if it is the sole fixed location of the trade or business) or if it is used as a licensed day care facility. (See the "Questions and Answers" later in this chapter for more details on this topic.)

If you maintain your office in a separate structure, for example, a garage, then the rules are less strict.

In this case you may claim a deduction if you use the structure regularly and exclusively in your trade or business. In other words—and this is the important point—the building does not have to be your principal place of business.

Another important rule: If you are employed by someone else, you must maintain your home office for the convenience of your employer—or you do not get a deduction.

◆ 𝒠XAMPLE

Assume you are an attorney with a downtown firm and you sometimes use your den to catch up on your reading and occasionally to meet with clients. Does your den qualify as a home office?

No, and here is why. You do not use it regularly and exclusively to conduct your law business, and it is not your principal place of business. Your principal place of business is your downtown office. Also, you use it only occasionally to meet clients—not regularly.

Now, assume you are a typist employed by a company to perform word processing. The company requires you to work at home full-time because no space is available for you in the company's building. You set up shop in what used to be your child's nursery.

You have already cleared one hurdle—the office is for the convenience of your employer. Now, you have only one more hurdle to get over.

If you use your office exclusively as your principal place of business—that is, you do not use it as a den, say, during the evening—you are entitled to deduct the appropriate costs. (See Chapter 9 for more information on rules governing deductions for employee business expenses.)

✪ 𝒞AUTION

If you're audited, the IRS may ask you to prove you maintain your home office for the convenience of your employer. Keep in mind it is not enough that your home office is "appropriate and helpful" to your employer. You should ask your employer to write you a letter specifying your home office is essential and is maintained at his or her request.

✪ 𝒞AUTION

Some taxpayers may use a home office to conduct more than one business. The Tax Court has ruled that for any of the home office expenses to be deductible, each business must qualify for home office deductions. In other words if one of the businesses fails to qualify, none of the home office expenses are deductible, even though the other businesses qualify.

In this case the taxpayer used his home office for two purposes—in connection with his employment and for work done as an independent contractor. Because employment-related use wasn't for the convenience of the employer, the court ruled that expenses attributable to that use weren't deductible. The court treated this use as personal use. The use of the office for work done as an independent contractor couldn't be regarded as exclusive business use since the office was also used for personal purposes. Accordingly, none of the expenses attributable to the office were deductible.

In the past, some taxpayers used another part of the tax law to bypass the requirement that a home office serve as their principal place of business. They would lease a part of their home to their employer. Then they would deduct the costs associated with the leased space but they would not use the home office rules to justify their write-offs.

Rather, they used the section of the tax law that allowed them to deduct expenses for rented space. Now, however, the tax law specifically forbids this practice.

Here's why. Congress worried that employees would get around the restrictions on home office deductions by arranging to have a portion of their salary paid in rent. The legislators did not like these transactions.

➤.𝒯IP

Renting a portion of your home to your employer may still provide tax benefits, even though you may not deduct your expenses.

◆ EXAMPLE

You accumulate passive losses from an investment in a limited partnership. The rules say you may deduct passive losses only to the extent of your passive income. Rental activities are almost always considered passive, so you may be able to generate passive income by renting your home office. (See Chapter 19 for more on passive losses.)

In order to substantiate this transaction you must charge a fair and reasonable rent, you should have a written lease, and you should use the rented space exclusively for business.

The diagram below will help you determine whether you may claim a home office deduction.

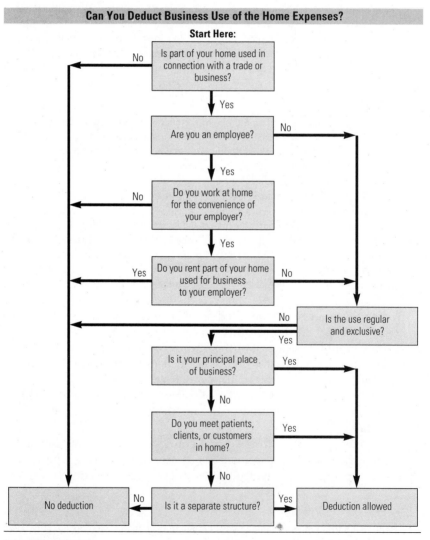

Can You Deduct Business Use of the Home Expenses?

Start Here:

Is part of your home used in connection with a trade or business? → No

Yes ↓

Are you an employee? → No

Yes ↓

Do you work at home for the convenience of your employer? → No

Yes ↓

Do you rent part of your home used for business to your employer? — Yes / No

Is the use regular and exclusive? — No / Yes

Is it your principal place of business? — Yes

No ↓

Do you meet patients, clients, or customers in home? — Yes

No ↓

Is it a separate structure? — No → No deduction / Yes → Deduction allowed

Source: IRS Publication 587

FIGURING THE DEDUCTION

The law imposes a strict limit on the total amount of home office expenses you may deduct, even if you meet the various qualifying tests. It says you may not use the cost of maintaining a home office to create or increase a loss from your business and therefore reduce your other, unrelated income.

Specifically, the law says you must first reduce your gross business income by the sum of the portion of mortgage interest and property taxes attributable to your home office space and the *direct expenses* attributable to your business. (These are expenses you would incur even if you did not have a home office.) Then, it says, your deduction for home office expenses (first operating expenses, then depreciation) may not exceed this "net" amount.

◆ *Ẽ*XAMPLE

As an accountant just out of school, you decide to work from a basement office in your St. Louis home. In your first year you earn $20,000 in client fees. The mortgage interest and taxes on that part of your home you use for your office add up to $4,000. The expenses for your part-time secretary, phone answering service, stationery, and so on—everything but the home office expenses we noted at the beginning of this chapter—come to $12,000. Operating expenses, such as utilities, come to $2,000, and your depreciation expense totals $3,000

Here's the home office deduction computation:

	Year 1
Gross business income	20,000
Mortgage interest and taxes (home office)	(4,000)
	16,000
Direct business expenses	(12,000)
Net income	4,000
Operating expenses (home office)	(2,000)
	2,000
Depreciation expense (home office)	(3,000)
Income/(loss)	(1,000)

You may not use these expenses to reduce your taxable business income below zero, so $1,000 of depreciation is disallowed for that year.

Here is a break, though. You may carry this unused office expense deduction forward to offset your business income in future years.

Assume in the second year of your accounting practice you earn $30,000 in fees, have mortgage interest and taxes of $4,000 on that part of your house you use for your home office, rack up $10,000 in direct expenses for telephone, secretarial help, and so forth, and have home office expenses of $7,000 (including depreciation). Here's year two's calculation:

	Year 2
Gross business income	30,000
Mortgage interest and taxes (home office)	(4,000)
	26,000
Direct business expenses	(10,000)
	16,000
Home office expenses ($7,000 current and $1,000 prior year carryover)	(8,000)
Income	8,000

In this case you may deduct the entire $8,000 of home office expenses, giving you taxable income in your second year of only $8,000.

Do not worry about deducting the portion of your mortgage interest and property taxes attributable to your home office or your direct business expenses. These are always deductible in any event. They just serve—as demonstrated in the computations above—to limit your home office deductions.

Thus, as a homeowner you are always entitled to deduct your mortgage interest and property taxes. And if you are operating a business, you may deduct direct business expenses even if they create a loss. But you may not use home office expenses to increase a loss.

◆ EXAMPLE

Assume your gross business income before you deduct your home office expenses adds up to $8,000. Say, too, that interest and taxes attributable to your home office come to $10,000. Under the rules you may not use home office expense deductions to reduce your net income below zero.

You would write off $8,000 to reduce your gross income to zero. Then you would write off the remaining $2,000 of interest and taxes as itemized deductions.

You may also deduct your direct business expenses—secretarial wages, office supplies, and so forth—that are not exclusively related to your home office.

You may not, however, write off any other home office costs—utilities, maintenance, and so on—since you may not use these costs to increase the loss from your business (but, as noted, you may carry your home office expenses forward to offset your business income in future years).

✍ CAUTION

If you're audited, expect the IRS to ask you to prove the amount claimed for your home office. Maintain documentation of all your expenditures—utility bills, canceled checks, and so on.

QUESTIONS AND ANSWERS

Q.   I'm a physician and I maintain an office downtown. I don't use my home office to meet with patients, but I do telephone patients from my home office in the evening, and I do use the office exclusively for business. Am I entitled to a write-off?

A.   Sorry, but the IRS will not allow you to take a deduction. The reason is that your home office is not your principal place of business. Also, you do not meet there with patients face-to-face (phone calls do not count).

Q.   I'm a musician and am employed by an orchestra. I practice in our spare bedroom because there is no place to practice at Symphony Hall. May I claim a deduction?

A.   In most cases your employer's principal place of business is your principal place of business, but you are an exception to this rule.

Because your employer does not provide you with practice space, and practicing is essential to maintaining your skills, you may be entitled to a deduction. However, you must overcome the presumption that the Symphony Hall is your principal place of business. How much time is spent at each location should be considered. In addition, remember you must use your spare bedroom regularly and *exclusively* as a practice room.

Q.   I maintain an office in my eight-room home. Do I write off one-eighth of the expense of maintaining my home?

A.   You may, if all eight rooms are approximately the same size. Otherwise, you may calculate the percentage of floor space your home office occupies.

Q.   I operate a day care center and use the basement of my home exclusively for this purpose. May I claim a home office (i.e., day care) deduction?

A.   Yes. You are also entitled to a deduction if you use your home regularly to provide day care for children or people who are elderly or handicapped. When it comes time to calculate your deduction, you must take into account the amount of space your day care operation occupies.

Say you use 30 percent of the floor space of your home for day care. You are entitled to write off 30 percent of the expense of operating your home. You may deduct 30 percent of your heating bills, 30 percent of your cooling bills, 30 percent of your home insurance bills, and so on.

Congress carved out an exception to the exclusively-for-business rules for day care center operators. If, for instance, you use your living room and kitchen as a day care center only during the day, you may still claim a home office deduction. But you must operate a licensed facility.

You are subject to the same rules as the day care center operator above— plus one other rule. You must take into account how much time you use your home for day care and how much as a residence, and you deduct only those costs attributable to the day care.

Here is how it works. Assume you use 30 percent of your floor space for day care and your business uses this space 10 hours a day Monday through Friday and 6 hours on Saturday for a total of 56 hours each week.

During the remaining 112 hours, your family uses the space. You may write off 10 percent of the cost of operating and maintaining your home; that is, 30 percent of your floor space times the 33 percent of time you use the house for your day care business.

Q.   Where on my tax return do I claim a deduction for my home office?

A.   File Form 8829, "Expenses for Business Use of Your Home," with your return to support your deduction. The amount determined on Form 8829 carries over to other forms that must be filed with your return, depending on your employment status.

If you are self-employed, write off your home office on Schedule C of your Form 1040. If you are employed by someone else, claim your home office deductions on Schedule A, with Form 2106 attached, as a miscellaneous itemized deduction subject to the 2 percent floor. That is, you may deduct only those expenses that, when added with other miscellaneous expenses, top 2 percent of your adjusted gross income. (See Chapter 9 for the details on how to write off miscellaneous deductions.)

Q.   I claimed a home office deduction for the past 10 years and I am planning on selling my house. Are there any tax implications?

A.   If you claim a home office deduction and plan to sell your home, there may be tax implications at the time of the sale. It depends on whether you are entitled to claim a home office deduction in the year you sell your home. And the key word here is *entitled.*

If you are not entitled to claim a write-off that year, you may roll over the entire gain from your house into another home and defer paying taxes on your profit.

If you satisfy all the rules and you are entitled to claim a home office deduction in the year you sell your house, you are taxed on that portion of your gain attributable to that part of your home you used as a home office.

Assume, for example, that the cost of your house plus improvements is $125,000 and you sell it for $150,000. From the time you purchased your home until you sold it, you used 10 percent of the floor space in your house as a home office.

You allocated $12,500 of the cost of your home to your home office. Over the years you claimed depreciation deductions of $5,000.

The net gain on the sale of your house is $30,000 ($150,000 less your cost of $125,000 reduced by depreciation of $5,000).

The IRS says you may roll over a portion of this gain, tax-free, into a new house. But, since you were entitled to a home office deduction in the year you sold your house, the portion of your gain allocable to your home office is taxable.

Here's how to calculate this taxable gain.

You allocate the sale proceeds between the office and nonoffice portions of your home. Remember, you allocated 10 percent of the cost of your house to your home office.

You use this same 10 percent to allocate the proceeds from the sale of your home. That is, you allocate $15,000 of your sale price to your home office (10 percent times $150,000).

Your taxable gain on the sale comes to $7,500 ($15,000 less $12,500 cost reduced by $5,000 depreciation). You may roll over the remaining $22,500 of your gain into a new house. (See Chapter 15 for more information on the tax implications of selling your home.)

If you are planning to sell your home, put pencil to paper to decide what is worth more to you:

- Claiming a home office deduction in the year you sell your house and forgoing the gain deferral attributable to the home office portion, *or*
- Not claiming a home office deduction and rolling over that portion of your gain on the sale attributable to your home office.

If postponing the gain gets you more, violate the home office rules. For example, do not use your home office exclusively for business.

That way you are not entitled to claim a home office deduction in the year of the sale. You lose the deduction, but you get to postpone the gain on that portion of your house.

Note: This strategy should work, but it is not free from doubt that the IRS will accept it upon audit. If this situation applies to you, obtain professional tax advice.

17

$\mathcal{G}$ETTING THE MOST FROM YOUR VACATION HOME

- Is your second home vacation property, rental property, or some combination of the two?
- How do the tax laws differ for each type of property?
- How do you calculate any gain or loss associated with the property?

When it comes to vacation homes, you have to ask yourself this question: What do I really want from my vacation home? A place the family and I can use whenever we like? A place I know I can always escape to? Or is my primary consideration keeping costs down?

If getting away from the madding crowd is your primary goal, then tax consequences are a secondary issue.

But in either case you must know the rules so you can make an informed choice and avoid an unexpected tax bill.

The tax treatment of a second home varies, depending on how you use your retreat. Is it strictly for personal use? Do you rent it? To whom? And for how long?

The information in this chapter will help you understand the differing tax treatment depending upon your choice of how you use the property.

WHAT IS A VACATION HOME?

As far as the IRS is concerned, your second home is either a vacation home used exclusively by you and your family, rental property, or some combination of the two. How the IRS treats the house depends on which classification applies.

Although the sections just ahead cover the details, here is an overview of the tax differences among these three categories.

A vacation home you use personally most of the time gets the same tax treatment as your first home, even if you rent the property to others for as many as 14 days a year.

If your vacation home is treated as a second home, you may deduct your mortgage interest and property taxes as itemized deductions, but you may not deduct other expenses, such as repairs and utilities. And the same restrictions that apply to the deductibility of mortgage interest on your first home apply to the second. (Chapter 5 explains these rules.)

➤ 𝒯𝙸𝙿

If you rent out your home for fewer than 15 days, the rental income you collect is tax-free. Of course, in this situation you cannot claim any deductions related to the rental of the vacation home beyond mortgage interest and property taxes as noted above.

When you sell your vacation home, it doesn't qualify for the same tax breaks as your principal residence. That is, any gain is immediately taxable to you.

Rental property is very different. You get income from renting the property, and you generally may deduct most of the expenses you incur, utilities and repairs, for instance, from that income. You may also depreciate the property (i.e., deduct a portion of its cost each year).

Combination property gets different treatment depending on how many days you rent the property and how many days you use your vacation hideaway.

𝒞AUTION

Just one day one way or the other, as you will see when we get to the details, can make a big difference in your tax bill.

DEFINING THE DIFFERENCE

Since for tax purposes the differences between a personal vacation home and rental property are great, the tax code is very precise about which is which. If you intend to rent your second home and take advantage of the tax deductions that renting brings you, these distinctions are important to you.

The tax law says you may classify your second home as rental property as long as you do not occupy it for more than 14 days in the year or for more than 10 percent of the total number of days that it is rented at fair market value for the year, whichever is greater.

If, in other words, you rent your second home at the going rate for 300 days, you could use the home yourself for as many as 30 days, and it would still qualify as rental property.

𝒞AUTION

What happens if you occupy it for 31 days? You may still claim a deduction for mortgage interest and taxes allocable to your personal use of the home, but you are limited on the deductions you may take for mortgage interest and taxes allocable to rental use, operating expenses, and depreciation.

The IRS is strict about what it considers personal use. Under these rules, you have used your home for personal purposes if on any part of any day your vacation home is occupied by you or:

- A person who has an equity stake in the property.
- A spouse or blood relative (meaning your parents, children, siblings, and grandparents).
- A person with whom you have a barter arrangement that allows you to use another dwelling.
- A person to whom the vacation home is not rented at "fair market value," which according to the law is the going rate for other, similar homes in the area.

Even if you charge a relative, or someone with an equity interest in the property, a fair rent, the IRS still considers this personal use.

◈ ℰXAMPLE

Assume you own a vacation home in upstate New York. You rent it to your sister, a relative, for the going rate, $1,500 for 10 days.

Next, as part of a barter agreement you allow your friend Bob to occupy your vacation home for 11 days. In exchange you use his home in California for eight days.

Finally, you rent your vacation home to your father's boss for 10 days and charge only half the fair market rental.

How many of these days are personal days? By IRS rules, all 31 count as personal use days.

What constitutes a day? When you are counting, do it the way hotels do: each 24-hour period.

Assume you occupy your vacation home from Saturday afternoon through the following Saturday morning. For IRS purposes you have used your house for seven days—even though you were on the premises for part of eight calendar days.

The law does contain one exception to the general rule on renting to relatives. Let's say you rent your property at fair market value to a relative who uses the house as a principal residence—a condo for your parents, for instance. The IRS does not consider this use personal use.

◈ 𝒯IP

There may be a way to reduce the rent you charge relatives. Consider this Tax Court case.

The court allowed a taxpayer to reduce by 20 percent the fair market rent he charged his parents. The court ruled the reduced rent was fair because it reflected the amount the taxpayer saved in maintenance and management fees by renting to such trustworthy tenants.

❂ 𝒞AUTION

If you donate time in your vacation home to a charity, you may have to claim that time as personal use time. In one ruling the IRS held that a week's use of a vacation home the owner donated to a charity auction counted as personal use of the home. The reason? The owner did not charge the bidder at the auction—the renter—a fair rent. Instead, the bidder paid the rental to the charity. To make matters worse, the owner could not claim a deduction for a charitable contribution because a gift of the right to use property is not deductible.

➣.𝒯IP

If you want to donate use of your vacation home to a charity auction, rent your home for a week at its fair market value, then donate the rent to charity. That way you get a deduction for your contribution and avoid using up personal use days.

REPAIR AND MAINTENANCE VISITS

Anyone who owns a vacation home knows that such homes require repairs and maintenance. If you stay at the house while doing the repairs, the IRS will not count these as personal use days. Your "principal purpose" in staying there must be to make repairs or perform maintenance chores.

◈ 𝒮XAMPLE

Assume you own a mountain cabin that you rent during the winter. You and your spouse arrive at the cabin late Thursday evening. The point of the trip: to prepare the cabin for the rental season. But the two of you are tired.

So you enjoy dinner by the fire, then turn in early to get plenty of rest for the days ahead. You work on the cabin all day Friday and Saturday. Your spouse helps for a few hours each day, but spends most of the time catching up on paperwork.

By Saturday evening the work is done. You spend the rest of the evening relaxing, then head home shortly before noon on Sunday.

Since the principal purpose of your trip was for maintenance, none of these days are counted as personal days. They are all maintenance days.

❂ 𝒞AUTION

In an audit the IRS may probe to make sure your "principal purpose" was indeed repairs and maintenance. An auditor will look at the frequency with which you did your chores, the amount of time you spent on these activities, and the presence and activities of friends. If the auditor sees that you claim to spend most of your time at your home doing maintenance but you always bring along companions, he or she may argue that the purpose of your activities was not for maintenance and repair. Accordingly, the IRS might count those days as personal use, which may result in a loss of deductions.

⊘.𝒯ιP

Keep a log of your repair and maintenance days. Write down when you arrive, how much time you spend on various tasks, and what kinds of work you perform. That way you can prove how you spent your time should the IRS ever question you.

RENTAL PROPERTY

What is rental property worth to you tax-wise? Probably a lot of deductions. Let's take a look at the types of expenses you may deduct from your rental income.

Advertising and Commissions. Say you own a mountain cabin in West Virginia and you enlist the help of a local real estate agent to keep the property occupied. Each time he or she signs someone up to rent your cabin, you pay a commission.

Under the rules you may deduct these commissions directly from your rental income. You may also deduct advertising expenses.

Property Taxes and Mortgage Interest. You may deduct state and local property taxes that are assessed on your rental property. You may also deduct mortgage interest. (Of course these same costs may be deductible even if your vacation home does not qualify as rental property; that is, you use it as a personal residence.)

(See Chapter 5 for more on deducting interest expenses. See Chapter 8 for more on deducting state and local taxes.)

Operating Expenses. Deductible operating costs include utilities, maintenance, insurance, and any other expenses, such as professional fees and repairs. You may also deduct any supplies, a receipt book, say, that are normally deductible for profit-oriented activities.

Depreciation. You probably can reduce your taxes by depreciating your vacation home.

If you began renting your house after 1986, you may recover its cost by depreciating it over a 27.5-year period.

You may also claim depreciation deductions on furniture and appliances in your vacation home. The post-1986 rules allow you to depreciate these items over seven years. (See Chapter 18 for the details on depreciation.)

Of course you do not get a deduction without incurring an expense, and as owners know, maintaining rental property *is* expensive. Furthermore, the passive investors may be limited in terms of the amount of rental loss that may be deducted in any given year.

Passive investors in rental property may deduct rental losses, but only against income generated by other passive investments, limited partnerships, for instance. If you have no income from other passive investments, you have to postpone claiming your deductions from the vacation home you operate as rental property until you do have passive income or dispose of the property. If you actively participate in the rental activity, you may be entitled to a special exception that would allow you to deduct all or a portion of the loss you incur. Real estate professionals may also be entitled to additional deductions. (For more information on these rules, see Chapter 19.)

MIXED USE: ALLOCATING EXPENSES

There are two categories of mixed-use property. In the first, you may make personal use of your vacation home within the 14-day or 10 percent limits and still claim most of the deductions you would get for rental property.

If your use falls into this category, your property—in the eyes of the IRS—is not a personal residence. It's rental property and the rules won't allow you to write off as mortgage interest any interest allocated to your personal use. The IRS treats the interest as nondeductible personal interest expense, the same as credit card interest, for instance. Note that if your personal use is less than 14 days or 10 percent of total use, chances are most of your interest expense will be deductible as rental expense.

Property taxes, of course, are fully deductible. (See Chapter 4 for more information on deductions.)

In the second mixed-use category, your personal use of the house exceeds 14 days or the 10 percent limit, and the tax treatment your house receives is substantially different.

The portion of your interest, taxes, and expenses allocated to rental use is only deductible to the extent of your rental income. In other words if your second home falls into this category and you post a loss from renting the house, you may not deduct that loss currently against your other taxable income. Assuming this type of property qualifies as a second residence, you may write off any mortgage interest allocable to personal use as an itemized deduction. And of course you may deduct the personal portion of the taxes.

❖ ℭAUTION

If your property falls into this second mixed-use category, you must deduct your "rental" expenses in a certain order:

- First, you deduct advertising and commission charges;
- Then, property taxes and mortgage interest;
- Next, your operating expenses; and,
- Finally, depreciation.

Why is the order important?

The IRS requires you to deduct the expenses (with the exception of advertising and commissions) that you are allowed to deduct in any case against rental income first. You may deduct your other expenses only if you still have rental income left over after these deductions are made.

➲.📐P

You may carry forward to future tax years any expenses you may not deduct current-ly—subject to all the limits we have described, of course.

🌣 ℭAUTION

If you own a third home and use it as both a residence and rental property, different rules apply. The portion of your mortgage interest allocated to personal use is not deductible as mortgage interest because the IRS lets you treat only two homes as personal residences.

Rather, the interest allocated to personal use is treated as personal interest and is not deductible.

Interest allocated to the rental use is deductible to the extent of rental income less advertising, commission charges, and taxes, as discussed above.

No matter which mixed-use category your second home falls into, you must allocate expenses. Be careful. This rule holds true even if you use your home yourself just one day of the year, New Year's Day, say, or the Fourth of July. You now must allocate one day's worth of your vacation home's total expenses to personal use. The IRS makes no exceptions to this rule.

The allocation formula, however, is simple. Here is how it works.

X	=	The number of days you actually rented your property at a fair market value.
Y	=	The number of days you used the property for any other purpose. (Do not count days it was standing vacant, and do not count any repair or maintenance days.)
Allocated expenses	=	Your total expenses (including property taxes and mortgage interest) for the year multi-plied by the fraction: X divided by the sum of X and Y.

The product of this allocation formula is the amount you may allocate to rental use.

WHAT A DIFFERENCE A DAY MAKES

Now let's use a couple of examples to figure the allocation of expenses. The examples also show the big difference just one additional day of personal use can make in the tax cost of owning your second home.

Assume the following facts: Your principal residence is in Connecticut, and you also own a vacation home in New Mexico, which you actively participate in renting.

You took out a mortgage to buy the home in New Mexico, and the interest expense totals $4,000, taxes are $2,000, operating expenses (utilities and maintenance) equal $2,000, and depreciation comes to $5,000. After you subtract commissions, you realize rental income in 1995 of $7,500 for the year, and your adjusted gross income is $80,000.

EXAMPLE A:

You rent the house at a fair rental value for 126 days. You use it for family vacations for 14 days, and you spend 4 days there to take care of repairs and maintenance.

The IRS figures you used the house for 140 days (126 rental and 14 personal). The four days you spent on repair and maintenance are not included in your total use days.

You may allocate 90 percent—that is, 126 divided by 140—of the costs associated with the house to its rental use.

Since you used the house yourself for only 14 days, and since your AGI is $80,000, the rules allow you to claim a loss up to $25,000. (Any remaining loss is subject to the general passive loss rules.) You compute rental income and expenses as follows:

Rental income	$7,500
Less expenses:	
Taxes (90%)	(1,800)
Mortgage interest (90%)	(3,600)
Operating expenses (90%)	(1,800)
Depreciation (90%)	(4,500)
Rental income/(loss)	**$(4,200)**

You may also deduct the other 10 percent of your property taxes, or $200, as an itemized deduction on Schedule A of your Form 1040. The remaining interest, however—the part allocated to personal use—is classified as personal interest and is not deductible. So in total you have deductions against your normal taxable income of $4,400: $4,200 plus $200.

EXAMPLE B:

Assume in this case that you increase your use of the house by just one day, bringing your personal use to 15 days for the year.

Since 15 days exceeds the maximum 14-day limit and is more than 10 percent of the total rental days (126 days), your vacation home is now classified as a residence.

As a result your deductions for costs allocated to rental use—that is, 126 divided by 141, or 89 percent—may not exceed the rental income you received. Furthermore, you must write off expenses allocated to rental use in the following order:

- Advertising and commissions.
- Property taxes and mortgage interest.
- Operating expenses.
- Depreciation.

On the plus side, the IRS counts the portion of mortgage interest you allocate to your personal use of your home as deductible, just like the interest expense on your principal residence. You may write this amount off on Schedule A of your Form 1040.

Therefore, in this instance, rental income and expenses are:

Rental income	$7,500
Less expenses:	
Taxes and interest (89%)	(5,340)
Limit on other deductions	2,160
Operating expenses (89%; not limited since less than the $2,160)	(1,780)
Limit on depreciation deduction	380
Depreciation (89%; $4,450 in reality but limited to $380)	(380)
Rental income/(loss)	**$ 0**

The result: You had a loss of $4,070, but you can't claim it currently. The reason: Your expenses cannot exceed your rental income. You may, however, still deduct the remaining 11 percent of property taxes and interest, or $660.

As you can see, using your house more than the maximum days allowed can cause your taxes to rise sharply. That extra day's use in our example cost you $3,740 in deductions (the difference between the $4,400 in deductions in Example A and the $660 in Example B). But remember, you may carry forward the excess not currently deductible—in this case, $4,070—to future tax years.

There is an alternative method for allocating taxes and mortgage interest (approved by the courts, but not the IRS) that you may use. Sometimes it works to your benefit.

How? It reduces the amount of interest and taxes allocated to the rental portion, giving you room to use more of your other expenses as deductions against rental income. In turn it increases the amount of interest and taxes allocable to personal use, giving you a bigger itemized deduction.

Under the alternative method, you divide the number of rental days by the total number of days in the year. You use the resulting percentage to determine the portion of mortgage interest and property taxes you deduct against rental income.

The percentage you calculate under the alternative method is smaller than the percentage you figured earlier. That is because the earlier method required you to divide the number of rental days by the number of days the property was actually in use.

So the alternative method usually results in greater savings. But to be sure you have to perform both calculations with your own numbers and compare the results.

EXAMPLE C:

Assume the same facts as in Example B, but allocate interest and taxes using this alternative method.

Rental income	$7,500
Less expenses:	
Taxes and interest (allocated based on the ratio of rental days to total days in the year, 126/365 x $6,000)	(2,071)
Limit on other deductions	5,429
Operating expenses (89 percent x $2,000)	(1,780)
Limit on depreciation deduction	3,649
Depreciation ($4,450 [89 percent x $5,000] in reality but limited in current year to $3,649)	(3,649)
Rental income/(loss)	**$ 0**

The remaining taxes and interest (239 divided by 365 times $6,000 or $3,929) are deductible as itemized deductions.

In this situation the alternative method works out much better for you. It gives you $3,929 in tax and interest deductions compared to $660 using the other method. In addition, the disallowed loss that must be carried forward is reduced to $801 (total depreciation of $4,450 less $3,649 allowed).

✿ CAUTION

Since the alternative method is approved by courts, not the IRS, you may be more likely to be challenged on this issue. Make sure you keep accurate records to support your use of this method.

The flowchart on page 150 will help you determine the tax treatment of your second home.

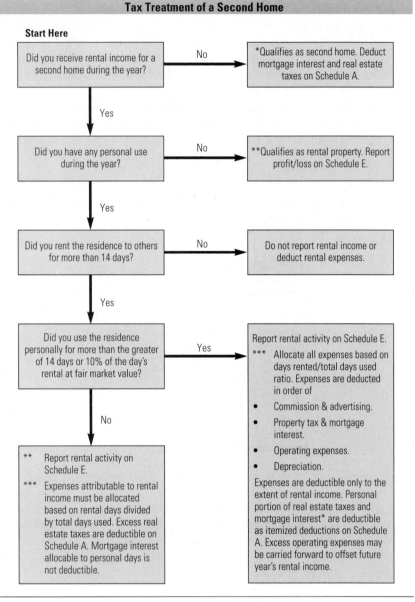

Tax Treatment of a Second Home

Start Here

Did you receive rental income for a second home during the year? → **No** → *Qualifies as second home. Deduct mortgage interest and real estate taxes on Schedule A.

Yes ↓

Did you have any personal use during the year? → **No** → **Qualifies as rental property. Report profit/loss on Schedule E.

Yes ↓

Did you rent the residence to others for more than 14 days? → **No** → Do not report rental income or deduct rental expenses.

Yes ↓

Did you use the residence personally for more than the greater of 14 days or 10% of the day's rental at fair market value? → **Yes** → Report rental activity on Schedule E.
*** Allocate all expenses based on days rented/total days used ratio. Expenses are deducted in order of
- Commission & advertising.
- Property tax & mortgage interest.
- Operating expenses.
- Depreciation.

Expenses are deductible only to the extent of rental income. Personal portion of real estate taxes and mortgage interest* are deductible as itemized deductions on Schedule A. Excess operating expenses may be carried forward to offset future year's rental income.

No ↓

** Report rental activity on Schedule E.

*** Expenses attributable to rental income must be allocated based on rental days divided by total days used. Excess real estate taxes are deductible on Schedule A. Mortgage interest allocable to personal days is not deductible.

---

* Mortgage interest expense, in this situation, can be deducted only if this is a second home. If you have more than two residences that fit these requirements, you must elect which residence will be the "primary" home and which will be the "second" home. (See Chapter 5 for more on interest deductions.)

** Rental activity losses are limited by AGI limitations and rules regarding active management of rental property. (See Chapter 19 for more on rental activity rules.)

*** Several court cases have concluded that taxes and interest may be allocated to the rental period in the proportion of rental use days to the total days in the year rather than in proportion of rental use to the actual period of usage. (See discussion above.)

QUESTIONS AND ANSWERS

Q.   In addition to my principal residence I own a small houseboat. Does my boat count as a vacation home?

A.   The IRS is quite liberal when it comes to defining a vacation home. It does not much matter if you have an A-frame in the woods or a townhouse in the city.

Any dwelling unit, even a boat or house trailer, that contains basic living accommodations—kitchen, bathroom, and sleeping space—qualifies as a vacation home. So if your boat is equipped with a bunk, a head, and a galley, you are all set.

A word of warning, however. The $25,000 passive activity rental exception only applies to real estate; a boat is not real estate, even if you do use it as a vacation home. (See Chapter 19 for more information on these rules.)

Q.   I own three homes. May I deduct mortgage interest on all of them?

A.   No. If you have three or more homes, you may claim the mortgage interest deduction on only two of them, your principal residence and one other. You decide which one—and you may change your mind from year to year.

The mortgage interest on other homes gets the same tax treatment as interest on personal loans. The interest is classified by how you use the money. For example, if your mortgage proceeds go to purchase common stock, the interest is investment interest.

You will want to put pencil to paper to figure out which house—in addition to your principal residence—you should designate as your second home in order to collect the maximum interest deductions.

Q.   I rent my second home only 10 days each year. The rest of the time my family and I use it personally. What rules apply to my situation?

A.   There is good news and bad news. On the plus side if you rent your second home for 14 days or less during the year, the rental income is yours tax-free.

The trade-off is that the only deductions you get to take are for mortgage interest and property taxes—no maintenance or repair costs and no depreciation.

But this could be a really good deal if your second home is in a location that commands sky-high rents for a very short period of time, the host city for a national political convention, for example. Rent it out for fewer than 15 days and enjoy the income—tax-free.

18

WHAT YOU NEED TO KNOW ABOUT DEPRECIATION

- How does depreciation differ for real and personal property?
- Can you maximize the advantage of the $17,500 expensing election?
- What are the luxury automobile limitations?

Depreciation rules are something that anyone with business property, including rental property, must understand. What is depreciation all about? Writing off a certain amount each year until you have written off the amount you paid for your property. In this way the government allows you a deduction for the use and wear and tear your business assets receive over the years.

In this chapter we cover many depreciation rules—which can be quite complex—and suggest strategies to make them work for you.

PERSONAL PROPERTY CLASSES

Personal property is a term the tax rules use to describe depreciable business assets other than real estate. (*Real property*—real estate—is discussed later in this chapter.) The law assigns personal property, both new and used, to one of six classes. These classes really describe *recovery periods*—that is, the length of time it takes to "recover" (i.e., deduct) your investment in these assets.

Recovery periods range from 3 to 20 years. Below is a listing that shows examples of property included in various recovery periods.

Three-year property: Special tools.

Five-year property: Light trucks, automobiles, computer equipment, typewriters, calculators, and copiers; assets used in research and development, oil and gas drilling, construction, and the manufacture of certain products such as chemicals and electronic components.

Seven-year property: Office furniture and fixtures and most other machinery and equipment.

10-, 15-, and 20-year property: Only a small number of assets, including land improvements, such as drainage pipes.

If you have any doubt about which class a particular asset falls into, contact your tax adviser.

ACCELERATED DEPRECIATION

You may depreciate your business assets—except those in the 15- and 20-year classes—using the *200-percent-declining-balance method* (also known as the *double-declining-balance method*). You may also opt for the *150-percent-declining-balance method* for all classes of personal property; however, you must generally use longer recovery periods under this method.

Both methods are types of *accelerated depreciation,* which means you get to write off greater amounts in the first years of ownership.

In fact, in the first year of an asset's life, the 200-percent-declining-balance method yields deductions that are twice the amounts you would get using the *straight-line method.* (The straight-line method produces the same write-offs from year to year.)

In each subsequent year, however, the 200-percent-declining-balance method lets you deduct progressively smaller amounts until at some point the write-offs you calculate under that method become the same or smaller than your annual deductions figured under the straight-line method based on the remaining useful life of the asset. At that point you are required to switch to the straight-line method to finish depreciating your property.

The 150-percent-declining-balance method, which is used for assets in the 15- and 20-year classes, is, as expected, one and one-half times the straight-line depreciation in the first year of an asset's life.

You have a choice when the time first comes to calculate write-offs on your business assets. You may use IRS-approved formulas (discussed below), or you may use the depreciation tables published by the IRS.

You may obtain a copy of these tables from your tax adviser or local IRS office. But even if you use the tables, you should understand the conventions, or rules, incorporated in them that apply to depreciation.

IMPORTANT CONVENTIONS

A *half-year convention* applies in depreciating personal property. This convention provides for depreciation for just half the taxable year in which you place personal property in service (i.e., put it to use).

Moreover, the half-year convention applies regardless of the date you actually begin using your asset during the taxable year. So the first-year deduction is one-half the amount you would take for a full year of depreciation.

✪ 𝒞AUTION

The tax law does not want taxpayers who place a large number of assets in service during the last quarter of the year to claim a full six months' depreciation, so it imposes a special 40 percent rule. This rule provides that you cannot use the half-year convention if, of all personal property that you first place into service during the year, more than 40 percent of it is placed in service in the last quarter of the year.

You must instead use a *midquarter convention* for all personal property you place in service during the year, even those assets you place in service *before* the last three months. The midquarter convention assumes that you placed your assets in service halfway through the quarter in which you actually put them into use.

When you have to use the midquarter convention, you may end up with smaller total depreciation deductions than you could claim under the half-year convention.

BY THE NUMBERS

The following example shows how the 200-percent-declining-balance method of depreciation and the half-year convention actually work.

◆ 𝒺XAMPLE

You buy a new car on January 1, 1995. You use the car only for business. The car, which falls into the five-year class, costs $10,000.

You depreciate it using the 200-percent-declining-balance method. To figure the first year's write-off, you divide $10,000 by five years and get $2,000.

Your depreciation deduction equals two times the amount you would write off using the straight-line method, which, as we have seen, allows you to deduct the same amount each year. In this case you multiply $2,000 times 2 and get $4,000. But the half-year convention allows you to write off only one-half of this amount, or $2,000, in the first year of ownership.

In the second year you depreciate your car by $3,200. This number is obtained by dividing the remaining *un*depreciated value of the car, $8,000, by the depreciation period, five years. You get $1,600. Now since we are using the 200-percent-declining-balance method, multiply this amount by 2. The result: $3,200.

Follow the same formula to calculate how much you may depreciate the third year under the 200-percent-declining-balance method: $10,000 minus $2,000 minus $3,200 equals $4,800; $4,800 divided by 5 equals $960; now you multiply by 2 to get $1,920 depreciation in the third year.

For the fourth year: $10,000 minus $2,000 minus $3,200 minus $1,920 equals $2,880, divided by 5 equals $576. And $576 times 2 equals $1,152.

As mentioned earlier, at some point during your car's depreciation life, straight-line depreciation begins to yield the same or a greater write-off than the 200-percent-declining-balance method. In our example that point is in the fourth year.

To figure straight-line depreciation:

Simply divide the remaining *un*depreciated cost of your car ($2,880) by the total number of years remaining in its five-year useful life (2½, because of the half-year convention). The answer, $1,152, is the same as you would get using the 200-percent-declining-balance method.

And you will see that in year five your straight-line depreciation of $1,152 tops the $691 you would get using the double-declining-balance method.

The sixth year will yield a deduction of $576, which represents a half-year of straight-line depreciation.

So in the fourth, fifth, and sixth years, you will switch to the straight-line method of depreciation until you have written off your entire $10,000 purchase price.

To save you the trouble of calculating when it is time to switch from the double-declining method to straight-line depreciation, consult the following chart. (**Note:** This chart uses the half-year convention.)

When to Switch	
Recovery Class	Year to Switch
3-year	3
5-year	4
7-year	5
10-year	7
15-year	7
20-year	9

EXPENSING VERSUS DEPRECIATING

You are allowed to deduct up to $17,500 of the amount you spend each year to acquire depreciable personal property. This is known as the small business expensing election.

To illustrate how this tax break works, assume you are in the restaurant business and you buy tables and chairs for $25,000.

The law allows you to depreciate the furniture over seven years. But the expensing rules give you another option. You may deduct $17,500 of the purchase price this year and then depreciate the remaining $7,500.

✪ *C*AUTION

Be aware of two pitfalls. First, the $17,500 annual ceiling is reduced dollar-for-dollar for every $1 in personal property you place in service in any one year over the first $200,000. So if you place $201,000 worth of assets in service, you may expense only $16,500. Second, the total amount of property that may be expensed for any tax year cannot exceed the total amount of taxable income derived from the active conduct of any trade or business during that tax year.

LUXURY AUTOMOBILE LIMITATIONS

The law caps the depreciation deduction you may claim for "luxury cars" used for business.

Your depreciation deductions are limited during the normal five-year recovery period on business automobiles purchased in 1995 costing more than $15,300.

For example, you bought a new car in 1995 and you use it exclusively for business. The automobile costs $20,000. The law caps your depreciation write-offs at $3,060 in year one, $4,900 in year two, $2,950 in year three, and $1,775 in each succeeding year.

Maximum Annual Depreciation				
Year Car Placed in Service	Year 1	Year 2	Year 3	Year 4
1991	$2,660	$4,300	$2,550	$1,575
1992	2,760	4,400	2,650	1,575
1993	2,860	4,600	2,750	1,675
1994	2,960	4,700	2,850	1,675
1995	3,060	4,900	2,950	1,775

Under this schedule you would have to keep your car for nine years before your car would be fully written off.

The law is even more strict if you use your automobile less than 100 percent of the time for business. Say your business use adds up to 75 percent. Your depreciation deductions are capped at $2,295 in year one (75 percent times the $3,060 ceiling), $3,675 in year two, $2,213 in year three, $1,331 in year four, and so on.

✪ ℰAUTION

The $3,060 cap also applies to the $17,500 expensing allowance. Therefore, the $17,500 expensing allowance cannot be used to boost your first-year write-off for your car.

DEPRECIATING REAL PROPERTY

Unlike personal property, which may fall into one of six different property classes, real property (i.e., real estate) is assigned to one of only two classes—residential rental property and commercial property.

For real property placed in service after May 12, 1993, you write off the cost of residential rental property over 27.5 years and commercial property over 39 years. You write off only the cost of the building, not the land under it, since as far as the law is concerned, land does not deteriorate.

In addition, instead of using the accelerated methods of depreciation allowed for personal property, the law requires you to use the straight-line method when it comes to depreciating real property. In other words, you write off the same amount each year with the exception of the first and last years.

The law also provides that you must abide by a so-called *mid-month convention*. This rule, which goes for both residential and commercial investments, means that you figure your first year's depreciation deduction from the middle of the month in which you place your property in service. The mid-month convention applies even if you place your property in service on the first, or the last, day of the month.

◆ *E*XAMPLE

You and a colleague buy a small office complex on August 1, 1995, in a nearby suburban development. The property costs you $500,000—$400,000 for the building and $100,000 for the land.

You spruce up your property and put it on the rental market on September 1, 1995. How much may you now write off on your 1995 tax return?

Even though the complex was placed in service on September 1, the midmonth convention says the property is placed in service on September 15. So in 1995 you may deduct 3½ months in depreciation write-offs, or $2,991.

Here's how it adds up. You take the cost of your building, $400,000, and divide it by 39 years, the number of years over which you must depreciate commercial property. Then you divide the result, $10,256, by 12 months and multiply by 3½ months—$2,991.

While the midmonth convention may seem unfair, it can actually work to your advantage. The reason? You're entitled to a half-month's depreciation no matter when during the month you place your property in service—even if, in the above example, it is September 30.

ALTERNATIVE DEPRECIATION METHOD

Under some circumstances, the law requires you to use an alternative method to depreciate your property—one that is usually less generous.

You must use the alternative method for certain "listed property," including luxury automobiles and computers used no more than 50 percent in your trade or business. And you must use the alternative method when you finance your property with tax-exempt bonds or when the property is used outside the United States.

To figure depreciation under the alternate method, generally you use the property's class life as specified in the *alternative depreciation system (ADS)*. If your asset doesn't have a class life specified in the ADS system, use 12 years. For residential rental real estate or commercial property, use 40 years.

Then you depreciate your property using the straight-line method. The half-year, midquarter, or midmonth conventions apply as discussed earlier.

In some cases the law *requires* you to use the alternative depreciation method. You may also *elect* to use the alternative depreciation method for any class of property. If elected, the alternative depreciation method applies to all property in that class placed in service during the year. In the case of real property, you may elect to use the alternative method with respect to any single property. Remember, though, that the alternative method periods are usually longer than the regular recovery periods.

Cellular telephones are "listed property" that are subject to the special depreciation limitations and other restrictions. So if you use a cellular phone or other similar telecommunications equipment no more than 50 percent of the time for business, you must determine depreciation based on the alternative depreciation system instead of the more accelerated, general system.

In addition, if an employee buys a cellular phone that he or she uses for business, no deduction for any business use is allowed unless the employee's use of the equipment is for the convenience of the employer and is required as a condition of employment.

⊛.🖋️ꟼ

To safeguard the deduction, ask your employer for a letter stating that your cellular phone is for your employer's convenience and is required as a condition of your employment.

Finally, to claim any deductions for cellular phones or any other listed property, you must comply with the IRS's record-keeping requirements.

ALTERNATIVE MINIMUM TAX

When computing your alternative minimum tax (AMT), your depreciation deduction must be recomputed. You must use a modified version of the alternative depreciation method. Instead of the straight-line method, you generally use the 150-percent-declining-balance method for all property other than real property. For real property you continue to use the straight-line method; however, you must use a 40-year recovery period.

Keep in mind that these are general rules. If you made the election to use the alternative depreciation method as your regular depreciation method (an election discussed above), then you would not use the 150-percent-declining-balance method when computing your AMT. Likewise, if you elect to use one of the other depreciation methods discussed below, special rules apply to your AMT depreciation calculation.

For more on calculating your AMT see Chapter 20.

OTHER METHODS

There are two other depreciation methods available for personal property. First, you may elect to use the straight-line method over the regular recovery period for any or all classes of personal property. If you elect this method, then you don't use the 150-percent-declining-balance method when computing your AMT.

Second, you may elect to use the 150-percent-declining-balance method for regular tax purposes and switch to straight-line at some point; however, this method generally requires using longer recovery periods. As you recall, you must use the 150-percent-declining-balance method for AMT purposes. Therefore, you would have no difference between your regular and AMT depreciation.

⮞.𝒯ip

Why would you want to use one of these alternative depreciation methods? Many taxpayers just find the straight-line method easier to use. Other taxpayers may want to use the 150-percent-declining-balance method to compute personal property depreciation for their regular tax and for AMT. That way they do not have to make two calculations. Similarly, when you use the 40-year method for real property, you don't have to add back to your AMT income the difference between the depreciation write-offs you took over 27.5 years or 39 years and those you took over 40 years. (See Chapter 20 for more information on the AMT.)

QUESTIONS AND ANSWERS

Q.   My partner and I opened a flower shop on June 1, 1995. That same day we purchased a small van to make deliveries. We paid $10,000 for the van. Our partnership's tax year ends on December 31. May we claim the half-year convention?

A.   Your partnership was in business only seven months in 1995. In other words, you had a short taxable year, and the IRS has special rules for calculating depreciation in a short taxable year.

First, you do not use the half-year convention in the same way we described earlier. Instead, you compute your depreciation from a "deemed placed-in-service-date," which—for property subject to the half-year convention—is the midpoint of your short taxable year, or September 16, 1995.

You then allocate your annual depreciation amount over the number of months in your short taxable year, beginning with the deemed placed-in-service date.

Your depreciation deduction for the van adds up to $1,167. That is, the $10,000 purchase price divided by 5 years equals $2,000; $2,000 times 2 (for the 200-percent-double-declining-balance method) equals $4,000 (the first annual depreciation amount); $4,000 times 3.5/12 (because you allocate the annual amount over the number of months from the deemed placed-in-service date) equals $1,167.

For the 1996 taxable year you calculate your depreciation using either the allocation approach we just described or a simplified method. Under the allocation method, you take the remaining 8.5/12 of the $4,000 first annual depreciation amount, or $2,833, plus 3.5/12 of the second annual depreciation amount of $2,400 ($10,000 minus $4,000 equals $6,000; $6,000 divided by 5 times 2 equals $2,400), or $700. The result: $3,533.

Under the simplified method, you take your adjusted basis of $8,833 (that is, your cost of $10,000 minus 1995 depreciation of $1,167) and divide by 5 years, then multiply the result by 2 (for the 200-percent-declining balance method). The result is the same: $3,533.

Usually the two methods give you the same depreciation amount, with two exceptions: the year you sell the asset or in a second short year, when using the simplified method results in a smaller amount.

Note, however, that if you use your personal automobile in your trade or business, you may be subject to the limitations on luxury automobiles ("listed property") discussed earlier in this chapter.

Q.   I am employed by a large corporation. I bought a personal computer so that I can do some of my work at home. Am I entitled to a depreciation deduction?

A.   The law is strict when it comes to writing off computers. It allows you to claim a deduction for your computer only if it is required for your job. In other words, you must need the computer to perform your job properly. And it must be for the convenience of your employer, *not* for your convenience.

So if you have access to a computer at work, you will not be able to write off the cost of your home computer, even if you use it to do some work at home.

Another rule you should know, and this one applies to self-employed people as well: You may depreciate your computer using accelerated depreciation or claim the expensing allowance only if you use your computer more than 50 percent of the time for business.

What if you fail to meet the 50 percent test? The rules allow you to claim a depreciation deduction, but you must use the straight-line method, not the accelerated method. In addition, you may not opt for the expensing allowance.

Q.   I want to use the $17,500 expensing allowance. How do I go about it?

A.   You opt for the expensing allowance simply by taking it. You take your deduction for these expenditures—up to $17,500, of course—on Form 4562, the same form that you use to calculate and claim depreciation deductions.

Q.   My partner and I own a trucking company. This year we bought several open-road trucks. The total cost was $204,000. We decided to use the expensing allowance. I also own and operate a locksmith business, and I bought a

van this year for $15,000. May I claim the full $17,500 expensing allowance on the van in addition to the $17,500 our partnership claimed?

A.   No. The rules provide that a taxpayer may not claim an expense allowance of more than $17,500 in any single year.

In your situation, your partnership may claim an expense allowance of only $13,500—not $17,500. The reason? It purchased property that added up to more than $200,000—$204,000. (The $17,500 allowance was reduced by $4,000 to $13,500.)

Your half of the $13,500 expense allowance comes to $6,750. So you may claim an expense allowance of only $10,750 on the purchase of the van; that is, the $17,500 expense allowance ceiling less the $6,750 expense allowance from your partnership. You may depreciate the remaining cost of $4,250.

The partnership reports your share of the expense allowance on Schedule K-1, the same form that lists your share of income, losses, and credits from the partnership. You note the amount of the expense allowance reported on the Schedule K-1 on Form 4562, which you attach to your personal return.

Q.   I am a 50 percent partner in three separate partnerships. Each has elected to take the full $17,500 expensing allowance. My three K-1s show that I should report $26,250—$8,750 for each partnership. May I deduct this amount on my individual return?

A.   No, you may deduct only $17,500. The $17,500 expensing limitation applies both to the partnerships and to you individually. And you would permanently lose the additional $8,750 deduction.

If you are a partner in several partnerships and expect your total share of expensing allowances to exceed $17,500, voice your concerns to the general partners. That way one or more of the partnerships may decline to elect the expensing allowance, and you will not lose any of the deductions to which you are entitled.

Q.   We bought a new home, but we are holding on to our old one and plan to rent it. What depreciation period do we use?

A.   The length of time over which you depreciate your house depends on two factors: when you purchased your home and when you placed it in service as rental property.

If you bought your house after 1980 and you began renting in 1987 or later, you depreciate it over 27.5 years. But if you bought it before 1980 and began renting it after 1980, *you must follow the depreciation rules that were in place at the time of your purchase.*

Q.   We converted our house into rental property in a depressed market. What is the basis of the house for purposes of depreciating it as rental property?

A.   The IRS requires you to value your property at the lower of your cost basis or the fair market value when determining the amount of the annual depreciation. In a depressed market, you may have to depreciate the rental property using a value less than cost.

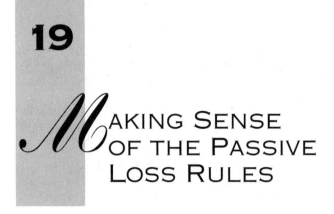

19

*M*AKING SENSE OF THE PASSIVE LOSS RULES

- How is a passive activity defined?
- What strategies help you avoid the passive loss rules?
- Are all rental investments passive activities?

Did you know that if you invest in an activity that generates losses, you may not be able to deduct those losses on your tax return? Special rules limit the amount of loss you can claim in a tax year if the losses are from *passive activities*. These rules aren't always easy to grasp. In this chapter we will define passive activities and examine the rules surrounding them.

WHO IS AFFECTED BY THE PASSIVE ACTIVITY RULES?

When our national legislators passed the law governing passive activities, their intent was to discourage tax shelters, but the rules went far beyond that simple goal.

The rules affect nearly every person engaged in business. If you're a shareholder in an S corporation, a shareholder in a closely held or personal service corporation, a self-employed person, a partner in a partnership, or a beneficiary of a trust or an estate, you can't ignore the potential impact of these rules.

You're also affected if you own rental real estate or rent out other types of property such as videotapes, hotel rooms, or tools. And as a result you may face burdensome restrictions and paperwork requirements.

WHAT'S A PASSIVE ACTIVITY?

In the eyes of the IRS a passive activity—subject to the rules we're about to discuss—is any trade or business activity in which you invest but aren't a material participant (i.e., are regularly, continuously, and substantially involved in its operations) or rental activities for most people. (See the discussions regarding rental activity exceptions below under "Rental Activity Exceptions" and "Special Rules for Real Estate Professionals.")

✿ CAUTION

Because limited partners almost never materially participate in managing the trade or business of the partnership, limited partnership investments are almost always passive.

Another important point is that passive activities can generate two kinds of income.

One is passive income, which is income from a trade or business or certain rental activities. The other is *portfolio income,* which includes interest, dividends, annuities, royalties, and so on. The law also says that income from personal services—that is, payment you receive for services rendered—and retirement plans is nonpassive income.

Although this might seem confusing at first, the character of the income is important. Why?

Passive activity losses may offset only passive activity income. Your passive losses may not reduce taxable income from nonpassive sources—salary or portfolio income, for instance.

◆ EXAMPLE

As a doctor in private practice you invest in a real estate limited partnership in 1994. In 1995 the partnership produces a $10,000 loss. Meanwhile, income from your medical practice adds up to $120,000, and your interest income from other investments is $5,000.

Because your real estate limited partnership is a passive investment, its resulting losses can't offset your nonpassive or portfolio income.

So your adjusted gross income (AGI) comes to $125,000.

WHAT'S PASSIVE WHEN IT COMES TO RENTAL ACTIVITIES?

Prior to 1994 the IRS considered all rental investments, with the exceptions discussed below, to be passive regardless of whether you materially participate.

After 1993, because of tax law changes, there is some relief from the passive loss rules for certain rental real estate activities for real estate professionals. Generally, these provisions aim to relieve the burden on real estate professionals hurt by the Tax Reform Act of 1986. These special rules are discussed later in this chapter.

Apart from these new special rules and the exceptions discussed below, passive rental activities include any investment that generates income from payments for the use of tangible property, rather than for personal services.

Included, then, are most real estate rentals, equipment leasing, and rentals of airplanes or boats—as long as no significant services (flying or fishing lessons, for example) are provided in making the property available to your customers.

RENTAL ACTIVITY EXCEPTIONS

The tax law provides several narrow exceptions to the passive activity rules for businesses whose main activity is renting either personal or real property.

✷ ℭAUTION

When your rental investment meets one of the exceptions, your income doesn't automatically escape passive characterization. Instead you determine whether you must treat your business as a passive activity by running through the material participation rules (described later in this chapter).

Exception 1—The Average Rental Period of Your Property Is Seven Days or Less.   You usually determine the average rental period by dividing the total number of days you have rented the property by the number of rental periods. (But the calculation becomes more complicated if you charge more rent for some units in the same complex—for example, you collect more for the handful of chalets nearest the slopes of your ski resort.)

A rental period is defined as a period during which a customer has a continuous or recurring right to use the property.

This exception exempts most hotels, motels, and bed and breakfasts from the rental property rules, as well as such businesses as short-term auto rentals, tuxedo rentals, and video cassette rentals.

Exception 2—The Average Rental Period Is 30 Days or Less and You or Someone You Hire Provides Significant Personal Services to Your Rental Customers.   Examples of rentals of this type include resort accommodations.

✷ ℭAUTION

Significant personal services do not include routine repair, maintenance, security, and trash collection services or services required for the lawful use of the property. In addition, significant personal services must be performed by individuals, so telephone and cable services don't qualify.

In determining what services are significant, the IRS takes into account all relevant facts and circumstances. These include the frequency of services provided, the type and amount of labor required to perform the services, and the value of the services relative to the amount charged for the use of the property.

Exception 3—Extraordinary Personal Services Are Provided by or on Behalf of the Owner of the Property without Regard to the Average

Period of Customer Use.   The IRS included this exception so that operations such as hospitals wouldn't be subject to the rental activity limitations.

What are extraordinary personal services? They're services provided in connection with a customer's use of the property, but the "rental" is incidental to the receipt of the services. For example, a patient in the hospital is renting the bed, but the bed rental is merely incidental to the major service of the visit, which is hospital care.

Exception 4—The Rental of the Property Is Treated as Incidental to a Nonrental Activity of the Taxpayer.   Take, for example, a developer who has constructed a condominium. During the marketing period some of the units are temporarily rented. Under these circumstances the rental won't be considered a rental activity. Note that the developer may of course also qualify for any of these exceptions or for the special rules for real estate professionals discussed below.

Exception 5—Property Is Customarily Made Available during Defined Business Hours for the Nonexclusive Use of Various Customers. A golf course, for example, might qualify under this exception. While golfers pay a fee to use the course, the course is available during defined business hours and for the nonexclusive use of various customers.

Exception 6—Property You Provide to a Partnership or S Corporation Isn't Rental Property if You Own an Interest in That Partnership or S Corporation.   This rule generally applies to any property you may own that you provide to your business. And it can include buildings and equipment.

SPECIAL RULES FOR REAL ESTATE PROFESSIONALS

Losses and credits from rental real estate activities in which the "real estate professional" materially participates are generally not subject to the passive loss limitations if certain eligibility requirements are met. These requirements focus on demonstrating "material involvement" in the real estate businesses for which you perform services, including minimum annual time commitments.

Generally, an individual is eligible for the real estate professionals exception if:

- More than half of all the personal services the individual performs during the year are for real property trades or businesses in which the individual materially participates *and*
- The individual performs more than 750 hours of service per year in those real estate activities.

A real property trade or business means any real property development, redevelopment, construction, reconstruction, acquisition, conversion, rental, operation, management, leasing, or brokerage trade or business.

◆ *Ĕ*XAMPLE

Jim spent 1,200 hours working as a self-employed real estate broker during the year and 800 hours employed as an insurance salesman. In addition, Jim spent 200 hours managing four houses that he rents and performs substantially all the services related to the management and maintenance of the houses. Jim suffered a $40,000 rental loss on the houses during the year.

Because Jim materially participated in real estate trades or businesses for more than 750 hours (in fact, 1,400 hours) and more than 50 percent of his time spent performing personal services was in real estate trades or businesses (1,400/2,200), Jim may deduct the full $40,000 loss related to the rental real estate activities.

✿ *Ĉ*AUTION

Personal services you perform as an employee are not treated as performed in a real property trade or business unless you own at least 5 percent of the business. And if you do not own at least 5 percent of the business, such services will effectively count against you in determining if more than 50 percent of your time was spent in real estate trades or businesses.

Material involvement or material participation has the same meaning as under the general passive loss rules discussed below (i.e., the taxpayer must be involved in the operations on a regular, continuous, and substantial basis). Also, as under the general rules, an interest as a limited partner in a limited partnership generally is not treated as an interest in which a taxpayer materially participates.

➘ *Ť*IP

This is a limited relief exception designed to be available only to real estate professionals. The passive loss limitations (discussed above) continue to apply to all other taxpayers.

✿ *Ĉ*AUTION

Because of the eligibility requirements that limit the availability of the relief, it may be difficult for many individuals not already qualifying to modify their circumstances sufficiently to become eligible.

The relief is available to married couples as long as one of the spouses separately satisfies the more-than-half and the more-than-750-hour service requirements. If at least one spouse meets these service requirements, the activities of either spouse or both spouses will count toward meeting the material participation requirement.

✦ℰXAMPLE

Tom is a 25 percent owner of a real estate brokerage business in which he worked as an employee for 900 hours during the year. Tom also worked as a bookkeeper for 600 hours. Tom's wife, Cindy, manages an apartment building she owns and spent 550 hours during the year managing the building. The apartment building suffers an $80,000 rental loss for the year. Since Tom materially participates in the real estate business for more than 750 hours *and* more than 50 percent of the personal services he performs are in real estate activities, all of the real estate losses from rental real estate activities of both Tom and Cindy in which either or both are considered to materially participate are deductible in full on their joint return. Thus, the $80,000 loss is deductible in full.

✪ ℭAUTION

Rental real estate losses are deductible only if at least one spouse materially participates in the activity. In the above example, if neither Tom nor Cindy materially participated in the operation of the apartment building, it would fall under the general rental real estate rules discussed earlier in the chapter (i.e., the loss would be passive).

PASSIVE TRADE OR BUSINESS

What constitutes an activity when it comes to your involvement in one or more trades or businesses?

The activity rules require you to first determine whether your involvement with numerous (or more than one) trades or businesses constitutes a single activity or multiple activities.

How do you determine whether these trades or businesses are a single activity or multiple activities?

Current rules call for the application of a so-called facts and circumstances test to identify and segregate businesses into separate activities.

To determine whether multiple trades or businesses qualify as a single activity or multiple activities, these five factors are given the greatest weight:

- Similarities and differences in the types of businesses.
- The extent of common control of the businesses.
- The extent of common ownership of the businesses.
- The geographic location of the businesses.
- The interdependencies of the businesses.

The interdependencies of the businesses can be based on the extent to which the businesses purchase or sell goods between or among themselves, involve products or services that are normally provided together, have the same customers, have the same employees, or are accounted for with a single set of books and records.

◆ℰXAMPLE

You own part of a bakery and part of a movie theater in Rochester, New York, and part of a bakery and part of a movie theater in Philadelphia. Depending on the relevant facts and circumstances, you may group all four businesses into a single activity, split them into two activities (i.e., a movie theater activity and a bakery activity, or a Rochester activity and a Philadelphia activity), or treat the businesses as four separate activities.

◆.𝒯IP

You can probably group these activities in a manner that is most advantageous to you as long as you can substantiate that the grouping is an appropriate economic unit. However, grouping a movie theater and a bakery together probably requires more interdependence than just location. If the businesses have the same customers or employees, or are accounted for with the same set of books and records, the argument that they comprise an appropriate economic unit will be easier to substantiate.

A few special rules apply. You can't group rental activities with nonrental activities, and you can't treat the rental of personal property and the rental of real property as a single activity (unless the personal property is provided in connection with the real property). There are exceptions to these special rules, so consult your tax adviser.

❂ 𝒞AUTION

Once you have grouped your businesses into activities, you must continue to use that grouping unless the original grouping was clearly inappropriate or there has been a material change in the facts and circumstances that makes the original grouping clearly inappropriate.

❂ 𝒞AUTION

If the IRS believes you grouped businesses in a way designed to sidestep the passive activity rules, the IRS may regroup them.

◆.𝒯IP

Since rental real estate is usually passive (subject to the aforementioned exceptions), it usually is desirable to treat each rental property as a separate activity. The reason? When it comes time to dispose of or sell the units, you can use all the suspended losses (losses greater than passive income) attributable to these units you've accumulated. The same is true, of course, with nonrental real estate activities. (We discuss the treatment of suspended losses later in this chapter.)

◆.𝒯IP

What if you dispose of substantially all of an activity? You may be able to treat the disposed portion as an activity separate from the portion you retained. Doing so may allow you to take additional deductions in the year of disposition for losses attributable to the disposed portion that were limited (suspended) by the passive activity rules in prior years.

MATERIAL PARTICIPATION

If you pass the *material participation* test, your trade or business (or your rental activity that fell into one of the exceptions) will not be classified as passive. You materially participate in a rental activity or a trade or business if you're involved in its operations on a "regular, substantial, and continuous basis."

The IRS has devised seven tests to help you determine whether you're a material participant in an activity. If your involvement satisfies just one of these, you're a material participant. If you don't satisfy any, your investment is passive.

Annual Material Participation Tests

1. More than 500 hours of participation.
2. Substantially all participation.
3. More than 100 hours of participation and not less than anyone else.
4. More than 500 hours worked in several activities with more than 100 hours in each.
5. Material participation in any 5 of the last 10 years.
6. For personal service businesses, material participation in any three previous years.
7. Facts and circumstances.

✪ *C*AUTION

It's not enough to satisfy one of the tests in just any one year. The IRS requires you to reevaluate your participation annually. You may be a material participant one year and a passive investor the next.

Test 1—More than 500 Hours of Participation.   If you spend more than 500 hours in an activity during the year, you're a material participant for the year. You may count any work that you do in connection with the activity, even if it is not the type of work normally done by owners, as long as it is not performed to circumvent the passive activity rules.

Moreover, say your spouse also performs the work of an owner or performs work not ordinarily done by an owner, but the work is not done to avoid the passive activity rules. You may add his or her participation to your own for purposes of this rule—and the other material participation tests outlined in this chapter.

➲·*T*IP

It doesn't matter that your spouse isn't a part owner of the business or whether the two of you file a joint return for the year. If the total hours the two of you worked tops 500, you meet the requirements of the first test, and your investment isn't subject to passive activity rules.

◆ ℰXAMPLE

Patrick and Meghan, a married couple, together put in more than 500 hours of work managing a restaurant that Meghan owns.

They meet the requirements of Test 1. But if Patrick's work had consisted of dishwashing, a job that owners don't usually perform, and the purpose of his taking on this task was to avoid the passive loss rules, his hours wouldn't count toward the 500-hour threshold.

✿ 𝒞AUTION

For purposes of all seven tests, you are not allowed to count the number of hours you spend in your capacity as an investor, unless you're directly involved in the day-to-day management of the business.

What's the role of investor? The IRS says it includes studying and reviewing financial statements, preparing or compiling summaries or analyses, or monitoring the finances or operations of the business in a nonmanagerial capacity.

Test 2—Substantially All Participation. If your participation, or the participation of you and your spouse, represents substantially all of the participation by anyone in an activity for the year, including nonowners, you're a material participant.

Test 3—More than 100 Hours of Participation and Not Less than Anyone Else. This test has two parts. First, you must spend more than 100 hours during the year operating the business. Second, you must spend more time than anyone else, including nonowners, working in the business.

Test 4—More than 500 Hours Worked in Several Activities with More than 100 Hours in Each. This test itself isn't complicated, but it can have unexpected consequences. The test says that if you spend more than 100 hours on each of two or more activities and a total of more than 500 on all of them, you're a material participant in each of those business ventures.

But that could be bad news. Why? Maybe you wanted one of the activities to give you passive income or losses.

◆ ℰXAMPLE

Joseph, a full-time attorney, invested in several real estate limited partnerships. He expects these investments to lose money for several years.

Joseph is also a general partner in two other, very profitable separate activities—an auto parts store and a dry cleaning business.

He spends about 300 hours per year in the auto parts store and about 250 hours per year in the dry cleaning business. Both businesses have several full-time employees.

Joseph hopes to write off the passive losses from his real estate investments against the income from the dry cleaning and auto parts businesses.

After all, he figures, he isn't involved in either of the businesses for more than 500 hours, and others spend more time than he does working there.

But Joseph has a problem. He has satisfied the fourth test since his participation in each of these businesses comes to more than 100 hours and his total participation tops 500 hours.

So, as far as the IRS is concerned, he's a material participant in both the auto parts store and the dry cleaning business. And the income from these businesses isn't passive. The result? Joseph can't use his passive real estate losses to offset the income from his two part-time businesses.

What if you invested in two businesses and both are posting a profit and your time spent on both of these activities doesn't exceed 500 hours? A special rule applies if you have profits.

If you participate 140 hours in one business and 160 hours in the other, under test 4, you aren't a material participant. But because of the special rule your profits aren't passive either. The IRS treats them as nonpassive income because you spent more than 100 hours participating in each business and the businesses were profitable, and you may not use these earnings to offset any of your passive losses.

What happens if, instead, the two businesses are operating in the red? You lose again because the losses will now be treated as passive losses.

Test 5—Material Participation in Any 5 of the Last 10 Years.

If you've been a material participant in a business for any 5 of the immediately preceding 10 years, the IRS considers you a material participant in the business for the current year—no matter how small your actual involvement.

This rule is designed to prevent people from shifting income from the passive to nonpassive category—or vice versa—just to reduce their tax liability. The following example shows how that tactic might work.

◆ *E*XAMPLE

Joe is the sole owner of Joe's Tool and Die, a very profitable sole proprietorship. He's also an investor in several real estate limited partnerships.

These limited partnerships produce sizable losses, which Joe wants to offset against the profits from his business.

Joe worked full-time in his business since he started it 10 years ago. But he has decided to reduce the amount of time he spends at the tool and die company beginning in the current year so he can pursue other opportunities.

Since Joe reduced his involvement, he thought his income from the business would be passive. Unfortunately, he meets the fifth test.

He has been a material participant in the business since he started it, or 9 out of the last 10 years. Consequently, even though he doesn't materially participate in the business currently, the IRS treats him as a material participant.

Test 6—For Personal Service Businesses, Material Participation in Any Three Previous Years.
Say you have materially participated in a

personal service business—law, engineering, accounting, architecture, health, consulting, performing arts, actuarial science, and so on—in any three preceding years. What are the tax consequences?

Under this test you're considered a material participant for the current year and into the future.

Therefore, once you've been a material participant in, for instance, an architectural firm for *any* three years, any income you receive from the firm in the future is nonpassive no matter how few hours you toil for the firm.

The IRS considers residual fees, for instance, that inactive partners might receive from a personal service firm as nonpassive income.

Test 7—Facts and Circumstances.   This test is easy to state, but difficult to apply. It says simply that the facts and circumstances in any specific case will be the final determinant of whether you are a material participant.

Unfortunately, the IRS hasn't issued much guidance on how it will look at facts and circumstances. Still, it does have a few guidelines.

First, you may not automatically add, as time spent in the business, the number of hours you devote to management. You may include your management hours only if no one else performs and gets paid for managing the business, and no one else spends more time than you managing the business.

Second, you must devote at least 100 hours to the business during the year to qualify under the facts and circumstances test.

If your participation comes to fewer than 100 hours, you're out of luck for this test—the tax law says you aren't a material participant in the business regardless of any other facts and circumstances.

❖ *Є*XAMPLE

> Assume you are the sole owner of a small company that provides word processing services. Your business is organized as an S corporation, and it is the only company in which you have an ownership interest. Your son works full-time for the business and is in charge of the day-to-day operations, but you are actively involved in consulting, arranging financing, and monitoring the corporation's financial success. You spend about 400 hours a year in these efforts. In fact, your financial analysis is used regularly in the actual decision-making process of the business. In 1995 your business reported a loss. Do you report this loss as a passive loss?
>
> The answer? It depends. You spent only 400 hours a year on the business—that is, you fail to meet the 500-hour material participation test.
>
> The only material participation test that you might pass is the facts and circumstances test. As mentioned above, the IRS has yet to issue guidance on what criteria would allow the losses to be treated as nonpassive for purposes of the facts and circumstances test.

➤.*Т*IP

> Although the law doesn't require it, anyone who anticipates that material participation could be an issue would be smart to keep a daily log of the hours he or she puts into a business. If the decision is a close call, the log could tip the balance.

LIMITED PARTNERS

What about limited partners? Can they materially participate in a business? Generally no, because state laws normally prohibit limited partners from being active in a business. And limited partners who do become active risk losing their limited liability.

Since limited partners do not normally participate in limited partnerships, the material participation tests don't apply.

Exceptions exist, though. The first exception deals with the first test, the 500-hour test. Even limited partners are material participants if they put 500 hours or more into the business.

The second exception relates to tests 5 and 6. If a limited partner meets either the any-5-of-10-years test or the any-3-previous-years test, he or she is a material participant regardless of the limited partner designation.

A third exception applies to people who are both general and limited partners in the same activity. The IRS considers them, on balance, to be general partners who must go back through tests 1 through 7 above to determine whether they are material participants.

LOSSES

Losses incurred in the current year from passive activities are good for offsetting your profits from other passive activities.

But what if you don't have profits from passive activities? You may carry your passive losses forward and use them to offset passive income in future years. The passive losses that you carry forward are called suspended losses. And you must keep track of suspended losses from each of your passive activities from year to year.

◆ℰXAMPLE

The year is 1995, and you have invested in three limited partnerships—A, B, and C. All these partnerships are passive investments and under the tests are considered separate activities.

Partnerships A and B each generate $10,000 in losses this year. But Partnership C rewards you with a $5,000 profit. In total, you lost $15,000 on passive investments— that is, $10,000 plus $10,000 (or $20,000) minus the $5,000 profit.

The passive loss rules won't allow you to deduct your $15,000 on your current tax return. So you carry forward the suspended loss to future years.

The losses from Partnerships A and B are used *pro rata*—meaning in proportion— against C's $5,000 passive income, resulting in $7,500 of suspended loss you can carry forward for each partnership, A and B.

To do the calculation: Multiply the suspended loss of $15,000 by the ratio of each partnership's loss to their total losses.

Partnership A's suspended loss is $7,500—that is, $10,000 (A's loss) divided by $20,000 (A's loss plus B's loss), or 0.5 times $15,000.

Now, say the year is 1996. Partnership A earns a $20,000 profit. Partnership B once again generates a $10,000 loss, and Partnership C posts another $5,000 profit. You have a net $15,000 profit for the year ($20,000 from A plus $5,000 from C minus $10,000 from B).

You carry forward your total $15,000 loss for 1995 from partnerships A and B and apply it against 1996's $15,000 profit. The result? You've reduced your income from passive investments in 1996 to zero.

You may carry forward these suspended passive investment losses indefinitely.

Moreover, when you sell a passive investment, the law allows you to use (deduct currently) all suspended losses from the activity you sold right away. You use these losses to offset not only your passive income but then any other income, including earned income, or wages, and portfolio income as well.

You add suspended losses from an activity you dispose of this year to any current losses from the same activity and any losses you recognize at the time you dispose of the activity. All these losses will be allowed in full, first as an offset against any net income or gain from all your other passive activities, then as an offset against any income including wages and portfolio income.

◆ EXAMPLE

The year is 1996 and you sell Partnership A (see above example) to your neighbor Lisa on June 30.

For the first six months of 1996, Partnership A produces income of $2,000, and when you sell, you realize a gain of $1,500. Partnerships B and C don't produce any income or loss during 1996. Your only other source of income: your $120,000 salary.

You may use all your suspended loss from Partnership A in 1996 to reduce your income. But you must determine the suspended losses you're allowed as follows:

- Start by adding the following: the amount of your suspended loss from the previous year (in your case, $7,500 from 1995); the amount of your loss from the current year (none); and the amount of loss you realize when you dispose of or sell the activity (none).

- Now subtract from the result your net income from all your passive activities (in your case, $3,500).

- You may use the resulting amount—$4,000 loss—to offset your salary.

What about the $7,500 suspended loss from Partnership B? It's still suspended and will carry forward to 1997. You may not deduct it in 1996 against your salary. The reason? You didn't dispose of your interest in B.

❍ CAUTION

What if selling your passive activity results in a loss and the passive activity was a capital asset? In this case the loss on the sale is treated both as a passive loss for purposes of the passive loss rules, including determining your passive loss limitation for the year, and as a capital loss subject to the capital loss rules, including determining the allowable capital loss deduction for the year. (See Chapter 14 for more information on capital losses.)

PASSIVE INCOME GENERATORS

If you have substantial passive losses from old tax shelter investments, consider investing in passive income generators, or PIGs.

A PIG may generate a positive cash flow as well as taxable passive income.

Among the more common types of PIGs are limited partnerships that operate ongoing, profitable businesses—a ski resort, golf course, or conference center, for example.

The benefit of these investments is that the income they generate is passive, and you may use your passive losses to offset this passive income.

How do you know which PIGs might make sense for your circumstances? First, many PIGs are syndicated—that is, they're offered to the public through public offerings—and are actively marketed by brokers. However, special rules may limit the benefits from such syndicated offerings. These rules are covered in the Questions and Answers section about master limited partnerships later in this chapter.

Once you've decided that a passive income generator may help you at tax time, compare a specific PIG to other investments and consider the investment merits of the PIG exclusive of any associated tax benefits.

Using the same methods, compare rates of return. Also take a look at how the deal and the promoter stack up against others in the same industry. Make sure to include in your analysis any fees that might be involved in buying or selling both investments.

If you're interested in investing in PIGs, you should have no trouble finding them. Your investment adviser, stockbroker, or financial planner will know the names of some of these partnerships. You may also run across names of PIGs in financial publications.

OTHER OPTIONS

Here's a useful strategy if you own a profitable corporation that isn't organized as a personal service corporation or an S corporation.

Transfer ownership of investments that generate passive losses to your corporation. The reason? The law allows a corporation to use passive losses to offset its regular business income, and it makes no difference if the corporation is closely held.

⊘ 𝒞AUTION

This strategy doesn't make sense if your passive investments generate income (not losses) currently or will do so in the not-so-distant future. That's because the income a corporation earns is taxed twice—once at the corporate level, then again when the income is passed along to you in the form of dividends.

Another drawback is that if the investment has phantom income, such income may be triggered upon transfer. We discuss phantom income in the Questions and Answers section later in this chapter.

⊙.🎵P

If you're the owner of a profitable corporation but don't materially participate in business operations, you may want to elect S corporation status.

Since you don't materially participate, your income from the S corporation is passive, and you can use your passive losses to offset profits from your S corporation.

Remember, you add together income and losses from all your passive investments. So if you find yourself locked into some older investments that you expect will generate passive losses, follow the obvious strategy: Invest in vehicles that generate passive income. You may then use this income to offset your losses.

✿ 🎵AUTION

Make sure your investments make economic sense apart from the tax benefits.

ACTIVE PARTICIPATION IN RENTAL REAL ESTATE ACTIVITIES

You may also qualify for a special exception designed to help the "moderate-income" taxpayer avoid the passive loss rules if the taxpayer does not otherwise qualify for the passive loss special rules for real estate professionals discussed above.

This exception allows you to deduct rental real estate losses of up to $25,000 from your regular income under three conditions: you meet certain income guidelines, you actively participate in the operation of your rental property, and you own at least 10 percent of the real estate.

As long as your adjusted gross income (AGI) is $100,000 or less—figured before you subtract any rental or passive losses—you may deduct from your ordinary income up to $25,000 in rental losses from residential or commercial rental property.

But you lose the deduction for part of the loss if your income falls between $100,000 and $150,000. You're not entitled to any deduction at all if your AGI tops $150,000.

What if your AGI is between $100,000 and $150,000?

You must reduce the $25,000 limit by 50 percent of the amount by which your AGI exceeds $100,000.

◆ XAMPLE

Your AGI comes to $140,000—that is, it tops $100,000 by $40,000. So you multiply 50 percent times $40,000 and subtract the result—$20,000—from $25,000. In your case you may deduct $5,000 in rental losses from your regular income—as long as you actively participate in managing the property and own at least 10 percent of it. What if your losses top $5,000? You treat the excess the same as you treat other passive losses (i.e., you may carry over the remainder as a suspended loss).

You should know, though, that this $25,000 limit applies in the aggregate to all your rental property. No matter how many rental buildings you own, the loss you claim, which offsets regular income, may not exceed the $25,000 total. There are no exceptions to this rule unless you qualify for the special rules for real estate professionals.

If you are married but file separately from your spouse, special rules apply to reduce the $25,000 limitation. (See your tax adviser if the reduced limitation may apply to you.)

GIFTS

When you give away an interest in a passive activity to a friend or relative, you lose your right—forever—to claim (deduct) suspended losses allocated to that interest. Instead, the recipient of your generosity must add these suspended losses to his or her basis—which is otherwise determined by reference to your basis—in the investment.

What if, later on, the recipient sells the investment at a loss? Then, for purposes of determining the donee's loss, his or her basis is limited to the fair market value of the interest on the date you made the gift.

So if the fair market value at the time of the gift is less than the donee's basis (including the suspended losses), part or all of the suspended loss will be lost forever as a deduction.

However, if the donee sells the investment at a gain, the fair market value of the interest on the date you made the gift is ignored. In this case the donee's gain will be figured using the donee's basis, which is determined by reference to the donor's basis and the donor's suspended losses.

◆ XAMPLE

Alex owns an interest in a limited partnership that he gifts to his sister Samantha. Alex had a basis of $1,000 and suspended losses related to the limited partnership of $5,000 on the date of the gift; thus, Samantha's basis is $6,000. The fair market value on the date of the gift is only $4,000. If Samantha later sells the interest for $3,000 (assuming no other activity that would have impacted Samantha's basis), the basis for determining her loss is limited to $4,000 (the fair market value on the date of the gift). Thus, $2,000 of Alex's original basis and suspended losses is lost forever.

However, if Samantha sells the interest for $7,000, the basis for determining her gain is $6,000. Thus, all of Alex's original basis and suspended losses are utilized, resulting in a $1,000 gain.

Moreover, sales you make to related parties—relatives, your closely held corporation, and so on—will also not let you immediately use your suspended losses. You carry forward the losses until the related party disposes of the investment in a taxable transaction, at which time you may deduct your suspended losses allocated to that investment.

◆ 𝓔XAMPLE

You sell your limited partnership interest to your father. You won't be able to use suspended losses from the partnership when you make the sale. Instead, you continue to carry these losses forward as suspended losses until your father sells the investment to an unrelated party, at which time you may deduct the suspended losses.

What if you generate passive income from other activities before your dad sells the investment? In that case you can use the suspended losses of the activity you sold your father to offset the passive income of the activities you still own.

INTEREST EXPENSES

The law says that if an investment is a passive activity, interest expense on loans associated with that activity isn't subject to the personal or investment interest limits.

You may write off such passive activity interest only to the extent of your passive activity income. If you report no passive activity income, you may not claim a deduction.

But you may carry forward your passive activity interest indefinitely. In other words, you may use the interest you carry forward to offset passive income in future years. And in the year you dispose of a passive activity, you may deduct all passive activity interest that you hadn't been able to deduct before. In essence this passive activity interest expense is treated just like it was a passive loss.

What does this rule mean? When you borrow money to purchase a passive activity, the interest expense is passive activity interest expense and is offset against your income or loss from the activity to determine your net passive income or loss from the activity.

The one exception to this rule: passive activities that report portfolio income, such as a real estate partnership that earns interest income on its excess cash reserves. In these cases you must classify a portion of your interest expense (to the extent of your portfolio income) as investment interest, and it is subject to the investment interest limits.

◆ *Ɛ*XAMPLE

You're a new limited partner in ABC Partnership in 1995. And for 1995, you have a passive loss before interest expense of $10,000. In addition, the ABC Partnership itself incurs $2,000 in interest expense (that is not incurred in its trade or business) allocable to you. ABC reports no portfolio income.

The partnership isn't required to treat any of its interest as investment interest. The entire $2,000 is added to your passive loss for the year. You don't need to treat this amount separately as investment interest on your return.

What if ABC did have portfolio income? In this case the partnership must trace the debt proceeds and allocate the interest expense accordingly. If all (or a portion) of the debt proceeds that generated the interest expense was used by ABC to purchase securities, all (or a portion) of the $2,000 of interest expense must be allocated to the portfolio income. ABC would then report this amount—to the extent of your portion of the portfolio income—as investment interest separately to you. And you would have to treat it as investment interest expense on your return.

What if you loan money to the partnership or it loans money to you? Proposed regulations would permit you to treat a portion of the interest income generated by such lending transactions as passive income, rather than portfolio income.

Usually, losses you take from your passive investments won't have an impact on your investment interest limitations. (See Chapter 5 for more information about interest deductions.)

CREDITS

The same rules that apply to passive losses apply to credits from passive activities. You may use tax credits passed along to you by passive investments only to offset the tax on the net income from your passive investments.

◆ *Ɛ*XAMPLE

You would owe $50,000 in tax if you disregarded your net passive income. But you would have to pay $80,000 if you took into account both your net passive income and your other taxable income.

So the amount of tax that you attribute to your passive income comes to $30,000, and you're allowed to take any credits from your passive investments that don't top $30,000.

This provision applies mostly to a tax shelter that passes along such tax credits as energy credits, rehabilitation credits, and research and development credits.

Like losses, you may carry forward suspended and unused credits to a future tax year. However—unlike losses—you can't use credits to offset tax on earned income and portfolio income when you sell your investment.

In these cases, however, you may increase your basis by the amount of any suspended credit to the extent of the original basis adjustment before you sell. Basis adjustments were required, for example, when claiming the rehabilitation tax credit. This provision gives you a lower gain or higher loss when you sell your property. You may no longer carry forward the suspended credit to offset tax on passive income.

QUESTIONS AND ANSWERS

Q.   Last year I invested in a building, and this year I lost my only tenant. It is virtually impossible for me to sell the building or convert it for use by someone else. Is there some way I can dispose of it so I don't have to treat my loss for the year as passive?

A.   Yes, you can abandon the property. The law also considers so-called abandonments as dispositions that let you escape the passive loss limitations. So you may claim your entire loss in the current year. The law can be tricky, though, when it comes to abandoning property. If you plan to go this route, consult your tax adviser beforehand.

Also, if you abandon your building, the suspended loss rules let you take all the losses you have been carrying forward in the year the abandonment occurs.

How do you abandon an investment?

Your building is considered abandoned if you can prove that you originally had a profit motive for investing in the building, and the property became useless. You must also show that you have permanently deserted the building and discontinued trying to rent or sell it.

Just not using the building—or a decline in its value—isn't conclusive evidence that you have abandoned your property. You must show that you have actually forsaken it. For example, the IRS would consider cutting off utilities, boarding up windows, and canceling insurance as proof of abandonment.

Q.   My accountant says I should look into "paired investments." What are these vehicles, and are they appropriate for me?

A.   Only you can decide whether an investment is right for your circumstances, but paired investments do hold appeal for many investors.

What are they? As their name implies, they are limited partnerships with two distinct businesses. One business generates income and, hopefully, cash. The other business generates losses—at least for tax purposes—to offset that income.

Paired investments are just another variation on the tax shelter theme. Therefore, invest in one of these vehicles only if it makes economic sense.

Q.   I owned a limited partnership interest in a piece of rental real estate. We sold out in 1985 on an installment-sale basis, and I am still receiving income. Is this income passive?

A. The answer is yes. The tax law treats the income as passive, even if the passive loss rules weren't in place when you sold your partnership. However, any interest income received would be treated as portfolio and not passive income.

Q. I have heard about master limited partnerships or publicly traded partnerships. How do I treat income and losses from these partnerships for tax purposes?

A. Interests in master limited partnerships—that is, MLPs or publicly traded partnerships—are traded on public exchanges, just like shares of stock. So they're much more marketable and much more liquid than other types of partnerships.

Originally, these publicly traded partnerships were thought to provide passive income to investors with passive activity losses. These investors could then use the losses to offset their income. The partnerships came under congressional scrutiny, not only because they offered this opportunity to save on taxes, but also because they paid no tax and had characteristics of a publicly traded corporation. Instead, the individual partners paid tax on their share of any profit.

Unfortunately, as a result of subsequent congressional action, net income from publicly traded partnerships is treated in a similar manner as portfolio income. That means you may not use this income to offset passive losses from other investments.

What's worse, losses from publicly traded partnerships are treated as suspended losses, and you may subtract these losses only from net income from the partnerships. But you may claim any unused suspended losses when you dispose of your interest in the partnership.

Moreover, the IRS taxes publicly traded partnerships formed after December 17, 1987 as corporations. So profits and losses no longer flow through to the partners.

There is, however, an exception to the corporate treatment rules. If 90 percent of the partnership's gross income comes from interest, dividends, real estate rents, gains from the sale of capital assets, income or gains from certain oil and gas activities, and gains from the sale of certain trade or business assets, the IRS will still treat the MLP as a partnership.

Q. Given the dramatic change in the tax-shelter rules, does it still make sense to highly leverage my investments?

A. Generally, no.

It used to make sense to leverage your deal to the greatest extent you could. It paid to borrow as much money as possible because you could obtain significant deductions with only a minimal cash investment. Also, you could deduct fully the interest you paid on any borrowed funds.

Now, however, you may want to minimize leverage in your passive investments to reduce your interest expense. When you do minimize leverage and cut your interest expense, you may end up creating passive income or perhaps even breaking even in operations or at least reducing your passive losses.

Also, it's possible that your investment will produce positive cash flow in excess of the passive income. This can happen as a result of noncash deductions, such as depreciation and depletion, that don't require a cash expenditure.

Q.   I invested in an oil and gas limited partnership and sold it at a loss. If this loss is a capital loss, how is it treated for tax purposes?

A.   The capital loss rules take precedence over the passive loss rules in determining what losses you may take on your return when you sell your passive investment. (See Chapter 14 for a discussion of capital gains and losses.)

Let's say that you sell your entire interest in your oil and gas limited partnership in 1995. As a result, you have a $10,000 long-term capital loss. Your investment also produced $5,000 of suspended passive losses in prior years. And in 1995, your investment brings you $3,000 in passive income. You have no other capital gains or losses.

The law allows you to claim only $3,000 in capital losses in one year. You must carry forward any remaining losses. So the long-term capital loss you deduct in 1995 is $3,000, and the capital loss you carry forward adds up to $7,000.

But you may also claim in 1995 your $5,000 in suspended passive losses. And this $5,000 offsets the $3,000 in income you realize in 1995 from your partnership. Moreover, you may use the remaining $2,000 in losses to offset your wages or portfolio income. The reason: You have disposed of your passive investment.

Q.   What is phantom income?

A.   In the past, tax shelters were structured so that investors could deduct tax losses in the early years of ownership. But these deductions usually diminished over time, and at some point in the future the shelter often began producing income. But usually this income was not accompanied by any cash, so the income was effectively only a paper profit. Paper profit not accompanied by cash became known as "phantom income."

A shelter that generates no further losses and may produce taxable income but doesn't generate cash (i.e., a shelter that produces phantom income) is known in investment circles as a "burned-out" shelter. Although the phantom income generated by this burned-out shelter usually occurs when you sell or dispose of the shelter, you must report on your return an amount of income on the sale or disposition that exceeds—often by a considerable amount—the sales proceeds you actually receive. In other words, the phantom income effectively represents a "reversal" of those tax-shelter deductions you took in prior years.

Phantom income from a passive activity is, in fact, passive income. If you find yourself with a burned-out shelter producing phantom taxable income, consider a new investment that generates passive losses to offset the phantom income, if you have no other passive losses to offset the phantom income. But make sure any new investment makes economic sense apart from the tax benefit.

Also consider selling the investment, but be aware that you'll usually have to sell at a deep discount. And besides incurring a discount on the sale, disposing of the investment itself usually creates taxable—and phantom—income for you as noted.

Selling the shelter, however, may help you minimize the amount of phantom income that you'll have to report on your tax return.

Q.   I own some rental property that I actively participate in managing, but I don't qualify for the exception for real estate professionals. Now I am thinking about investing as a limited partner in a rehabilitation deal. May I claim both losses up to $25,000 from my rental property and the credit equivalent of $25,000 from the rehabilitation partnership?

A.   Unfortunately, the answer is no. You may deduct from your ordinary income no more than $25,000 a year in combined losses from rental real estate and credit equivalents. How do you calculate how much you may write off?

Here is an example. Say you report a $25,000 loss from an apartment building you manage yourself. You post a loss of $5,000 from a real estate limited partnership, but you record a $15,000 gain from a research and development limited partnership.

The rules require you first to count up all your losses from rental properties in which you actively participate; in your case, the total comes to $25,000. Then you add up any profits and subtract your losses from your profits. Since you posted no profits, you are left with a $25,000 loss.

Next, you add up your gains from passive investments: $15,000 in your case. Then you subtract your losses from passive activities: $5,000. The result: $10,000 is your net passive income.

Now subtract your $25,000 of rental losses from your $10,000 of passive income. The result—$15,000 loss—is the amount you may write off on your return as a rental loss. But remember: You may deduct rental losses up to $25,000. So if you also invest in a rehabilitation partnership, you may write off as much as $10,000 in credit equivalents.

Q.   I am in the situation you describe above, but I have exhausted the $25,000 limit and still have losses and credit equivalents left. What do I do?

A.   You may carry these losses and credit equivalents forward for use in future years. But even then you are subject to all the limits we described earlier, including the $25,000 ceiling on rental losses.

Q.   I subtracted my passive losses from my passive income, and I came out $23,000 in the red. I also have a loss of $2,000 from my rental property in which I actively participate. May I deduct this entire $25,000 loss from my regular income?

A.   No. The rules say you may deduct passive losses only from passive income. You subtracted your passive losses from your passive income and you are still $23,000 in the red.

But the news is not all bad. You may carry forward this loss to future years. And you may deduct your $2,000 rental loss, as long as your AGI falls within the limits we have described.

However, if you demonstrate material involvement as a real estate professional, you will be able to fully deduct these losses.

Q.   I own a condo—part of a 200-unit complex—in Denver. It is a full-service building, with a housekeeping staff and a switchboard. Each year I

put my unit in a rental pool that rents the condos by the week. A team of employees hired by our management group takes care of advertising, renting, and maintaining the units. And I limit my personal use of my condo to 14 days. What rules apply to my situation?

A.   The tax law does not consider your condo a rental unit for purposes of the $25,000 rental exception to the passive loss rules. The IRS would view your condo as a hotel or motel.

Why? You rent your unit to "transients," that is, people who stay in a place for fewer than 30 days. Moreover, your association provides "significant services," among them maid service and a telephone switchboard.

But even if your condo did qualify as a rental unit, you would fail the "active participation" test. The reason: Your management group runs the rental operation and makes the final decisions.

So you are only a "passive" investor. And any loss you post is subject to the passive loss rules—that is, you may deduct these losses only against passive income.

20

CALCULATING THE ALTERNATIVE MINIMUM TAX

- What is the alternative minimum tax (AMT)?
- Does the AMT impact other tax years?
- Are there strategies to avoid or minimize AMT liability?

Through the use of deductions, deferrals, and credits, you may reduce the tax bite on even a substantial income to a relatively small number. However, you should be aware of a separate tax system called the *alternative minimum tax*, or AMT for short. The idea behind the AMT is that no matter how successful you are at cutting your tax bill, the IRS is still going to see to it that you pay your fair share.

As noted, the AMT is a tax system separate from the regular tax system. First you calculate your tax under the regular system. Then you calculate it under the AMT system.

You compare the two results and pay the higher one. Not everyone is required to pay the AMT, but if you have claimed many deductions in the categories listed below, you may be an AMT candidate:

- State and local real estate taxes, income taxes, and personal property taxes.
- Passive investments, such as oil and gas limited partnerships, and real estate.
- Interest on a refinanced mortgage if the amount refinanced is greater than your original mortgage (interest on the excess amount over your original debt).
- Home equity interest (where the loan proceeds are not used to improve your home).
- Miscellaneous deductions.

Other circumstances may also make you liable for the AMT. For example, you may have exercised incentive stock options (ISOs) or invested in what are known as *private-activity bonds.* (State and local governments issue these bonds to raise money for private purposes.)

♻ *C*AUTION

If you just can't tell whether you will be subject to the AMT, there is only one way to know for sure. You must "run the numbers."

This chapter discusses the AMT in four steps:

Step 1: Determining income subject to the AMT.
Step 2: Explaining an exemption that may help you offset some AMT taxable income.
Step 3: Understanding tentative minimum tax and the minimum tax credit.
Step 4: Providing strategies to minimize the AMT.

STEP 1: AMT INCOME

The first step is to calculate exactly how much of your income may be subject to the AMT. This amount is called alternative minimum taxable income, or AMTI. To begin, take your regular taxable income and make the following adjustments.

STANDARD DEDUCTION AND PERSONAL EXEMPTIONS

The AMT rules do not allow you to claim the standard deduction—the one taxpayers claim who don't itemize. Nor may you take the deduction for personal exemptions. So you must add these items back.

ITEMIZED DEDUCTIONS

The regular tax system allows for many itemized deductions that the AMT prohibits. Therefore, when calculating your AMTI, you must add most of these deductions back to your regular taxable income. The items you must add back are:

- Real estate and personal property taxes,
- State and local income taxes, *and*
- Medical expenses that total less than 10 percent of your AGI. (As you may recall, for regular tax purposes, you may deduct medical expenses that exceed 7.5 percent of your AGI.)

In addition to these items, you must add back those other miscellaneous deductions—professional dues and tax preparation fees, for instance—

that you deducted under the regular tax system.

The law does allow some itemized deductions. You may continue to deduct under the AMT:

- Investment interest that does not exceed your investment income and home mortgage interest (however, see below for deductibility of interest on a refinanced mortgage or home-equity loan),
- Charitable contributions,
- Casualty losses,
- Gambling losses, *and* certain other miscellaneous itemized deductions not subject to the 2 percent limitation.

➤.☂TIP

Keep in mind that although you may not deduct any investment interest in excess of investment income, you may still get a benefit when it comes to investment interest expense. You may carry forward indefinitely, until you use it up, any of this expense that you're unable to use for AMT purposes in the current tax year.

Also, the rules are different when it comes to interest you incur when you refinance your home mortgage. Under the AMT you may deduct interest only on that part of the refinanced mortgage that does not exceed your outstanding mortgage before you refinance.

✪ ☂AUTION

If you take out a home-equity loan to avoid the rules that prohibit deducting personal interest, the AMT rules may prohibit you from deducting this interest. You usually may not deduct interest on home-equity loans for AMT purposes. (See Chapter 5 for the rules on deducting interest.)

➤.☂TIP

However, as noted earlier, the law does allow for an exception to this rule. If you use the money you receive from the home-equity loan to pay for major home improvements or renovation, the interest is deductible for AMT purposes.

Of course, if you use the proceeds of a home-equity loan (or any other loan for that matter) for investment purposes, the interest may be deductible as investment interest (see above). And any interest attributable to a loan used for business purposes—whether a home-equity loan or otherwise—is deductible for AMT purposes as business interest.

✪ ☂AUTION

If you buy a luxury boat, and it qualifies as a second home, the interest on the money you borrow to purchase the boat is deductible under the regular tax system. However, you may not deduct this amount under the AMT system because, according to the AMT rules, a boat doesn't qualify as a second home. However, if the boat is your principal residence (i.e., not a second home), the interest is deductible for AMT purposes.

➲.𝒯ɪP

Due to recent tax law changes, a deduction is now allowed for both regular tax and AMT purposes for charitable contributions of appreciated capital gain property equal to the fair market value of the contributed property.

➲.𝒯ɪP

The 3 percent floor on itemized deductions discussed in Chapter 4 does not apply for AMT purposes. Therefore, all itemized deductions allowable for AMT purposes—for example, cash contributions to charity—are fully deductible.

PASSIVE ACTIVITIES

Passive activities come in many forms. Investments in limited partnerships or certain taxpayer rental properties are considered to be *passive investments*. (See Chapter 19 for more information on passive activities.)

The IRS considers any investment passive if it constitutes a trade or business in which you do not materially participate.

Under the passive activity rules (which are generally the same for both regular tax purposes and AMT purposes), you can deduct losses from passive activities only to the extent you have income from other passive activities. You may carry any nondeductible losses forward to future years and use them to offset future years' passive income.

Only in the year you sell or otherwise dispose of your interest in the passive activity will the losses you've carried forward be deductible against other income (for example, wages, interest, and dividends). In addition, any loss you may incur when you dispose of the interest is similarly deductible in the year of the disposition.

✪ 𝒞AUTION

It is important to realize that the loss you may have from a passive activity that is deductible for regular tax purposes is not necessarily the same as the loss that is deductible for AMT purposes.

Why? You may write off some items, such as depreciation deductions, faster for regular tax purposes than for AMT purposes.

✦𝒞XAMPLE

You invested in a real estate limited partnership that you do not materially participate in that produces a regular tax loss of $800 in 1995. Because you have no other passive income, you won't be able to deduct the passive loss for regular tax purposes.

Some of the $800 loss occurred because the property owned by the partnership was depreciated using an accelerated method. The AMT rules say that you may depreciate property using only the straight-line method, which gives you a lower depreciation deduction in the early years that the property is owned.

The partnership recalculates its depreciation deductions for AMT purposes. Instead of the $800 loss reported to you for regular tax purposes, it reports $200 of income for AMT purposes.

You would also have an $800 passive loss carryover from 1995 for regular tax purposes, but no AMT passive loss carryover.

STOCK OPTIONS

The big advantage of incentive stock options (ISOs)—options granted to an employee by his or her employer to buy company stock—is that when you exercise them, you usually pay less for the stock—sometimes much less—than the stock's fair market value. According to the tax code, this difference between the price you pay and the stock's fair market value— the "bargain element"—is not subject to regular tax. However, the difference is treated as an "adjustment" for the AMT.

An adjustment is an item that receives *different* tax treatment under the regular tax rules than under the AMT rules. It is similar to an AMT "preference." A preference is an item that usually receives *favorable* tax treatment under regular tax rules, but not under AMT rules.

In the year you exercise your options, you are generally required to add back the bargain element to your AMT income. The difference also becomes part of your stock's cost basis for AMT purposes. Therefore, when you finally sell the stock, your gain—for AMT purposes—is less than for regular tax purposes.

◆ *E*XAMPLE

In 1986 your company granted you 1,000 ISOs at an option price of $11. You exercise the options early in 1995. The fair market value of the stock when you buy it comes to $61 a share. So for AMT purposes you have a tax "preference" of $50,000—the difference between the option price ($11,000) and the fair market value ($61,000). By late 1996, you're ready to sell the 1,000 shares, which you do for $71 a share. Your gain for regular tax purposes totals $60,000—an amount equal to $71,000 less your option price of $11,000.

But you face a different situation for AMT purposes. Here your gain totals only $10,000—$71,000 less your AMT basis for the shares, $61,000 (the $11,000 option price plus the $50,000 bargain element you had to add to your AMT income in 1995).

When you calculate your AMT income in 1996, you subtract the $50,000 difference in the gain for an AMT gain of $10,000.

◈ *T*IP

You should never put regular tax or AMT considerations before economic considerations when it comes to investment decisions. If it makes economic sense to exercise your options now, then you should exercise them.

DEPRECIATION

You must adjust (either increase or decrease) your income for AMT purposes for the difference between the depreciation you claimed for regular tax purposes and depreciation you calculated using the alternative method of depreciation. (See Chapter 18 for calculation of depreciation for AMT purposes.)

❖*E*XAMPLE

In January 1993 you bought the land and building where you have an office. The price came to $125,000. You allocate $100,000 to the cost of the building and $25,000 to the cost of the land.

When you file your 1995 return, you write off depreciation for the building using the straight-line method over 31.5 years. In 1995, your depreciation deduction is $3,175.

For AMT purposes you depreciate the building under the alternative method. Under this method you depreciate real property (the building) using the straight-line method over 40, not 31.5, years. So your depreciation deduction is $2,500. The difference between the two methods—the amount you must add back to your income for AMT purposes—totals $675.

Assume that 32 years have gone by, you are still the owner of the building, and you've fully depreciated it for regular tax purposes.

Under the AMT rules you may still deduct $2,500 each year in years 33 through 40. You no longer must add back depreciation; instead, you are allowed to claim an additional deduction from your AMT income.

❖*C*AUTION

There is one exception to this rule. It applies to real property placed in service before 1987. In calculating your AMT, you must add back to your regular taxable income the excess of the depreciation you claimed using the accelerated method over the old straight-line depreciation. However, you are not allowed later to subtract the difference between the straight-line method and accelerated depreciation.

OTHER PREFERENCE AND ADJUSTMENT ITEMS

A number of other *preference* and *adjustment items* apply to the AMT.

Interest on Tax-exempt, "Private-Activity" Bonds Issued by State and Local Governments after August 7, 1986. You pay no tax on the income you collect from these bonds under the regular tax system. But you may have to pay tax under the AMT. However, the AMT rules let you write off interest expense you incur to buy these bonds to the extent of your tax-exempt income generated by these bonds. The regular tax rules, by contrast, do not let you deduct this interest.

Excess Intangible Drilling Costs that Total More than 65 Percent of the Net Income from Productive Oil and Gas Wells. The adjustments you must make when you own shares in oil and gas partnerships are quite complicated, so we strongly advise you to consult with your tax adviser if these are part of your investment portfolio.

Research and Experimental Expenditures.   For purposes of the regular tax system, you may write off these expenses in the year you incur them. The AMT rules, however, require you to capitalize the R&E expenses—that is, deduct them over several years. In this case you must deduct them over 10 years.

You deduct 10 percent of the R&E costs each year of the 10-year period. This holds true even though you already deducted them in full for regular tax purposes.

⊘.𝒯ıᴘ

You may avoid treating R&E expenses as an adjustment item by amortizing all or a portion of them for regular tax purposes and deducting them over 10 years.

This strategy, of course, is far from perfect. When you employ it, you get a much smaller deduction each year for regular tax purposes. Therefore, you should run the numbers to see which method of treating these costs saves you the most tax.

Now you've made all the adjustments to your regular taxable income and accounted for all tax preference items. The result is your AMT income, or AMTI.

STEP 2: EXEMPTIONS

Fortunately, the law allows you to reduce your AMTI by these exemptions:

- $45,000 for married taxpayers filing a joint return,
- $33,750 for single taxpayers, *and*
- $22,500 for married taxpayers filing separate returns.

⊘ 𝒞ᴀᴜᴛɪᴏɴ

However, you may have to reduce your exemption if your AMTI is high. You reduce it by 25 percent of the amount by which your AMT income exceeds:

- $150,000 for married taxpayers filing jointly.
- $112,500 for single filers.
- $75,000 for married taxpayers filing separately.

 Therefore, you will not be allowed any exemption if you and your spouse file jointly and your AMTI exceeds $330,000. As a single taxpayer your ceiling comes to $247,500.

❖ EXAMPLE

You and your spouse file jointly and your AMTI comes to $213,725, well over the $150,000 threshold for married taxpayers filing jointly.

So you must take your AMTI of $213,725 and subtract $150,000. The answer: $63,725. Then multiply this amount by 25 percent. The result comes to $15,931. Next, subtract $15,931 from the $45,000 AMT exemption to arrive at $29,069. So your exemption falls from $45,000 to $29,069.

STEP 3: TMT AND MTC

TENTATIVE MINIMUM TAX

The AMT calculations are almost finished. So far, you've figured out your AMTI and adjusted it by the appropriate exemption amount. To compute your alternative minimum tax, simply take your adjusted AMTI and multiply it by the AMT tax rate of 26 percent for adjusted AMTI up to $175,000, and 28 percent for adjusted AMTI in excess of $175,000. The result you obtain—after you subtract any foreign tax credits the law allows, recomputed for AMT purposes—is your tentative minimum tax (TMT).

Now compare your TMT to your regular income tax. (Again, first take any allowable foreign tax credits.) If your TMT is larger than your regular tax, you must pay the difference—the AMT—in addition to your regular tax.

MINIMUM TAX CREDIT

You must also calculate what's known as the *minimum tax credit* (MTC). The MTC is a credit for taxes you paid earlier under the AMT system that you would not have paid under the regular tax system.

The reason for this credit is that some of your AMT liability may be the result of the AMT accelerating certain income. In other words, the AMT rules sometimes require you to report income before you would have to for regular tax purposes. One example is paper profits you "realize" when you exercise ISOs.

Since, under the AMT system, you pay taxes on this income earlier than you otherwise would under the regular system, you have already paid a portion of your regular tax liability. In a later year the MTC can reduce your regular tax liability by the amount of AMT taxes you paid in prior years.

In computing your AMT income you've made adjustments to your regular taxable income that fall into one of two categories:

- Deferral items, or
- Exclusion items.

What's the difference?

Deferral items, as the name suggests, will not reduce the amount of regular tax you owe permanently. They only defer your tax liability until later.

Exclusion items are AMT preferences and adjustments for which you never have to pay regular taxes that you attribute to these items. Exclusion items are the following:

- Standard deduction.
- Personal exemptions.
- Medical and dental expenses.
- Miscellaneous itemized deductions.
- Taxes.
- Interest expense.
- Depletion.
- Tax-exempt interest.
- Gains on the sale of certain small business stock.

Everything else counts as a deferral item (e.g., an incentive stock option "bargain element" when exercised).

To calculate your MTC, you must recalculate your AMT using only the exclusion items listed above. Your MTC equals the difference between this adjusted AMT and the AMT calculated using both the exclusion and deferral items (limited, of course, to the total AMT you paid for the year). In other words, your MTC is the amount of AMT attributable to deferral items only.

You may carry this credit forward indefinitely (although you may not carry it back) to offset your regular tax liabilities in the future. You may reduce your regular tax, however, only by the amount that it exceeds the TMT in the year you carry forward the MTC.

◆ *Ɛ*XAMPLE

In 1994 you pay $16,000 in AMT. The entire amount you pay results from your exercising incentive stock options, which count as a deferral tax item. So the $16,000 now qualifies as your MTC carryover.

In 1995 your regular tax liability is $61,000 and your TMT is $59,000. Therefore, you may use $2,000 of that $16,000 MTC carryover from 1994 to reduce your 1995 tax payment.

If you must pay the AMT year after year or your AMT liability and your regular tax bill are similar, the minimum tax credit doesn't help you much at all.

STEP 4: STRATEGIES

It is important to think about both short-term and long-term strategies when you plan for the AMT. Your short-term strategies should involve accelerating or deferring income and deductions. But you must also consider the impact of the minimum tax credit. For your long-range planning you must focus on the kinds of investments you make.

◈ *E*XAMPLE

Over the last five years you've invested heavily in real estate limited partnerships. In fact, these are practically your only investments. You suspect you may have to pay the AMT either this year or in future years. What should you do? It may make sense for you to shift your money into corporate bonds, say, or stocks or mutual funds. The reason? These investments don't have any effect on the AMT.

➤.*T*IP

In the realm of long-range planning: Focus on the kind of tax treatment you elect for rental property and other depreciable assets. You may choose, for regular tax purposes, the longer alternative method of depreciation. If you do, you won't be required to add to your AMT income the difference between accelerated depreciation and alternative depreciation.

Of course, you may not have this opportunity when it comes to AMT adjustments and preferences from limited partnership investments. With these investments, you usually don't have much influence over decisions.

➤.*T*IP

You should always be aware that you may be liable for the AMT. Then run the numbers each and every year.

You should also project your tax situation two years out. That's because the actions you take this year affect your AMT situation next year. Obviously, making these calculations can be burdensome.

Remember, you can't wait to worry about the AMT until you're ready to send in your tax return. The rules say that you must pay certain amounts to the IRS through withholding and estimated tax payments. You may have to pay more in estimated taxes if you're subject to the AMT. (See Chapter 26.)

QUESTIONS AND ANSWERS

Q.   Let's say I sell property I placed in service in 1993. Will I have the same gain or loss for regular tax purposes and for the AMT?

A.   No. You are depreciating your property by a different method for the AMT. So you end up with a different AMT basis—that is, your adjusted cost or your cost less depreciation—which, in turn, affects your gain or loss.

Consider this example. Say you purchased a building on May 1, 1993, for $200,000. You sell it on June 1, 1995, for $250,000. For regular tax purposes your depreciation deductions for 1993, 1994, and 1995 amount to $13,227. For the AMT, however, your depreciation deductions total $10,417.

So your basis for the regular tax system is equal to $200,000 minus $13,227 of depreciation deductions, or $186,773, and your gain comes to $63,227. But your basis for AMT purposes totals $200,000 minus $10,417, or $189,583.

So your AMT gain comes to $60,417. And your AMTI is reduced by $2,810—the difference between $63,227 and $60,417—in 1995.

Q.   I overpaid my state income taxes in 1994 and received a refund in 1995. I know I have to report my refund as income for regular tax purposes in 1995 since I took the deduction in 1994. But how do I treat it for AMT purposes?

A.   As we've seen, the tax law will not allow you to deduct state and local income tax payments for AMT purposes. Accordingly, you don't have to report any state and local tax refunds as income when you calculate your AMTI.

Q.   I've run the numbers for 1995 and 1996. It looks like I'm subject to the AMT in 1995 but not in 1996. What is the best course of action for me?

A.   At a minimum you want to make sure you calculate your 1995 MTC so you know what amount is available to offset your regular tax in 1996. As we've seen, MTC is generated only by deferral items.

Run the numbers. Ask your tax adviser to help you divide your deductions into two categories: deferral items and exclusion items.

One strategy to consider is to postpone until 1996 paying expenses that you may claim as deductions. If you pay these expenses in 1995, you may get a smaller tax benefit if the item was deductible for AMT purposes (for example, charitable contributions). Or you could waste potential deductions if the items weren't deductible at all for AMT purposes (for example, state and local taxes).

Alternatively, try accelerating income into 1995 since it may be taxed lower under AMT than it would in 1996 under the regular tax rates; for example, take your bonus this year rather than next. Be aware, however, that each of these strategies must take into account the impact on, and the effect of, your MTC. In fact, these strategies *may* not save you any tax in the long run. So remember to project your regular tax and AMT situation at least two years out—and always consider the MTC consequences.

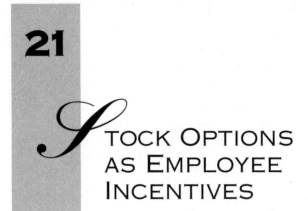

21

$\mathscr{S}$TOCK OPTIONS AS EMPLOYEE INCENTIVES

- What are the tax consequences of stock options?
- How do the rules affect the use of incentive stock options (ISOs)?
- How are stock appreciation rights (SARs) taxed?

It would be hard to imagine better business recruiting and retention tools than *stock options* and *stock appreciation rights.*

Both let employees share in the success of their employer, and from the company's perspective both boost employees' incentive to work for that success.

Some companies restrict options to top executives. Others spread this benefit down the line. Often, options are a negotiable part of a total compensation package.

You can use stock options and stock appreciation rights to your best advantage if you understand the tax rules that govern them. These rules are not difficult, but you have choices to make. This chapter helps you understand these rules so you can make those choices on a more informed basis.

HOW OPTIONS WORK

When your employer grants you a stock option, you've gained the right to purchase a specific number of shares of your company's stock at a specific price within a specific period of time. You don't have to buy, but you may—at your option.

One of the advantages of purchasing stock pursuant to an option your company grants you lies in the price you pay.

◆ $\mathscr{E}$XAMPLE

As a result of your outstanding performance last year, your boss gave you a bonus— an option on 2,000 shares of company stock.

The *option price* is $12 a share. The option price is the amount you pay for the stock when you *exercise* your option and in most cases is the *fair market value* of the stock on the date your option was granted.

Now, a year later, the *market price* of the stock has soared to $20 a share, and you decide to exercise the option. When you do, you pay $24,000—that is, $12 times 2,000 shares—for stock that is currently worth $40,000.

INCENTIVE STOCK OPTIONS

Options come in two varieties: *incentive stock options* (ISOs) and *nonqualified stock options* (NQOs). The difference lies mainly in the tax benefits provided by ISOs.

There's no regular tax due on an incentive stock option until you eventually sell or exchange the stock, and then only if you sell or exchange it for more than you paid for it. (You must hold ISOs for a specified amount of time if your profits are to be taxed as capital gains. See the section "Capital Gains" later in this chapter for the details.)

Generally with NQOs, on the other hand, there's an immediate tax bite when you exercise the option, as well as the tax you pay when you sell the stock at a profit.

Returning to the above example: If you were granted NQOs instead of ISOs, you would have incurred a tax liability when you exercised them. The IRS taxes you on the difference between the option price—$12—and the market price—$20—at the time you exercise the option. So you're taxed on $16,000 when you exercise your NQO, and this income is treated as ordinary income.

If you're able to sell the stock, say, a year later for $30 a share, you're taxed again, this time as capital gains on the difference between $20 and $30. With an ISO you're taxed just once for regular tax purposes when you finally sell the stock for $30 a share.

But with an ISO, the entire amount of your gain—that is, the difference between the $30 a share you receive at the sale and the $12 a share option price that you originally paid—is taxed as a capital gain. (For more information on capital gains, see Chapter 14.)

The advantage of the ISO is that you pay no regular tax until you actually realize a gain when you sell or exchange your stock, and all of that gain is treated as a capital gain.

With the NQO you generally pay tax on your *paper profit* as ordinary income when you exercise the option. That means you not only must have cash to buy the stock when you exercise an NQO, you also need the money to pay taxes due. (An amount normally must be paid to your employer to be remitted as withholding taxes.)

Fortunately, you do get to increase your *basis* in the stock—that is, the stock's cost to you—by the amount of your reported gain.

The *bargain element*—the difference between the price at which you buy your stock and the fair market value—on the exercise of ISOs is an adjustment when you compute your alternative minimum tax (AMT).

②.𝒯ₚ

> Timing is an issue. You may not want to exercise an ISO if it will throw you into an AMT situation. (See Chapter 20 for the details on the AMT.)

Which is the better deal? ISOs? NQOs? The answer is, it depends. You may be better off from a tax perspective with ISOs. But ISOs do come with a set of rules that can make them less desirable for other reasons.

ISO RESTRICTIONS

Specific rules and restrictions define an ISO. If a stock option doesn't conform, it is, by definition, an NQO and is automatically treated as such. Even if an option qualifies as an ISO, you may be able to treat it as an NQO if its terms give you that option; or, if you violate the rules, your ISO will be treated tax-wise as an NQO.

The following rules and restrictions apply to ISOs:

- Employee status.
- Option period.
- Fair market price.
- $100,000 ceiling.
- Order of exercise.
- Capital gains.
- Transferability.

EMPLOYEE STATUS

From the day you receive the ISO until three months before you exercise it, you must be employed by the company (or a related company) granting it.

So you may, if your employer's plan allows, exercise the option within three months after you leave the company and still obtain the favorable tax benefits.

But if you leave a company due to permanent and total disability, and if your employer's plan allows it, you have up to one year to exercise your ISOs. Sick leave or any other company-approved leave doesn't count, however.

What if you die? Your options remain ISOs and go to your *beneficiaries*—meaning the people you specify as your heirs—and they may, in turn, exercise them.

OPTION PERIOD

You must exercise your ISO within 10 years of the date it's granted, unless you own more than 10 percent of your company's stock. In that case the option period may not exceed five years.

Another rule you should know: The company must grant ISOs within 10 years of the date the shareholders formally approve the stock option plan or the plan is adopted, whichever is earlier.

FAIR MARKET PRICE

The ISO rules require that the option price not be less than the fair market price of the stock on the date the option is granted.

But a special rule applies to individuals who own more than 10 percent of a corporation's stock. In their case only, the option price must at least be equal to 110 percent of the fair market value of the stock on the date the ISO is granted.

$100,000 CEILING

Of all the ISOs you are granted after 1986, no more than $100,000 worth of stock (valued at the time the options are granted) may become exercisable for the first time in any one year.

If you violate this rule, the first $100,000 of optioned stock still qualifies as ISOs. But the remainder falls into the category of NQOs.

You calculate the first $100,000 of optioned stock that qualifies for ISO treatment by adding together your options in the order you receive them.

◈ *Ε*XAMPLE

Your company grants you two options that are first exercisable in 1995. The first—to purchase 6,000 shares at $10 a share, or $60,000—is exercisable on January 15, 1995. The second—to purchase 7,000 shares at $10 a share, or $70,000—is exercisable on July 15, 1995. In each case the stock has a fair market value of $10 a share on the day you receive the options.

The first option of $60,000 qualifies as an ISO.

So does $40,000 of the second option. The remainder of the second option ($70,000 minus $40,000, or $30,000) falls into the category of an NQO.

Understand, though, that the $100,000 limit isn't on the value of stock subject to options your employer may grant you. Your company may grant you any amount it sees fit.

Rather, the limit is on the amount of stock first exercisable by you in any year. The amount of stock is based on the value of the stock at the date of the option grant multiplied by the number of shares in the option.

◆ EXAMPLE

Your employer in 1995 grants you options to purchase $300,000 worth of stock. The entire amount would qualify as ISOs as long as the option states that you could only exercise $100,000 in 1995, and the second and third $100,000 worth in 1996 and 1997, respectively.

You don't have to exercise them at all, or you could exercise all three in 1997 and have all qualify as ISOs. But you may not *first* exercise more than $100,000 in any one year for them to qualify as ISOs.

What if your employer grants you an option to purchase $150,000 worth of stock in 1995, all of which can be exercised in the same year?

In this case, you should instruct your employer at the date of exercise to issue you separate stock certificates and to identify the certificates as an ISO exercise in the stock transfer records for $100,000 of the stock.

Otherwise, each share of stock will be treated as two-thirds acquired by ISO and one-third acquired by the exercise of an NQO. The separate designation will provide you with greater flexibility in recognizing income in future years.

ORDER OF EXERCISE

You must exercise ISOs granted to you before 1987 in the order they were granted. But you may exercise ISOs granted *after* 1986 in any order you like.

◆ EXAMPLE

You hold an option to purchase 2,000 shares of stock at $15 a share, another to buy 1,000 at $10 a share, and still another to purchase 5,000 at $5 each.

You received the $15-per-share option in July of 1986, the $10-per-share option in December of 1986, and the $5-per-share option in 1988. You may exercise the post-1986 option—the $5-per-share option issued in 1988—before the other two.

But you must exercise options issued before 1987 in the order they were granted. So you must exercise the July option before you exercise the December option.

CAPITAL GAINS

You may claim long-term capital gain treatment from gains on the sale of stock bought with ISOs only if you hold the shares for the later of more than two years from the date the option was granted or more than one year from the date the shares were actually transferred to you.

Otherwise, your gain—the difference between the option price and the amount you collected when you sold your stock—is taxed as ordinary income.

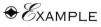
Example

You receive an option on July 3, 1995. You exercise the option six months later, on January 3, 1996. Under the law, in order to have your gain considered a long-term capital gain, you must hold the shares until after July 3, 1997—that is, two years after the option was granted to you.

If the holding period requirements are not met, the gain that would have been realized at the time the options were exercised is included as ordinary income in the year of the disqualifying sale. Gain for those purposes is the lesser of:

- The fair market value of the stock on the date of the exercise over the option price of the stock, *or*
- The amount realized on the sale of the stock over the adjusted basis (usually the option price) of the stock.

Transferability

There are a number of other requirements that must be met to make sure that your options will be treated as ISOs rather than NQOs.

Only you and your heirs may exercise ISOs. But you may not contribute your options to an IRA or other retirement plan. The IRS doesn't want you deferring gains on options even longer than the options themselves permit.

Tip

No one else, not even your spouse, may exercise your ISOs during your lifetime, and you may not assign options in a divorce settlement. Both sides to a divorce must devise a formula to compensate for the fact that much of an executive's wealth may consist of nontransferable stock options.

Caution

You may not sell your right to exercise an option or use the right as collateral for a loan.

With all the restrictions that apply to them, why might you still prefer ISOs to NQOs? Tax deferral is the best reason. As pointed out earlier you report no gain for regular tax purposes until you sell or exchange your ISO stock.

Tip

This and the fact that you may use company stock you already own to pay for ISO stock allows you to use a powerful strategy.

◆ *E*XAMPLE

You join a young company whose shares are selling for $2. At the time you come on board, you buy 1,000 shares of stock and receive ISOs for 5,000 shares at $2 a share. In five years the stock price hits $10, and you decide to exercise your option.

You do so by exchanging the 1,000 shares you bought earlier. Now, you own 5,000 shares worth $50,000 at the current market price, but your investment cost just the $2,000 you paid for that initial stock. And this transaction is not subject to the regular tax (but may be subject to the alternative minimum tax—see Chapter 20) until you sell the option shares.

Now let's say that you use this same strategy, but instead of paying with shares you bought, you pay with shares acquired under an ISO.

The same rules apply, but only if you have held the stock for more than two years after your ISOs were granted or more than one year after the shares were transferred to you, whichever is longer. Otherwise, the shares you exchange no longer qualify for treatment as ISOs.

If you have made a so-called *disqualifying disposition*—that is, you have disposed of ISO stock before meeting the holding period requirement, then you must pay tax on your profit—that is, the appreciation—at ordinary income rates when they are exchanged.

◈.*T*IP

The capital gain income that ISOs yield—besides giving you the benefit of the preferential tax rate ceiling on long-term capital gains—may be useful for other tax purposes. For instance, you may use these capital gains to offset your capital losses.

NQOs, however, have their place.

With NQOs you don't have to worry about the AMT. Nor do you have to worry about any of the special rules and regulations affecting ISOs, including limits on when you can exercise your options or sell the stock you have acquired.

STOCK APPRECIATION RIGHTS

At the beginning of the chapter we mentioned stock appreciation rights, SARs for short. With SARs you do not actually buy your company's stock. But you still profit from the stock's appreciation. SARs allow you to receive, either in cash or employer stock, the appreciation in the value of a share of employer stock over a certain period of time.

◆ *E*XAMPLE

Your company gives you a one-year SAR on 5,000 shares of stock when the market price is $2 a share. A year later the stock price has risen to $3. Thus, the appreciation of the SAR is $5,000 (5,000 shares times $1 appreciation per share).

You could get a check for $5,000 (less any withholding, of course). Or your company could give you $2,000 (again, less any income-tax withholding) plus 1,000 shares of stock valued at $3 a share. Either way, your total compensation comes to $5,000.

The gain is taxed at ordinary rates, just like the gain on an NQO. But unlike stock options, you never have to put up any cash of your own with an SAR.

Because you put up no cash with SARs, companies sometimes use them in tandem with ISOs to provide employees with the dollars they need to exercise their ISOs.

◆ *Example*

Your company grants you a one-year SAR on 5,000 shares of stock. At the end of the year it yields $1 a share, or a total of $5,000.

You receive a check for $5,000 minus federal income-tax withholding taxes.

Say, too, that along with your SAR your company grants you an ISO to purchase 1,800 shares of company stock at an exercise price of $2 a share.

You use the dollars you receive from your SAR at year-end to exercise your option. You're out of pocket only the additional taxes you pay on income from your SAR.

RESTRICTED STOCK

Where an employer gives or sells stock to an employee on the condition that the employee must work for the employer for a prescribed period of time, the stock is referred to as restricted stock. If the employee does not meet the length of service requirement set by the employer, the stock is usually sold back to the employer for the amount paid (if any). Oftentimes, the length of service requirement (i.e., vesting) takes place in installments over a period of time. The following example illustrates the tax consequences associated with restricted stock.

◆ *Example*

On May 1, 1995, your employer sells you 1,000 shares of stock, having a market value of $20 per share, for $5 per share. The sale of the stock is subject to the condition that you must continue to work for the company for a period of four years. If your employment terminates for any reason during this period, you are required to sell your shares back to the company for $5 per share.

Until you "vest" in the restricted stock (i.e., the length of service requirement is met), it is not considered to be compensation income for tax purposes. When the stock vests and is no longer restricted, a taxable event occurs. You recognize ordinary income equal to the spread between the value of the stock on the date the stock vests and the amount, if any, you paid for it. Thus, if the stock vests on December 31, 1995, when the market price is $21 per share, you must report $16,000 as ordinary income.

> **⊛.ℱ**P

An election is available that minimizes the tax consequences of restricted stock. Called a Section 83(b) election (after the section in the tax code), the election allows you to include in income, to be taxed at ordinary income tax rates in the year the restricted stock is issued, the difference between the fair market value (FMV) of the stock on the date the stock is purchased and the cost of the stock. The restricted stock must be received in connection with performing services (i.e., your job) for you to be eligible to make the election.

As a result of this election, when you fully vest and your stock is no longer restricted, you do not experience a taxable event. So if the stock appreciates between the date you purchase it and the date it vests, you do not report the appreciation as ordinary income. When you sell the stock, any gain—including the appreciation when the stock vested—is considered to be a capital gain, potentially resulting in a significant tax savings.

✿ 𝒞AUTION

You must make the Section 83(b) election within 30 days of your receipt of the restricted stock. Consult your tax adviser to determine if you can take advantage of this election.

QUESTIONS AND ANSWERS

Q. Are the rules different for a corporate insider?

A. If you're a corporate *insider*—an officer, a director, or a more-than-10-percent shareholder of a public company—you must conform to special requirements regarding ISOs and NQOs. Among these requirements is the so-called "six-month" rule imposed by the Securities and Exchange Commission (SEC), under which you may have to forfeit to the company profits realized from the purchase and sale of the company's stock.

Generally you will be subject to the six-month rule if you exercise or otherwise dispose of options within six months of the date the options were *granted* to you. However, most stock option plans don't allow you to exercise or otherwise dispose of your options within six months of the date they were granted, so the six-month rule will not apply in the usual case. If, under your company's stock option plan, you may exercise options within six months of the date of grant and you plan to do so, contact your attorney to determine whether the six-month rule may apply to you.

The SEC rule effectively imposes "restrictions" on when an insider may sell his or her company stock. Accordingly, the tax law generally does not require you to recognize your paper gain from the exercise of a stock option until the SEC restrictions on sale no longer apply. In the unusual case where the six-month rule is applicable and prevents you from selling the stock immediately after you exercise the option, an election, the so-called Section 83(b) election, is available that allows you to recognize the income as of the exercise date. When you make this election, you—as a holder of appreciating stock received as a result of the exercise of an NQO—maximize the portion of your total gain that ultimately is treated as a capital gain. If the situation is right, and you can benefit from this election, just be sure to make the election within 30 days of your option exercise. See your tax adviser for details on how to make the election.

As you can tell, insider regulations are quite strict and complex. You need to choose carefully when you exercise and when you sell your stock. If you're an insider, ask your tax adviser and attorney to help you evaluate your personal situation. Enlist their help as soon as you get an option. This way you won't unknowingly violate these rules and jeopardize your gain.

22

CONTRIBUTING TO A RETIREMENT PLAN

- What are the different benefits of IRA, SEP, Keogh, and 401(k) plans?
- Are there benefits to tax-deferred investing?
- How are annual contributions to such plans limited?

Putting money into what is commonly known as a qualified retirement plan, either your company's or your own, is one of the best ways to prepare for your financial future.

It is also a great way to reduce your current tax bill. Understanding your retirement plan options under the tax law is doubly important, but not necessarily easy.

The variety of retirement plans that qualify for special treatment under the tax law can be bewildering unless you understand that the underlying principle for most of them is the same: The money you put in now will not be taxed until you take it out at retirement.

Having said that, we must also warn you there are important differences between retirement plans. In this chapter we show you how the tax laws affect the ways you can put money into your retirement plan.

And we will simplify the distinctions among retirement plans—*individual retirement accounts (IRAs), Keoghs, 401(k)s,* and all the rest. This knowledge will allow you to make intelligent choices among the retirement plans available to you, whether you work for yourself or someone else.

TYPES OF PLANS

There are really only three types of retirement plans: those you create and contribute to yourself, those your company runs and contributes to, and those to which both you and the company may contribute. Most people may participate in more than one type of plan.

INDIVIDUAL RETIREMENT ACCOUNTS (IRAS)

IRAs are retirement plans that you create and to which you contribute. IRAs, unfortunately, are no longer as useful as they once were to individuals who are covered by employer-sponsored retirement plans. Still they are not totally without value.

The law allows you to contribute to an IRA the lesser of $2,000 or 100 percent of your compensation each year; $2,250 if you and your nonworking spouse file jointly.

But you may deduct this contribution only if neither you nor your spouse is covered by a tax-deferred retirement plan or your adjusted gross income (AGI) falls below a certain level.

Whether your annual contribution to an IRA is deductible or not, the account earnings still accumulate tax-free until you withdraw your money.

KEOGH PLANS

If you work for yourself, you should have a Keogh for saving and sheltering part of your self-employment income—Keogh plans are bona fide wealth-building tools.

To have a Keogh plan, you must be self-employed. In other words, you must have income from your own unincorporated business, such as a sole proprietorship or partnership. If you have employees, you generally must include them in your Keogh plan.

Having a Keogh does not preclude you from having an IRA, but you should know that a Keogh is a qualified plan under the tax law.

So if you set up an IRA, your income must fall within certain levels, or your IRA contributions are not deductible.

You may deduct your Keogh contributions, and you pay no tax on any earnings that accumulate until you begin to collect benefits, usually at retirement.

Keoghs come in two varieties: a *defined-contribution* plan or a *defined-benefit* plan. A defined-contribution plan allows you to contribute a specified amount—10 percent of your earnings, say—to the plan each year. To make matters more complicated, these plans themselves come in two varieties: *profit-sharing plans* and *money-purchase plans.*

You may contribute up to 15 percent of your self-employment income with a profit-sharing plan or up to 25 percent with a money-purchase plan. But in either case your contribution must not total more than $30,000.

You must subtract your contribution and your deduction for one-half of your actual self-employment taxes for the year to figure your net self-employment income. So in practice you are contributing only 12.12 percent of your self-employment income to your profit-sharing plan or 18.59 percent to a money-purchase plan. For 1995 these percentages are for self-employment income of less than $61,200. If your earned income tops this amount, the percentage varies slightly. Contact your tax adviser to determine how much you can contribute.

With a defined-benefit plan you contribute annually whatever amount is required to fund a specified retirement payout. The payout is fixed, and the contribution is based on actuarial tables for your life expectancy.

The only limit: The annual benefit after retirement may not top the lesser of $120,000 for 1995 or 100 percent of your average earnings for your three consecutive years of highest earnings.

✪ 𝒞AUTION

Your contribution cannot top your current annual income.

Many people avoid setting up a defined-benefit Keogh. The reason is that the paperwork and the cost of maintaining the plan are greater than with a defined-contribution plan. But for many people the benefits outweigh the hassles involved, especially if you are over age 45.

◆ ℰXAMPLE

You are 55 years old and currently earn $110,000 in self-employment income. The most you could put away with a defined-contribution money-purchase plan is approximately $21,000.

But say you want to fund a benefit of $59,000 (assuming your three consecutive years of highest earnings are at least $59,000) after you retire at age 65. Based on actuarial computations, you could put away as much as $31,661 this year in a defined-benefit plan—almost $10,700 more.

✪ 𝒞AUTION

If you have employees, you must provide them with comparable benefits, and you must weigh the cost of doing so with the benefits you will realize from the plan.

➤ 𝒯IP

To take advantage of a Keogh, you must create your plan no later than the last day of your taxable year, which for most people is December 31. But generally you do not have to make your actual contribution until the due date of your tax return, including extensions.

✪ 𝒞AUTION

You may not know it, but the tax law requires you to make contributions to defined-benefit plans quarterly. If you fail to do so, you must then make additional contributions to the plan to make up for the interest income you lost by not making your contributions on time.

If you do business as a sole proprietor, *you* set up your Keogh plan. But if you are a partner in a partnership, the partnership must establish the Keogh plan.

➤.*Tip*

Although the amount of your contribution to a profit-sharing plan may be more limited than it is for the other two types of plans, this type of arrangement does have one important advantage. You may vary the amount you set aside each year and are free to base your contribution on how well your business performs. In other words, if your business does poorly one year, you aren't required to make a contribution. You are even free to skip a contribution any year you like. By contrast, if you have a money-purchase or defined-benefit plan, you must make an annual contribution to the plan each year; otherwise, you may be subject to an excise tax.

➤.*Tip*

It is also possible to "pair" or combine a money-purchase plan with a profit-sharing plan. The advantages: You may, if you want, contribute and deduct a full 18.59 percent of your self-employment income. This enables you to fully fund a money-purchase plan and still have flexibility in the amount you *must* contribute each year.

Here is how pairing works. You set up a money-purchase plan to shelter, say, 8 percent of your income. Now you may contribute up to an additional 10.59 percent (for a total of 18.59 percent) to a profit-sharing plan.

The amount you put into the profit-sharing plan is entirely up to you. You may still protect from current taxation as much as $30,000, or 18.59 percent of your income, whichever is less.

➤.*Tip*

This paired strategy is desirable for people who want to set aside more than 12 percent of their earnings in a retirement plan but do not want to tie themselves to contributing a significant percentage of their incomes year after year.

EMPLOYER-SPONSORED RETIREMENT PLANS

Employer-sponsored retirement plans are created, and for the most part funded, by the company that employs you. As with Keoghs, employer-sponsored plans come in two types: defined-contribution plans and defined-benefit plans.

And as with all retirement plans, any earnings accumulating in employer-sponsored plans remain untaxed until you begin withdrawing funds at retirement.

HYBRID PLANS

There are several retirement plans that combine some features of employer-sponsored plans with the IRA concept. For instance, 401(k) plans are a hybrid.

Your employer will create and administer a 401(k) plan and may contribute to it. Employees use 401(k) plans much as they do IRAs—as a place to deposit a tax-deferred portion of their salary or wage income until they need to withdraw it, usually at retirement.

Another hybrid, the *simplified employee pension (SEP)* plan, is very similar to an IRA. An employer, rather than maintaining its own pension fund, makes contributions to the IRAs of its employees, and the employer may deduct its contributions. Moreover, you do not have to count your employer's contributions to your SEP as part of your income.

You may also, if your plan allows, make contributions to your own SEP, up to a cap of $9,240 (in 1995) or 15 percent of your compensation, whichever is less.

⮕.𝒯IP

If you missed the December 31 deadline for setting up a Keogh plan, consider an SEP instead. The deadline for establishing and funding an SEP is the due date of your tax return, including extensions.

♻ 𝒞AUTION

The IRS classifies as a 401(k) plan any partnership plan, no matter what type you think it is, that directly or indirectly lets individual partners vary the annual contributions made on their behalf. In this case the $9,240 limit will apply to the discretionary contributions you make.

ADVANTAGES OF IRAS

IRAs used to be among the best retirement saving plans around until Congress clipped some of their more generous features back in 1986. And now? They are still a useful part of many retirement portfolios with more limitations.

The greatest appeal of an IRA used to be that as long as you were not more than age 70½, the contributions you made—up to the $2,000 annual limit—were fully tax-deductible.

Today that is true for only two types of people: those who are not eligible for an employer-sponsored retirement plan or those whose incomes fall below specified levels.

If neither you nor your spouse is eligible for a company retirement plan, the rules governing your ability to make tax-deductible contributions to an

IRA were not affected by the 1986 tax law changes. Both of you are still free to write off IRA contributions equal to the lesser of your earned income or $2,000 a year ($2,250 if you have a spouse who does not work outside the home or who earns less than $250 a year).

But if your company has a retirement plan and you are an active participant in it, you may lose some or all of the deductibility of your annual IRA contribution.

For people with company retirement plans, the first test of IRA deductibility is income. You may still make a fully deductible IRA contribution as long as your joint AGI does not exceed certain levels.

In this case AGI is your adjusted gross income before you claim a deduction for your IRA but *after* you have deducted any losses from investments. Also, your AGI includes any taxable Social Security benefits you receive.

If you are covered by a retirement plan at work, you can take IRA deductions as shown in the table below.

| | | Married | |
AGI	Single/ Head of Household	Filing Jointly/ Widower	Married Filing Separately
Available IRA Deductions*			
$0–$10,000	Full	Full	Partial
10,000–25,000	Full	Full	None
25,000–35,000	Partial	Full	None
35,000–40,000	None	Full	None
40,000–50,000	None	Partial	None
50,000 +	None	None	None

* If you are covered by a retirement plan at work.

Figuring the partial deduction is easy. Just subtract your joint AGI from the $50,000 cap. Then divide the result by $10,000. That answer is the fraction of the maximum IRA contribution that you may deduct.

◆ *E*XAMPLE

Your joint AGI is $42,000. Subtract that amount from $50,000 to get $8,000. Divide $8,000 by $10,000 to get 80 percent. This is the percentage of the IRA base, $2,000, that you may contribute to an IRA and deduct, so you may deduct $1,600. (See the IRA deduction worksheet in the Appendix.)

Of course you are free to *contribute* the full $2,000, but do not count on a deduction for the extra $400.

The rules and the calculations for single people are the same, except that the income limits are different.

◆ *&*XAMPLE

A single person with a $30,000 AGI may deduct half of his or her maximum IRA contri-
bution (the $35,000 cap minus $30,000 of AGI equals $5,000, which, when divided by
$10,000, comes to 50 percent).

 P

The law allows you to contribute at least $200 to an IRA and write off the full amount,
as long as your calculation shows that your deductible contribution is limited to no
less than $10.

WHAT HAPPENS WHEN YOU FILE SEPARATELY?

It does not matter that only one spouse participates in another retirement
plan. If you file jointly, you are treated as if both of you do.

The same is true if you file separately, and another strict set of requirements applies. The IRA deduction for each spouse is phased out beginning
with the first $1 of AGI. When your AGI reaches $10,000, you cannot get
any deduction.

The rules are different if you are married, file separately, but live apart
from your spouse for the entire year. In this case the spouse who is not
covered by a qualified plan may contribute up to $2,000 to an IRA and
deduct the contribution. If you are an active participant in a plan, the
phase-out begins at $25,000.

◆ *&*AUTION

Whatever limit the rules place on the size of your or your spouse's annual deductible
IRA contribution, you will pay a penalty if you contribute too much.

If you exceed your contribution limit, the IRS will demand that you pay an excise tax
equal to 6 percent of the excess contribution. And as we will see later, you also face
a 10 percent penalty when you withdraw the money. You can avoid both these
penalties if you withdraw your excess contribution before you file your tax return for
the year.

WHAT IS ACTIVE PARTICIPATION?

As a general rule the IRS considers you an active participant in a defined-
benefit plan if the plan's rules say that you are covered, even if you decline
to participate. Just being eligible in one of these plans makes you an active
participant.

In the case of defined-contribution plans, you are considered an active
participant if any money is added to your account during the year. One
exception to this rule is allocations to your account in the form of investment earnings. If investment earnings are the only amount added to your
account, you are not considered an active participant.

How do you know if you're an active participant? One quick way is to look at your W-2 form. It provides a box for your employer to check. If this box is blank, though, you've got some work to do, and you'll need to familiarize yourself with the active participation rules.

Participation in any of the following plans can make you an active participant and not eligible to deduct your IRA contributions:

- Qualified pension, profit-sharing, or stock bonus plans, including Keogh plans.
- Qualified annuity plans.
- Simplified employee pension plans (SEPs).
- Retirement plans for federal, state, or local government employees.
- Certain union plans (so-called Section 501(c)(18) plans).
- Tax-sheltered annuities for public school teachers and other employees of charitable organizations.
- 401(k) plans.

Say you meet the eligibility conditions under your employer's defined-benefit pension plan, but under the plan rules you will not be credited with any contributions your employer makes on your behalf unless you contribute to the plan. Even if you do not make a contribution, and therefore are not credited with benefits, you are considered an active participant.

Furthermore, vesting has nothing to do with determining whether you are an active participant.

◆ *Example*

Your company offers a profit-sharing plan. You are an active participant once your employer contributes something to your account for the year. It makes no difference that you are not vested for five years.

The tax rules classify you as an active participant if you participate in a retirement plan for just part of the year.

◆ *Example*

You change jobs in November 1994 and move from Old Company Inc. to New Corp. You are not eligible for the New Corp. pension plan in 1995, so you make what you think is a tax-deductible IRA contribution for 1995.

However, Old Company's pension plan does not end its tax year until January 31, 1995. Therefore, you are eligible and "active" in that plan for the first month of the 1995 year. So the deductibility of your IRA contribution for 1995 may be limited depending on the amount of your AGI.

⊘.𝒯ₚ

You calculate your AGI *after* you make your Keogh contributions. Say, for example, you are self-employed and you and your spouse file a joint return. Your earnings from your business add up to $40,000, and the two of you report interest and dividend income of $5,000. You contribute $7,000 to a Keogh account. Under the rules, you may make a fully deductible $2,000 IRA contribution, because your joint AGI—$38,000 before you subtract your IRA contribution—is less than the $40,000 threshold amount.

SPOUSAL IRAS

You do not have to hold a job to have an IRA. A nonworking spouse may start a so-called spousal IRA, as long as both file jointly and the nonworking spouse's earned income totals less than $250.

If you meet these two requirements, each of you may open and make contributions to an IRA. Together, collectively, you may contribute as much as $2,250 in any single year. No more than $2,000 of that amount, however, may go to either account.

How much you write off on your tax return depends on your circumstances. You are subject to the same rules on deductibility as other taxpayers.

So how do you split up your contribution? The answer depends on your long-term objectives. If you want to keep your savings in an IRA as long as possible, make the greater contribution to the IRA of the younger spouse. If you want to get at your savings sooner, put it in the older spouse's account.

Another point to consider in deciding how to split up your contributions: Deposit the majority of the money in the account of the person who has the largest proportion of nondeductible dollars. That way, if that person withdraws part of his or her IRA funds from that account before age 59½, the amount subject to the 10 percent early withdrawal penalty will be minimized.

Of course, if your spouse's earned income exceeds $250, you do not lose out. Your spouse just opens his or her own IRA and contributes as much as 100 percent of his or her income (up to $2,000) to it.

⊘.𝒯ₚ

If you own your own business and your spouse helps out from time to time, consider paying him or her for services rendered. Your spouse may deposit all or part of his or her earnings in an IRA and claim a tax deduction for the contribution.

◆ 𝒠XAMPLE

In 1995 you pay your spouse $2,000 for bookkeeping services. She has no other income.
The two of you file a joint return listing AGI of $30,000. The result: Each of you may make a tax-deductible contribution to an IRA of up to $2,000.

✪ 𝒞AUTION

Make sure you pay your spouse with a payroll check. The IRS may not consider a deposit in a joint bank account as an actual payment of wages. And be prepared to show that your spouse's employment is genuine.

Remember, wages paid to a spouse are generally subject to Social Security taxes. In 1995 the combined rate is 15.3 percent; that is, 7.65 percent paid by the employee and 7.65 percent paid by the employer.

HOW MANY IRAS?

If you are eligible, it does not matter how many IRAs you have—one or a dozen. Set up as many as you like. But you should know that many institutions charge an annual maintenance fee for each IRA. The fees can run as high as $50, which can get expensive if you open lots of accounts.

The effect of these fees is to reduce the net return on your investments. The fees are deductible, but only if you pay them from non-IRA funds and only to the extent that they and all your other miscellaneous itemized deductions top 2 percent of your AGI.

The rules also allow you to borrow money to make an IRA contribution. The only question: May you deduct the interest on the loan?

The answer depends on whether the interest is classified as personal interest or investment interest, and the rules are not clear on this point.

You may not deduct any of your personal interest expense. You may deduct investment interest only from your investment income.

Choosing the Right Account and Manager

Who should manage your IRA, and what sort of investments should be in it? You may choose as the manager of your IRA the institution where you have an account: a bank, for instance, or a savings and loan or brokerage house, or you may manage it yourself.

As to what investments belong in an IRA, almost any investment vehicle makes sense, with just a few exceptions.

What you obviously do not want in an IRA are tax-free investments—municipal bonds, for instance. The yield on tax-free bonds is almost always lower than on taxable investments of comparable quality, and the beauty of an IRA is that it allows you to defer taxes on an investment's earnings. If the earnings are already tax-free, you lose. Here is how.

The income from tax-exempt bonds is tax-free; in other words, not subject to federal taxation. The income from an IRA is tax deferred; that is, you pay tax on it when you withdraw it. If you use IRA dollars to invest in tax-exempt bonds, income from those bonds is paid to your IRA, and when the income is withdrawn, it is taxed. In effect you have turned tax-free income into taxable income.

Among the IRA investments you should consider:

- Bank certificates of deposit (CDs) that pay market rates of interest. Deposits are insured up to $100,000 at most institutions.
- Money market mutual funds offered by brokerage houses and other financial institutions.
- Mutual funds of all types (except municipal bond funds).
- Stocks, including individual issues. You may, for example, open a self-directed IRA at a brokerage firm. You select the stocks you like and reinvest any dividends, thereby preserving the year-to-year tax-free feature of your IRA.
- Flexible-premium annuities offered by insurance companies. (These are known as individual retirement annuities.)

About the only investments the law says you may not make with IRA dollars are:

- Art objects,
- Antiques,
- Stamps,
- Other collectibles, *or*
- Gold or silver coins (except gold and silver eagle coins minted by the US Treasury and coins issued by a state).

Also, you may not use your IRA dollars for "self-dealing"; that is, you may not use IRA funds to purchase assets from yourself or from a company you own. For example, you could not use IRA dollars to purchase stock in a corporation you own.

What is more, you may not borrow from your IRA. If you do borrow from your IRA, the IRS treats the amount borrowed as if you had withdrawn it from your account.

Furthermore, you may not use your IRA as collateral for a loan. If you do, the IRS treats the amount you pledged as collateral as if you had withdrawn it from your account. What happens then? You pay tax at your normal rate on that amount of income, and if you are younger than 59 ½, you pay a 10 percent early withdrawal penalty, too.

Whichever investments you choose for your IRA, you are no more stuck with them than you are with non-IRA investment choices. As far as the IRS is concerned, you may buy and sell stocks and mutual funds, switch to CDs, or move into the money market as often as you see fit.

The institutions with which you place your IRA, however, may put the brakes on some of this activity. For instance a bank may penalize you by an amount equal to three months of interest if you withdraw funds early from a certificate of deposit.

You may withdraw and roll over your IRA from one institution to another without penalty just once each 365 days. So if you withdraw and roll over only part of the balance in your IRA, you are not allowed to withdraw and roll over the remainder until after 365 days later. But this limitation need not inhibit you if you have your IRA at an institution offering a variety of investment vehicles. You may switch among these vehicles as often as you choose.

If you maintain your IRA at a brokerage firm, you may, for instance, switch from stocks to mutual funds to bonds and back again without penalty. You do, of course, pile up commission fees and other transaction costs.

❧.𝒯ip

To avoid the once-every-365-days limit on withdrawals and rollovers, switch your funds using a "trustee-to-trustee" transfer.

You authorize the trustee of the institution that now holds your IRA dollars to transfer these funds directly to the trustee of another institution. Since you never touch the money—it goes from one institution to another—it technically is not a rollover. And it is not subject to the once-every-365-days limit.

❧.𝒯ip

The tax law says that your IRA may not lend you money, but there is a way to *effectively* borrow tax-free from your IRA for a short period of time using the rollover rules.

The law allows you to withdraw your IRA funds tax-free as long as it has been at least one year since your last withdrawal was rolled over. You pay no taxes and no penalties as long as the money is transferred back into another IRA within 60 days. The result: You may withdraw your IRA dollars, use the money for up to 60 days, then roll it over into another IRA— *all without any tax consequences.*

Here's something else you should know about such effective borrowing from your IRA. Up until now tax practitioners have assumed a rollover of an IRA must be from one IRA to another, but that's not what the IRS told a taxpayer we'll call Pat in a private-letter ruling.

Pat withdrew $1,500 from his IRA in 1990, then redeposited that amount in the same IRA 60 days later. He did that again in 1991.

The IRS says Pat is not subject to tax on the rollover. The IRS said in its ruling that "an individual" usually may take out IRA funds for his or her personal use and do so tax-free as long as he or she redeposits the funds in the same or another IRA in time.

This ruling applies only to the taxpayers involved, although these rulings do hint at the IRS's position on a given subject.

In the eyes of the IRS, IRAs you maintain at different institutions are considered separate accounts. What does it matter?

Say you maintain two IRA accounts, one at a bank, the other at a brokerage firm. On October 1, 1995, you withdraw and roll over the money from the bank to a mutual fund company.

Delighted with the mutual fund's performance, you decide—four months later—to withdraw and roll over the money from the brokerage firm to the mutual fund company.

Rest easy. You can do it without penalty. The reason: The 365-day rule applies separately to each account.

Alternatively, as discussed earlier, you could have the bank or brokerage firm transfer your IRA dollars from either one or both of the IRA accounts directly to the mutual fund and you would have accomplished the same result.

SHOULD YOU MAKE A NONDEDUCTIBLE CONTRIBUTION?

If you are not eligible, for whatever reason, to make deductible contributions to an IRA, should you make any at all? It is not an easy question to answer, even though the pros and cons of this decision are relatively straightforward.

The pros? The most obvious is that even though you may not deduct your annual IRA contribution, the earnings from your IRA investments accumulate and compound tax deferred. That means they build up faster than if you were paying tax on them every year.

The cons? Once you put money into an IRA, it is locked in until you reach age 59½ unless you are willing to pay a 10 percent penalty for early withdrawal.

The penalty applies to the deductible portion of your IRA contribution and to any earnings that have accumulated tax-deferred in your account. But you pay no penalty when you withdraw your nondeductible contributions.

And as discussed later, if your IRAs are made up of nondeductible contributions and either deductible contributions or tax-deferred earnings or both, a *pro rata* portion of any withdrawals will be considered to come from deductible contributions and tax-deferred earnings, which will result in that portion of the withdrawal being subject to the 10 percent penalty.

◆ ℰXAMPLE

Your account balance stands at $10,000. That amount consists of $7,000 of deductible contributions, $2,000 of nondeductible contributions, and $1,000 in earnings on your investments. So 80 percent of the amount withdrawn is subject to the 10 percent penalty: that is, $7,000 plus $1,000 divided by $10,000.

Of course, if you are almost 59½, early withdrawal probably will not be a problem. Go ahead and contribute to your IRA.

If you are young, say in your 20s, don't underestimate the long-term value of tax-deferred earnings on an annual contribution of $2,000. Consider making nondeductible contributions to an IRA. However, if your employer offers a 401(k) plan, contributions to it are usually a much better deal.

Some people feel that investing in tax-free bonds is a reasonable alternative to making a nondeductible IRA contribution, and they have a point.

The earnings from these bonds are tax-free, and you do not have to pay a penalty if you want to get at your money. Moreover, you are not limited to investing $2,000, or $2,250 for you and your nonworking spouse. But the bonds come with two potential drawbacks.

You can get locked into the bonds. If interest rates rise and the value of your bonds falls, you would have to take a loss to sell. So you are stuck with the bonds until maturity or until rates fall again.

The other potential problem with tax-free bonds is that, depending on the market, their yields are sometimes low compared to the after-tax yields of other securities. So they can be a poor investment.

Should you make a nondeductible IRA contribution? The answer depends on your circumstances. The key point is to take your personal situation into account. Lay out all the pros and cons each and every year before you make your decision.

*✪ C*AUTION

Remember, the option is time-limited. After the deadline passes for making this year's contribution, deductible or not, there is no changing your mind. Once missed, the opportunity is gone forever.

WHAT YOU NEED TO KNOW ABOUT 401(K) PLANS

The name 401(k) refers to the part of the tax code that describes these attractive retirement plans. Taking advantage of an employer-sponsored 401(k) is easy—and the benefits are substantial.

First, the money contributed to a 401(k) and the earnings that accumulate in it are tax deferred. That means your savings grow more rapidly than they would otherwise.

How much faster? Compare two investment plans, one tax-deferred and one not. With both plans you invest in the same mutual fund each year for 20 years. The fund earns 10 percent a year, and you reinvest these earnings, less any taxes due, in the account. Your marginal tax rate is 36 percent.

◆ EXAMPLE

To compare apples to apples, in the taxable fund you invest $9,240 (the maximum the law allowed in 1995 for tax-deferred plans) from your salary, less the $3,326 you owe the IRS in taxes, or $5,914 each year. At the end of 20 years this taxable fund has grown to almost $242,000.

But the tax-deferred fund is larger still—more than $582,000—for two reasons. You have been able to invest a full $9,240, since money earmarked for a 401(k) is not taxed currently, and you have not had to pay federal income tax on the earnings as they accumulated.

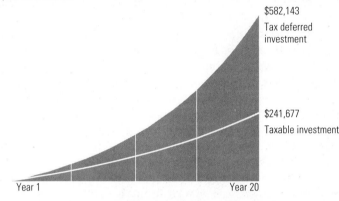

$582,143
Tax deferred investment

$241,677
Taxable investment

Year 1   Year 20

Tax-deferred, of course, does not mean tax-free. It only means that you do not pay taxes on the money contributed to a 401(k) or the earnings that pile up until you withdraw the funds.

Let's go back to our example. The true value of the tax-deferred fund is not $582,000 but $372,480; that is, $582,000 minus the $209,520 in income taxes you pay when you withdraw the money. Still, you come out about $130,480 ahead in your tax-deferred 401(k) fund.

A second benefit: The law allows your employer to help you build your 401(k) retirement fund. Many employers, in fact, contribute to employees' 401(k)s—up to a certain limit. It is almost like giving yourself a raise.

A 401(k) retirement plan is an attractive arrangement. But, as you might expect, Congress has established limits to keep it from becoming too attractive.

To get the most out of your 401(k), you need to know the rules. There are not many, at least when it comes to joining a plan.

If your company sponsors a 401(k) plan, signing up is simple. You authorize your employer to create an account for you and regularly deduct an amount from your pay.

If your salary adds up to $50,000 in 1995, you instruct your employer to subtract $400 a month from your pay and deposit it in a 401(k) plan.

When you get your W-2 form for the year, it will not show your entire $50,000 salary. Instead, it will report that you were paid $45,200: $50,000 less the $4,800 deducted for your 401(k). The $4,800 is treated as "deferred compensation" and is not reported as current income to you.

⟳ 𝒞AUTION

Although you do not currently have to pay federal income tax on the money that you contribute to your company-sponsored 401(k), this amount is still subject to Social Security tax in the year that you earn it.

WITHIN LIMITS

Not surprisingly, there are limits to the amount of money that you and your employer may contribute annually to a 401(k) plan. But these limits seem rather generous when compared, for instance, to the $2,000 cap on IRA contributions.

The government sets two limits on 401(k)s.

One caps the amount that you may contribute to your own retirement plan. The other restricts the amount that you and your employer together may contribute. The federal government adjusts both of these figures annually for inflation.

With planning you can ensure that your plan receives the maximum total contribution.

As far as the first limit is concerned, in 1995 the maximum amount an employee may salt away annually, tax deferred, in a 401(k) is $9,240; $9,500 in the case of a tax-sheltered annuity.

What is a tax-sheltered annuity? It is a kind of tax-deferred account for teachers, church workers, and employees of other nonprofit groups or institutions. It is usually sold by life insurance companies in the form of a contract that guarantees a payment to you at some future date, usually at retirement.

The second ceiling on 401(k)s limits the amount that you and your employer together may contribute to a 401(k) and all other defined-contribution plans. In 1995 the ceiling is $30,000 or 25 percent of your after-contribution salary, whichever is less.

◈ ℰXAMPLE

Your salary comes to $100,000 in 1995, and you contribute $9,240 to a 401(k). How much may your employer contribute?

	Salary	$100,000
Less:	Contribution to 401(k)	(9,240)
	After-contribution salary	90,760
Times:		25%
	Maximum employer and employee contribution (limited to $30,000)	22,690
Less:	Employee contribution	(9,240)
	Maximum employer contribution	**$ 13,450**

Would you be better off reducing your own contribution? First let's assume that your employer does not use a matching formula to tie its contribution to yours. Instead, it contributes a certain percentage of your compensation.

Now in the above example if you were to reduce your contribution from $9,240 to $5,000, your after-contribution salary would total $95,000 ($100,000 minus $5,000).

And 25 percent of that amount comes to $23,750.

By reducing your contribution, you have raised the maximum ceiling on the total retirement contribution for the year by $1,060 (the difference between $23,750 and $22,690). And you have also allowed your employer to increase its contribution.

The company may now chip in as much as $18,750 ($23,750 minus your $5,000 contribution). Less sometimes can be more.

QUESTIONS AND ANSWERS

Q.   Where should I invest my 401(k) funds?

A.   You really do not have much choice about where to invest your 401(k) plan dollars. Unlike an IRA where you have control of how your funds are invested, you must choose from among the options your employer offers for your 401(k) plan.

Some 401(k) plans limit you to a single investment option. Others let you split your account among two or more choices.

Q.   Does my participation in a 401(k) plan affect the level of other benefits I might receive?

A.   You will want to check with your employer to find out. Why? The value of some benefits—life insurance, for instance, and contributions to profit-sharing plans—is often tied to your total earnings. And what you get in these other benefits may vary depending on how the company tallies up your compensation.

The key point is this: Does the company reduce your compensation by the amount you have contributed to your 401(k)? Or does it add that amount back to your pay before calculating the value of your other benefits? Employers are *not* required to do the latter.

Ask your company about what procedure it follows.

Q.   What is the deadline for making a contribution to an IRA?

A.   For 1995 you may contribute to an IRA anytime after January 1, 1995, but no later than April 15, 1996—the due date of your annual tax return. (A calendar of important tax dates may be found in the Appendix.)

Q.   I have heard that there is a form that people who make nondeductible IRA contributions must fill out. Is my information correct?

A.   If you do make nondeductible IRA contributions, you must report the amount on Form 8606, "Nondeductible IRA contributions, IRA Basis, and Nontaxable IRA Distributions." This form is used to keep track of the nontaxable part of an IRA. You face a $50 penalty if you do not file it.

Q.   **I receive alimony and it is my only income. Does alimony count as earned income, so I can make a tax-deductible IRA contribution?**

A.   Yes. Alimony is considered earned income when it comes to calculating your IRA contribution.

23

WITHDRAWING MONEY FROM YOUR RETIREMENT PLAN

- Does it make a difference how you withdraw funds from a retirement plan?
- What tax savings strategies apply to withdrawals of retirement funds?
- Will penalties for early withdrawal be incurred?

If you are ready to withdraw money from your retirement plan, you should know the tax consequences of the options available to you. How and when you withdraw the funds can make a big difference in how much tax you will pay.

Whenever you begin to withdraw your funds, you really have just a few options. Depending on your retirement plan, you may usually take money out of your plan at retirement or before retirement. Further, you may usually take it out in one *lump sum* or spread your withdrawals over time. Each option has different tax consequences.

LUMP SUM WITHDRAWAL

The obvious disadvantage to taking your accumulated savings out of a retirement plan in a single lump sum is that you incur a big tax liability in the year you do so. But the tax law allows you to mitigate that liability somewhat by using a device called *five-year averaging.*

Five-year averaging can reduce the tax rate levied on lump sum withdrawals. Even though you pay your full tax in the year you receive your lump sum, you calculate the tax as if you received the money evenly over five years.

Here's how you figure your taxes on five-year averaging:

	Total lump sum distribution
Divided by:	5
	Taxable base
Times:	Applicable tax rate (using single taxpayer rates, not taking any other income or deductions into account)
	Current year tax on base amount
Times:	5
	Total tax owed in current year on lump sum distribution

This amount may be smaller than the tax you would pay if you subjected the whole amount to the standard tax computation in one year.

✪ 𝒞AUTION

You may use five-year averaging just once.

There are also conditions attached to lump sum distributions eligible for five-year averaging:

- The employee must have been a participant in the plan for five tax years before the tax year of the distribution (unless the distribution was paid out because the employee died).
- The distribution must total the full amount due the employee from all plans of the same type, for example, pension, profit-sharing, and stock bonus plans.
- The distribution must be paid in a single year.
- The distribution must be payable after the employee reaches age 59½, becomes disabled, dies, or terminates his or her employment.

✪ 𝒞AUTION

You cannot use five-year averaging in the case of lump sum withdrawals from IRAs and SEPs.

There are some special deals for individuals who were born before 1936. These individuals have an additional option open to them in dealing with lump sum distributions.

They may use five-year averaging or they may use *10-year averaging* rules. If they take this latter course, however, they must apply the tax rates that were in effect in 1986.

Moreover, these individuals do not have to wait until age 59½ to enjoy the benefits of averaging. However, if they receive a distribution before age 59½, they have to receive it because of separation from service.

➲.𝒯P

If you fall into this age category, the only way to know which option is the better tax choice is to do both calculations and compare the results.

❖ *C*AUTION

Anyone eligible to use 10-year averaging under this transition rule, however, must also be aware that if you use it on a lump sum distribution you receive before you reached age 59½, you may not use the averaging device (either 10- or 5-year averaging) ever again.

Part of your distribution may be considered to be a capital gain. If that is the case and you elect 10-year averaging, you may pay less tax because the maximum 1986 capital gain rate of 20 percent was less than the highest 1986 ordinary rate of 50 percent. If you find yourself in this situation, see your tax adviser *before* you withdraw your money.

PAYMENTS OVER TIME

Suppose you do not take your retirement plan benefits in a single lump sum. Your alternative is to withdraw the money in the form of an annuity—annual payments the size of which depends upon your life expectancy, or in some cases the life expectancy of you and your spouse or other beneficiary. (The IRS uses its Standard Annuity Tables to determine life expectancy.)

The payments are taxable unless you have made nondeductible contributions to the plan. If so—and this is true for many individuals—some part of each payment will be nontaxable. That part is based on the "exclusion ratio," and it reflects the portion of nondeductible contributions you have made to the total value of your retirement plan.

You may only continue to exclude that portion of your regular benefit payments from taxable income, however, until you reach your actuarial life expectancy. At that point, as far as the law is concerned, you have pulled all your nondeductible contributions out of the plan. Any payments that follow this statistical milestone will be fully taxable.

As a general rule, if you should die prior to your life expectancy and the annuity ceases, your estate is allowed a deduction for your unrecovered nondeductible contributions.

EARLY WITHDRAWALS

Under certain circumstances you may tap your retirement fund early, but you must comply with quite a number of restrictions to avoid paying expensive penalties on early withdrawals.

If for instance you leave a job before age 59½ and your employer requires you to take your pension benefits with you, you will incur a 10 percent early withdrawal penalty unless you roll the account over into an IRA or other qualified retirement plan within 60 days.

You may also avoid the early withdrawal penalty if:

- You use the distribution to pay for deductible medical expenses.

- You receive the benefits (after separation from service) in the form of an annuity spread over your life or the joint lives of you and your beneficiary. (Payments must be substantially equal and made at least annually.)
- You retire after reaching age 55 but before age 59½.

✪ 𝒞AUTION

Congress changed the rollover rules so that now if any part of a taxable distribution is not rolled over by the trustee directly to another qualified retirement plan, annuity, or IRA (i.e., a "trustee-to-trustee" transfer), that portion of the distribution will be subject to a 20 percent withholding rate. Furthermore, you will not be able to elect to avoid withholding on such amounts. Consult your tax adviser to learn about these rules before you make such withdrawals.

PENALTY ON EXCESS DISTRIBUTIONS

One point to keep in mind regardless of how you decide to withdraw your funds is the potential penalty you may incur for excessive distributions. If the total distribution you receive from all retirement plans, including IRAs, tops $150,000 in one year, you owe a 15 percent penalty on the excess. Special rules apply if the totally vested benefit in your retirement plan before August 1, 1986, was more than $562,500.

The penalty is assessed separately if you get a lump sum distribution and elect to take advantage of special income averaging rules. In this case the penalty is imposed only on the amount that exceeds $750,000.

➲.𝒯IP

If you think your yearly retirement benefits will exceed the limit, you may want to take some distributions early. Run the numbers and consult your tax adviser.

✪ 𝒞AUTION

This penalty applies whether you are over 59½ or not. However, the IRS will not also assess the 10 percent early withdrawal penalty (see below) on the excess distribution (i.e., you will be liable only for the 15 percent penalty).

IRA WITHDRAWALS

You may take your money out of an IRA at any time, but if you want to avoid a 10 percent penalty on withdrawals subject to taxation, you must wait until you reach the age of 59 ½. (Disabled individuals may make penalty-free withdrawals at any age.)

IRAs are different from all other tax-deferred retirement plans in one important respect. As a general rule, with other plans you may, for tax purposes, spread a lump sum withdrawal after age 59½ over five years despite the fact you get the money all at once. But—even though you pay the tax all in one year—you are taxed as if you had spread the withdrawal over a five-year period.

Not so with IRAs. Your lump sum withdrawal is taxed at ordinary income rates in the year you make the withdrawal. This rule is not a bar to lump sum withdrawals, but is a consideration you ought to keep in mind before deciding to take your IRA proceeds in a lump sum.

However you decide to withdraw IRA funds, you are going to owe some tax. Chances are at least some of the money you contributed to the IRA over the years was untaxed income (i.e., you probably received a deduction for at least some of the money contributed), and all the earnings from your IRA investments have been accumulating tax-free. These amounts get taxed upon withdrawal.

If by contrast the money you are withdrawing was taxed once, it is not taxed again. The way you apply this principle in figuring your taxes is pretty simple, too.

❖ *Ɛ*XAMPLE

You have had an IRA for 10 years. Now you begin withdrawing from it. For the first eight years you made tax-deductible contributions of $2,000 each year. Your total deductible contributions: $16,000.

During the last two years you also contributed $2,000 annually, but those were nondeductible contributions. Your total nondeductible contributions: $4,000.

Your IRA accumulated earnings of $10,000.

So altogether you have $30,000 in your account.

If you make a lump sum withdrawal, you owe tax on the $16,000 in deductible contributions and on the $10,000 in accumulated earnings. There is no tax on the $4,000 in nondeductible contributions. You are taxed on $26,000 of your $30,000 withdrawal.

But what if you want to withdraw just part of it, say, $4,000 in the first year? May you withdraw just the $4,000 that represents the nondeductible contributions you made and thereby escape paying income tax? No. In this case, $26,000 of the $30,000 in your IRA, or 87 percent, has been contributed or has accumulated tax-free. So 87 percent of any withdrawal you make that first year will be subject to tax. (Of course this proportion will change slightly from year to year as earnings continue to accumulate tax-free in your IRA while you make periodic withdrawals.)

The same rule of proportion applies even if you have several separate IRAs, some with mostly deductible contributions and others with nondeductible contributions. For purposes of computing the taxable proportion of any withdrawal you make, the IRS considers all of your IRAs to be one.

But remember, each spouse's contributions are grouped separately when it comes to withdrawing these funds.

➲.𝒯ɪᴘ

Once you reach age 59½, but before you reach age 70½, you may withdraw your IRA dollars anytime you choose and in any amount without penalty. Plan accordingly.

➋ 𝒞ᴀᴜᴛɪᴏɴ

As noted previously, if you take an extremely large distribution from your IRA, you may be subject to a 15 percent excise tax on excess distributions.

As we have seen, if you want your IRA money before you reach age 59½ and you are not disabled, you will pay a penalty—10 percent of the "untaxed" funds you withdraw. The same rule of proportion applies here as applied in the above example.

If 80 percent of the money in your IRA consists of deductible contributions and accumulated earnings, you pay a 10 percent penalty as well as regular income tax on 80 percent of any early withdrawal you make.

➲.𝒯ɪᴘ

You can avoid the penalty. Just take your distribution in the form of lifetime annual payments.

The law demands that these payments be of approximately equal amounts. Also, the payments must be based on your life expectancy or joint lives or life expectancies of you and your beneficiaries as determined by IRS tables.

Say, for instance, that you are 50 with a life expectancy of 33 years, according to the IRS tables. Your IRA contains $50,000. You may purchase an annuity contract that lets you take annual distributions of $4,340 (assuming an 8 percent interest rate) from the account without incurring a penalty.

Just as it discourages early withdrawals, the law also takes a dim view of late IRA withdrawals. The law requires you to begin pulling your accumulated IRA funds out before April 1 of the year following the year you reach age 70½.

Exactly how much you must withdraw depends on your life expectancy or, if you choose, the joint life expectancies of you and your beneficiaries.

If you do not withdraw the required amount, you pay a substantial penalty equal to 50 percent of the difference between the amount you withdrew and the amount you were required to withdraw.

◆ 𝒢XAMPLE

You are age 72. Based on your life expectancy, you must withdraw a minimum of $6,000 a year from your IRA. But in 1995 you made a mistake: you withdrew only $4,000.

What are the tax consequences? You pay a penalty that equals 50 percent of the difference between the amount you withdrew, $4,000, and the amount you were required to withdraw, $6,000. In this case you pay the IRS a penalty of $1,000, that is, 50 percent times $2,000.

◆ 𝒯IP

To get the maximum deferral from your IRA, consider naming your child or another younger person as beneficiary. That way your joint life expectancy will be quite long, and the amount you will have to take out of your IRA account will be much less than it would be otherwise. The IRS has limits that apply to the life expectancy you can use when your beneficiary is someone other than your spouse.

◆ 𝒯IP

Name your spouse as your beneficiary. A spouse—but not a child—can roll over an IRA he or she inherits from a deceased spouse. Now the spouse can avoid minimum withdrawal requirements until age 70½.

✪ 𝒞AUTION

Other individuals who inherit IRAs must withdraw the money within five years after the inheritance or must begin receiving annuity payments immediately; otherwise, they pay the 50 percent penalty.

✪ 𝒞AUTION

The above rules also apply to Keogh and SEP withdrawals.

WITHDRAWING MONEY FROM YOUR 401(K)

Two sets of rules govern withdrawals from 401(k)s.

One set is imposed by the federal government, the other by your employer, and you must abide by both when you make a withdrawal.

The rules imposed by your employer may never be more generous than those outlined in the tax law; but your employer's rules may be *less* generous. So familiarize yourself with the provisions of your employer's 401(k).

The IRS rules governing access to funds in a 401(k) plan are similar to the restrictions that apply to other retirement plans.

You may receive your money from your 401(k), without penalty, when you:

- Reach age 59½ regardless of whether you are working or not.
- Quit working after you reach age 55.
- Quit working before age 55 and your money is paid as an annuity.
- Die or become disabled.

If at any of these times you choose to make your withdrawal in a lump sum, you can likely reduce your taxes if the withdrawal is eligible for five-year averaging.

After you leave your job, you may receive your money in the form of an annuity, that is, periodic payments over your lifetime.

As for financial hardship, you may withdraw your money from your 401(k) if your employer's plan allows, but you still pay taxes and a 10 percent penalty. But the penalty doesn't apply if the hardship withdrawal is to pay deductible medical expenses. (See Chapter 7 for more information on writing off medical expenses.)

And your company may distribute the cash in the plan to you when your employment ends, regardless of your age.

In this case you have just 60 days to roll the 401(k) funds over into an IRA or other approved retirement plan. Any amount that you do not roll over is taxed as ordinary income, and you also pay a 10 percent penalty if you are younger than age 55.

✪ *C*AUTION

As previously mentioned, Congress changed the rollover rules for certain withdrawals so that now, if any part of a taxable distribution is not rolled over by the trustee directly to another qualified retirement plan, annuity, or IRA (i.e., a "trustee-to-trustee" transfer), that portion of the distribution will be subject to a 20 percent withholding rate. Furthermore, you will not be able to elect to avoid withholding on such amounts. Consult your tax adviser before you make such withdrawals.

If your employer's plan allows, you may withdraw your money from a 401(k) in the form of a loan. (That is generally not the case with other arrangements, such as IRAs.)

Borrowing from your 401(k) plan, while possible, has restrictions attached to it. Your loan, together with any outstanding loans, is limited to the lesser of: $50,000 or the greater of $10,000 or one-half of your vested 401(k) account balance. Moreover, the $50,000 limit is reduced by the excess, if any, of:

- The highest outstanding loan balance during the one-year period before the date of the new or extended loan, *over*
- The outstanding loan balance on the date you take out the loan.

◆ *E*XAMPLE

On January 1, 1995, the amount you have vested in your 401(k) comes to $100,000, and outstanding loans from your plan total $40,000. Eight months later, on September 1, you want to borrow more money. You've already paid back $15,000 of your loan, so your outstanding loan balance now totals $25,000.

Now you need another loan and want to know how much more you can borrow. The answer is $10,000—$50,000 less the current balance of your outstanding existing loan ($25,000), less the difference between the highest outstanding loan balance during the previous year ($40,000) and the outstanding balance of your existing loan ($25,000), or $15,000. What happens if you pay off the $40,000 balance by September 1? It makes no difference.

According to the rules you may borrow $10,000—$50,000 less the highest amount that was outstanding during the previous year ($40,000).

Also, you must repay the loan within five years unless you use the money to buy a principal residence. In that case, you may take as long as your plan allows, usually 15, 20, 25, or 30 years, the terms of typical mortgages.

However, the law requires you to repay your loan in equal payments, which you make at least quarterly over the term of the loan. The interest you pay on the loan must be "reasonable" (i.e., it must not be too low or too high).

✿ *C*AUTION

But whatever the interest is on such a loan, you usually may not deduct it even if the deduction would otherwise be allowed, such as mortgage interest. The legislators figured you should not be able to deduct interest that you are, in effect, paying to yourself.

You do get a break, though, if you took out a loan from your 401(k) plan before 1987. In this case you are allowed to deduct your interest under the interest tracing rules. For example, interest on a loan used to buy stock is classified as investment interest (see Chapter 5).

But if you took out a loan after 1986, the interest is not deductible, no matter how you used the money.

✿ *C*AUTION

When it comes time to take cash out of your 401(k), you are taxed on the amount of interest that you paid. It is treated in the same way as any other interest or dividends that accumulate on the amounts you have contributed.

✿ *C*AUTION

Say you leave a job and still have a 401(k) loan outstanding. If your plan requires repayment at the time you stop being an active participant in the plan—which in fact most plans do—your failure to repay the loan when you leave is a default. The amount of any defaulted loan balance will be treated as a distribution at that time.

In that case you pay taxes on the distribution, and what's worse, you'll pay the 10 percent early distribution penalty, unless you are one of the exceptions to the rule—such as you are age 59½.

QUESTIONS AND ANSWERS

Q.   Is there any point at which I must begin withdrawing funds from my retirement account?

A.   No matter what kind of retirement plan you have and how you decide to take the money out, the law requires that you begin withdrawing your benefits no later than April 1 of the year following the year you reach the age of 70½.

Failure to begin taking any of your benefits in time will subject you to a 50 percent penalty on the amount that is required to be distributed each year over the amount actually distributed.

24

WHAT YOU NEED TO KNOW ABOUT YOUR CHILDREN'S TAXES

- Are your children required to file tax returns?
- How does the tax treatment differ for children under and over 14 years old?
- What strategies are available to reduce your family's overall tax liability?

This chapter discusses when tax returns are required to be filed by or on behalf of your children. It also shows you how the rules on children's taxes (the so-called "kiddie tax" rules) may change your own tax strategies as a parent. Finally, this chapter discusses the rules governing trusts.

FILING REQUIREMENTS

The filing requirements for children are far from straightforward.

The rules say that dependent children with 1995 *unearned incomes* greater than $650, or with total gross incomes greater than the standard deduction, must file returns. (There are, of course, exceptions to this rule; these are discussed below.)

In 1995, the standard deduction is the greater of $650 or the amount of a child's earned income—up to a limit of $3,900. Both these figures are subject to an annual adjustment for inflation.

As a consequence, a child with modest unearned income and less than $3,900 in total gross income may still have to file a tax return.

❖ *EXAMPLE*

Molly received unearned income—from interest and dividends—of $400 in 1995. This is less than the $650 filing limit.

But she also earns $1,000 working at a summer job. Her standard deduction then is limited to the amount of her earned income—$1,000. But her gross income is $1,400—higher than her standard deduction. Molly has to file a return.

The following diagram will help you work through these rules.

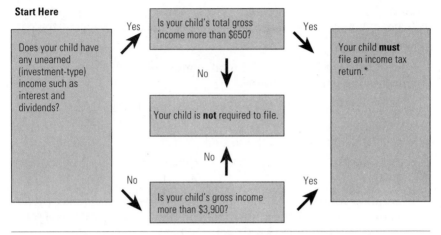

Start Here

Does your child have any unearned (investment-type) income such as interest and dividends?

Yes → Is your child's total gross income more than $650?

Yes → Your child **must** file an income tax return.*

No ↓

Your child is **not** required to file.

No ↑

No → Is your child's gross income more than $3,900? ← Yes

*Or, in certain cases, you may report the child's unearned income on your return (discussed below).

When you or your tax adviser calculate Molly's tax liability, you subtract the standard deduction, $1,000. The remainder is the amount subject to tax. Therefore, Molly must pay tax on $400 of her income.

Molly, a dependent of her parents, may not use the personal exemption, $2,500 in 1995, to reduce her taxable income. Only Molly's parents may claim her and take the personal exemption. (For more information on the personal exemption, see Chapter 3.)

REPORTING CHILD'S INCOME ON PARENTS' RETURN

You may report your child's unearned income on *your* return to avoid filing separately for your child. To do so you must file Form 8814, "Parents' Election to Report Child's Interest and Dividends," with your 1040.

You and your child must meet certain requirements, however:

- Your child must be under 14 years of age.
- The child's gross income can consist only of interest and dividends.
- The child's gross income must be more than $500 but less than $5,000. (Although logically these figures should be adjusted for inflation, they are not.)

So if your child has any earned income—from baby-sitting, for example, or running errands for the local drugstore—you may not report his or her income on your return.

✪ *C*AUTION

You may not make this election if your child has made estimated tax or withholding payments in his or her name and Social Security number.

If you do make this election, the tax law treats your child as if he or she had no gross income for the year. Therefore, your child will not have to file a return.

Instead, you include your child's unearned income on your—the parents'—return.

Here's how the IRS taxes the total amount of a child's unearned income on the parents' return:

- No tax on the first $500 of unearned income (thanks to the standard deduction).
- A flat 15 percent tax on the second $500 of unearned income.
- The balance of unearned income is taxed at the parents' highest marginal tax rate.

In addition you must treat any of the child's interest that is a tax-preference item for purposes of the alternative minimum tax (AMT) as if it belonged to you, the parent. (See Chapter 20 for more on the AMT.)

When you make this election, your investment income *should* increase by the amount of your child's unearned income for the purpose of determining your investment interest expense deduction. However, there is some uncertainty about this. Congress enacted this provision for administrative convenience, not to provide a tax benefit for investment interest expense. But it is possible to read the statute's language as giving you this unintended benefit.

✿ Caution

Including your child's income on your return will also increase your adjusted gross income for purposes of the limitations imposed on the overall deductibility of itemized deductions and personal exemptions, as well as those imposed on medical and miscellaneous itemized deductions.

✿ Caution

Your child's income may become subject to state income tax or to a higher state income tax if included in your return.

AGE 14 AS THE DIVIDING LINE

The tax law separates children into two groups: those who have reached the age of 14 and those who have not.

The distinction is a result of Congress's effort to significantly dilute tax benefits of a common tax-saving strategy known as income shifting. In the past, parents using this popular tactic would shift income to their children so it would be taxed at the child's lower marginal rate.

Parents may still use this strategy for children who are 14 years of age or older but not for their younger children, except for relatively modest amounts (i.e., not in excess of $1,300).

It does not matter when during the year your child turns 14. In fact, your child is taxed as a 14-year-old all year even if his or her 14th birthday is on January 1 of the following year.

FIGURING TAXES ON YOUR CHILD'S RETURN (PARENTS' ELECTION NOT MADE)

The net unearned income—that is, the income from investments, not from wages—of children under 14 is taxed at the higher of the parents' rate or the child's rate. (The parents' rate is almost always higher.)

This rule makes the calculation of younger children's taxes a bit complex. The key is to determine net unearned income.

The source of the unearned income makes no difference. It might come, for instance, from dividends on stocks given by grandparents or purchased with the child's own money, and the stocks may have been given or purchased long before Congress adopted this law in 1986. Nonetheless, the same tax rules apply. The net unearned income generated by the stock is taxed at the parents' rate or the child's rate, whichever is greater.

To calculate your child's net unearned income:

	Interest
Plus:	Dividends
Plus:	Capital gains
Plus:	Other unearned income
Equals:	Unearned income
Minus:	$650 taxed at child's rate
Minus:	Adjustments to income related to investment income (e.g., penalty on early withdrawal of savings)
Minus:	Greater of $650 or the child's itemized deductions associated with the production of investment income
Equals:	**Net unearned income to be taxed at parents' rate**

❖ *Ɛ*XAMPLE

Your 13-year-old, Rachel, earned $800 baby-sitting and raking leaves this year, and she received $2,000 in unearned income—interest and dividends from stocks and bonds you have given her over the years.

To compute her 1995 net unearned income, begin with the $2,000 in interest and dividends and subtract $650 because the first $650 of Rachel's unearned income, no matter what her age, is taxed at Rachel's rate, not yours.

Now reduce the remaining $1,350 in unearned income by the greater of $650 or any deductible expenses—in excess of 2 percent of Rachel's adjusted gross income (AGI)—related to producing that income. (In Rachel's case there were none.)

Therefore, take the $650 standard deduction and subtract it from her remaining $1,350 of unearned income. The result is that only $700 of Rachel's unearned income ($2,000 minus the $650 taxable at her marginal rate minus $650 from the standard deduction) is taxed at your marginal rate. The $700 is her net unearned income.

What about her wages? Any earned income—in this case, the $800 Rachel was paid for baby-sitting and raking leaves—is taxed at her rate, but Rachel pays tax on just $650 of her earned income.

The reason is that the law allows her to claim a standard deduction equal to the greater of $650 or her earned income (up to the $3,900 limit in 1995). So she is entitled to a standard deduction of $800—the amount she received for her work.

She has already applied $650 of her standard deduction against her unearned income. That leaves $150 that she can use to reduce her earned income. Subtracting this $150 from $800 results in $650, the amount of Rachel's earned income subject to tax.

Her tax liability on earned income comes to $98 (15 percent times $650). On her unearned income, however, she owes the IRS a total of $350—$98 from the $650 taxable at her 15 percent marginal rate plus $252 from the $700 taxable at her parents' rate (assuming you are subject to a 36 percent marginal rate). Her total tax: $448.

Here is a simple way of figuring the tax on your child's net unearned income—that is, the unearned income that will be taxed at your rate:

- First, calculate the net unearned income.
- Add it to your taxable income.
- Then calculate your tax.
- Next, calculate your tax without adding in your child's income.
- The difference between these two figures is the amount of tax due on your child's net unearned income.

✿ CAUTION

If you are the parent of more than one child under the age of 14, you must add all of their net unearned incomes to your taxable income. Then you calculate your tax again. If the result is an increase in your tax bill, you must allocate a *pro rata* portion of this increase to each of your children.

CHILDREN'S AMT

Children under the age of 14 may be subject to the alternative minimum tax (AMT) on their net unearned income in excess of $1,000 if their parents are. (Under current law, this dollar amount is not adjusted for inflation, although logically it should be.) So if you have to pay AMT, here is how to figure your child's tax:

- First, calculate the child's net unearned *minimum* taxable income. Basically, this calculation involves adding back certain preferences, such as miscellaneous deductions, and making certain AMT adjustments.
- Then add his or her unearned minimum taxable income to your AMT income.

If this increases your AMT liability, the amount of the increase is the amount your child owes in AMT.

✿ *C*AUTION

Remember that the child's AMT is in addition to his or her regular tax liability.

Children 14 and older will rarely be subject to AMT, but if you suspect that this might happen, consult your tax adviser to see how the child might avoid future AMT liabilities.

FURTHER CONSIDERATIONS

If a child's parents are divorced, his or her net unearned income is taxed at the rate of the parent who has custody. If the parents have joint custody, his or her rate is the same as the parent with the higher rate—just as it would be if his or her parents were married but filed separate returns.

If both parents are deceased, a child pays taxes at his or her own rate.

A child who is 14 or who turns 14 during the tax year pays tax almost like an adult in that a 14-year-old's marginal tax rate on unearned income depends strictly on his or her income level, not on the income of his or her parents.

However, older dependent children are entitled to claim a standard deduction of only $650—or an amount equal to their earned income if this amount is greater, up to $3,900—and they may not reduce their taxable income by their own personal exemption. As long as they are dependents, only their parents may claim that exemption.

WHY THE IRS WANTS YOUR CHILDREN'S SOCIAL SECURITY NUMBERS

The law requires you to list on your return the Social Security numbers of all of your children who are one year of age or older and for whom you claim a dependency exemption. It also requires each of your children to include your Social Security number on their returns.

The IRS uses these numbers to make sure that you do not claim deductions to which you are not entitled. For example, if you claim a personal exemption for your child, the IRS will check to see if your child is claiming one as well.

If you do not provide a Social Security number, the IRS may disallow the dependency exemption, which is worth a hefty $2,500 deduction. The IRS may also impose a penalty of $50 for each Social Security number you failed to include on your return.

Getting a Social Security number for your child is a simple process. Ask your local Social Security office for a copy of Form SS-5. Then fill it out and take it or mail it to the nearest Social Security office.

When you mail the application, include proof of your child's age and citizenship. A public birth certificate is the best evidence, but a hospital record of birth or a religious record showing age or date of birth is also acceptable.

Since you are applying on behalf of your child, you must prove your identity. Acceptable evidence includes a driver's license, church membership or confirmation record, U.S. passport, voter's registration card, or military record.

✪ 𝒞AUTION

The law also gives children under the age of 14 access to your tax return, which may be an issue for divorced parents. If you and your ex-spouse have joint custody of a child under 14, then, as mentioned earlier, the child pays the same rate on his or her net unearned income as the parent with the higher rate pays—just as he or she would if you were still married and filing separate returns.

The only way the child will know which parent has the higher rate is if he or she—and your ex-spouse—have access to your return. As a practical matter, there is not much you can do to avoid disclosure.

INCOME SHIFTING

The tax treatment of younger children means the opportunities for income shifting—moving income from a family member with a higher marginal rate to one with a lower marginal rate—are limited. However, some income-shifting opportunities are discussed below.

MAKING GIFTS TO CHILDREN
14 OR OLDER

Since the unearned income of children 14 years of age and older is taxed at the child's rate—which is usually lower than the parents'—shifting income to these children can produce tax savings.

◆ *Ɛ*XAMPLE

You invest $20,000 at 6 percent compounded annually for five years, and you are in the 36 percent bracket. You would have just $4,146 in after-tax earnings at the end of five years.

But let's say you and your spouse gave your 14-year-old son, Byron, the $20,000 and allowed him to make the same investment.

His earnings probably would be taxed at only 15 percent. So at the end of five years Byron would have after-tax earnings of $5,646—$1,500 more (36 percent) than your own.

Put another way, Byron's after-tax rate of return on the investment would be 5.1 percent compared to the 3.84 percent net rate of return that you were able to earn.

The result is that giving the $20,000 to Byron increased the *family's* net income by $1,500 over five years. The results would be even more dramatic if you were in the 39.6 percent bracket.

Probably the most sensible and simplest way to shift income to your children, regardless of their age, is through the Uniform Gifts to Minors Act (UGMA) or the Uniform Transfers to Minors Act (UTMA).

Under these acts, parents (or any other person) may give money to a child and keep those assets under a custodian's control.

You may select a member of your family, a legal guardian, or any adult you trust as the custodian. However, it usually is not a good idea for the donor—the person who gives the money—to serve as custodian.

The reason is that if the donor also acts as custodian and dies before your child reaches the age of majority, the money given your child is subject to estate tax. The situation may not be a bad one, though, if the donor's estate is small—less than $600,000.

You do not have to worry about legal fees in setting up an UGMA or UTMA account. Just go to a financial institution, such as a bank, and ask for the appropriate forms.

✷ *Ƈ*AUTION

Most states allow UGMA accounts but may not have adopted the revised UTMA provisions. You will have to check the law in your state.

➤.*Ɉ*P

The UTMA may make more sense if you want to make sure your child uses the account's assets for college.

With an UTMA account the custodian does not have to distribute assets until your child reaches 21, or even 25 in some states.

With an UGMA account, however, the custodian no longer controls the money when your child reaches majority, which is 18 in many states. Moreover, an UTMA account lets you invest in real estate. With an UGMA account you may transfer only money, securities, annuities, and insurance contracts. Transfers of other personal property and real estate are prohibited.

Shifting capital to your older children is an effective way of reducing the family tax burden. There are just two caveats, however.

First, you and your spouse may not give a child more than $10,000 each (other than money you give for support) in any year without facing a possible gift tax problem.

The distinction between a gift and support is not always clear-cut. The tax law provides that support items include food, clothing, lodging, medical expenses, baby-sitting costs, educational expenses, and so forth.

If you are exceptionally generous and buy Mary, your 16-year-old daughter, a $35,000 sports car, chances are the IRS will decide that the car is a gift. Although the courts have ruled that a child's transportation expenses count as support, the IRS would probably consider a $35,000 automobile excessive.

Second, once you have turned over cash to your child, it legally belongs to him or her—not to you. Legally, you cannot dictate how the money is spent.

If Byron decides to withdraw the $20,000 you gave him for college expenses and buy a car instead, legally he is free to do so.

However, giving gifts to children 14 years and older is still an attractive income-shifting device, but it is less effective for younger children.

You do, however, have alternatives when it comes to shifting income to younger children.

INCOME-SHIFTING TO YOUNGER CHILDREN

As long as a child is younger than 14, the government will tax most of the child's unearned income as if it were received by the parents.

However, this unfortunate rule does not mean that gift giving has lost all of its value as an income-shifting device to lower the family's overall tax burden. As previously discussed, the first $650 of the younger child's annual unearned income is not taxed at all, and the second $650 is still taxed at the child's lower rate.

Take advantage of these rules. It still makes sense to shift some income-producing assets to younger children, even if the tax savings are not dramatic.

◆ ℰXAMPLE

You give your four-year-old son, Robert, $8,000 and invest the money in a mutual fund that yields an 8 percent annual return. Your marginal tax bracket is 36 percent.

Since his annual dividend income is less than $1,300, Robert pays no tax on his first $650 of annual earnings and only 15 percent on the second $650. At the end of 10 years the $8,000 would have grown to $16,777.

Now assume you kept the $8,000, invested it in the same mutual fund, then gave the account to Robert when he turned 14.

You would pay tax on your annual earnings at 36 percent, so the account would have grown to only $13,181.

By taking advantage of this $1,300 break, your family would accumulate an additional $3,596.

And again, you would save even more if you were in the 39.6 percent marginal tax bracket.

Some other income-shifting devices are described below.

SAVINGS BONDS

Ironically, one of the best income-shifting devices for younger children comes from the government itself—US Savings Bonds.

If you redeem US Savings Bonds to pay educational expenses, the interest on the bonds is excluded from your gross income if certain conditions are met:

- The bond must have been issued after 1989;
- You, the purchaser, must be at least 24 years old before the date of issuance; *and*
- You must use the bond proceeds for qualified educational expenses incurred by you, your spouse, or dependents for higher education.

Qualified educational expenses include tuition and required fees that are over and above any scholarships, fellowships, employer-provided educational assistance, or other tuition-reduction amounts. Not eligible are expenses for any course or activity that involves sports, games, or hobbies unless the course is part of a degree program.

Also, the total proceeds of the redemption—that is, the principal and the interest—may not exceed the qualified educational expenses. If they do, you must multiply the amount of interest by a fraction, using the qualified educational costs as the numerator and the aggregate redemption proceeds as the denominator. Then you may exclude the resulting sum from your income.

You report the total amount received on Schedule B of your 1040 and then attach Form 8815, "Exclusion of Interest from Series EE US Savings Bonds Issued after 1989," to support the amount excluded.

✪ CAUTION

The law phases out the exclusion if your 1995 adjusted gross income falls within certain ranges—between $63,450 and $93,450 if you are married and file jointly and between $42,300 and $57,300 for single taxpayers. These ranges are inflation-adjusted in future years. If you are married and file separately, you may not take the exclusion, even if you meet all the conditions.

Even if you cannot meet the requirements for the exclusion, you should still consider Series EE Savings Bonds. Series EE bonds issued after April 1995 mature in 17 years, but you can continue to hold on to them and receive interest until 30 years after the date of issue. (Bonds issued between March 1993 and April 1995 mature in 18 years; different maturity dates apply for bonds issued prior to March 1993, but the 30-year holding option applies to all issues.)

You may purchase Series EE bonds with a face value as little as $50 or as much as $10,000 through banks and savings and loans, payroll deduction plans, the Federal Reserve, or the Bureau of the Public Debt. (The purchase price is one-half of the face amount.) There are no sales charges when you buy a Series EE bond. Also, if you keep the bond until it matures, you'll receive at the very least its full face value, and you may receive more.

The government guarantees that at maturity you will get at least twice the amount you paid for the bond, even if interest rates have dropped precipitously (this equates to an interest rate of approximately 4 percent). But if interest rates go up, you will collect more than the face value, and with the extended maturity dates, the interest on these bonds may continue to accumulate—tax deferred.

Unless you elect to report it annually, the interest on these bonds is not taxed until the bonds mature and you cash them in. (If you cash them in before they mature, any interest you have accumulated to date is taxed at the time you redeem them.) In addition, interest from Series EE bonds is not subject to state or local income taxes.

✪ CAUTION

Series EE bonds issued after April 1995 no longer provide a guaranteed minimum rate of return if redeemed prior to their scheduled maturity. In recent years, Series EE bonds were guaranteed to provide at least a 4 percent return, no matter when they were redeemed.

The new Series EE bonds will earn market-based interest rates, with no guaranteed minimum return if redeemed before their scheduled maturity. Also, the new bonds will earn short-term based rates only during the first five years, credited at six-month intervals.

The result: The new bonds are not quite as attractive as earlier Series EE bonds for long-term savers and if market interest rates fall below 4 percent. However, the option of being able to defer or possibly exclude some or all of the earnings remains, making Series EE bonds an investment that is still worth considering.

You can give your child cash and allow him or her to buy EE bonds, or you may buy the bonds in your child's name. The only requirement: Your child needs a Social Security number when you buy the bond or when you cash it in. If you put your number on the bond, the interest is taxable to you—unless you specify that the bond is a gift at the time you buy it.

✪ 𝒞AUTION

Do not list yourself as co-owner of your child's savings bonds. If you die before the bonds are cashed in, the bonds are included in your estate.

As mentioned earlier, there are two choices of when to report the interest income. The owner may report it annually. This is a good idea if the child's total annual unearned income is expected to be less than $1,300. Alternatively, the owner may report the interest when the bonds are redeemed. If your child reports the interest when the bonds are redeemed, and if at that time the child is 14 or older, the interest will be taxed at the child's lower rate, even though some of the interest was earned when the child was under 14.

If the owner of the bond chooses to report the interest annually but later decides that reporting it upon redemption would be better, the owner can switch only with the consent of the IRS.

You can file Form 3115, "Application for Change in Accounting Method," attached to your Form 1040, and file both forms by the due date of your return for the tax year of the change.

➲.𝒯IP

Under this procedure you can wait until you know your income for the year to decide whether to continue to recognize income annually or to defer the income until the bond matures or is redeemed.

✪ 𝒞AUTION

Once you have used this procedure to switch to deferring income, you cannot use it again for the next five years.

➲.𝒯IP

There is another type of saving bonds: Series HH. Although Series HH bonds are no longer sold for cash, they continue to be issued in exchange for Series EE bonds. The interest you earn from HH bonds is taxed annually, but you can defer the accrued interest from the Series EE bonds until the HH bonds mature.

However, with the extended maturity dates offered on EE bonds, it usually makes more sense to hold the EEs until their final maturity dates to continue to accrue tax-deferred interest.

GROWTH STOCKS

Growth stocks are shares issued by relatively fast-growing companies that probably are paying low or no current dividends. If there are no dividends, there is no tax to pay until your child sells the hopefully appreciated stock after he or she turns age 14.

Then the gain is taxed at the child's lower rate.

✪ 𝒞AUTION

Remember that with growth stocks you always face the possibility of losing some or all of your principal if the stock prices tumble. Therefore, before buying these investments you should carefully think through whether you want to take this risk with your child's education fund.

APPRECIATING PROPERTY

You may make a gift of any appreciating property to your child—land, collectibles, gold, coins, stamps, or art. He or she can then sell the property after turning 14, and the gain is taxed at his or her lower rate. However, consult your tax adviser regarding the gift tax consequences of doing this.

THE FAMILY BUSINESS

If you own a business and it is a sole proprietorship—that is, you report your business income on Schedule C of your Form 1040—you have an opportunity to shift income by putting your child to work in your business. You will reap a double tax benefit.

First, your child's wages are considered earned income, which is always taxed at the child's lower rate, regardless of his or her age.

Second, the wages you pay your kids are legitimate business expenses; therefore, they are tax-deductible.

✪ 𝒞AUTION

You have to be sure that the job is a legitimate one and that you can justify the salary you pay. Abuse—paying your 12-year-old $20 an hour to sweep up—may attract the IRS's attention.

There are two other benefits.

Under a special provision in the tax law, you do not have to pay Social Security taxes on your child's wages as long as he or she is under 18. (Neither does your child.)

Also, your child may open an individual retirement account (IRA) and shelter some or all of his or her earnings. A child may put the lesser of $2,000 or 100 percent of his or her earnings in an IRA and receive the full benefit of an IRA deduction, assuming, of course, that your child's AGI is less than $25,000. (IRAs are discussed in Chapter 23.)

The earnings of an IRA are tax-deferred—that is, your child pays no taxes on the earnings that accumulate until the money is withdrawn, usually at retirement.

Assume your child contributes $2,000 to an IRA in 1995 and deducts the full amount. Next he subtracts $3,900 for the 1995 standard deduction.

His deductions, then, add up to $5,900. So that means he could earn that much in wages in 1995 without paying federal income tax.

✪ 𝒞AUTION

An IRA is a long-range investment. If your child withdraws money before age 59½, he or she will have to pay income taxes and a 10 percent early withdrawal penalty.

✪ 𝒞AUTION

You will have to pay Social Security and unemployment compensation taxes on wages you pay your children if the family firm is a corporation or partnership (other than a family partnership). No such payroll taxes are required for sole proprietorships. In addition, your children will have to pay Social Security taxes on their wages. Obviously, doing so will serve to offset some of your income tax savings.

➤.𝒯IP

If the business is a family partnership, an exemption from payroll taxes on the child's wages will apply if a parent-and-child relationship exists between the child and each of the partners—for instance, where the mother and father are the only partners.

TAX-EXEMPT MUNICIPAL BONDS

Tax-exempt municipal bonds are issued by cities or states for local projects. They are free of federal income taxes, and if you buy municipal bonds issued in your own state, you usually do not pay state taxes either.

Therefore, purchasing one of these bonds for your child—or buying shares in a municipal bond fund—lets him or her avoid taxation altogether. (However, income on tax-exempt, so-called private activity bonds issued after August 7, 1986, is taxable for purposes of the alternative minimum tax.)

➤.𝒯IP

Buying municipal bonds or shares in a bond fund is not a way to shift income from one family member to another; it's a way to avoid taxation.

✪ 𝒞AUTION

Any gain realized when you finally sell a tax-exempt municipal bond is subject to tax. Only the interest generated by the bond is tax-free.

Therefore, you may want to give your child money to purchase these bonds. (Remember, you and your spouse each may give a child up to $10,000 a year with no gift tax consequences.) That way any capital gains are taxed at the child's rate (if the child is 14 or over) or up to a maximum rate of 28 percent.

With corporate or US Treasury *zero-coupon bonds*, the IRS requires you or your child to include a portion of the discount (called *original issue discount*, or OID) in your or your child's gross income each year, even though you do not receive anything until the bond matures. As a result, you or your child may have to pay taxes on this amount.

However, when you buy zero-coupon municipal bonds, you are not required to pay any tax because the rules on reporting OID do not apply to tax-exempt bonds.

⟩.𝒯ıP

Consider buying zero-coupon municipal bonds or bond funds in your child's name. Zero-coupon bonds are quite similar to US Savings Bonds. They are sold at a deep discount from their face value and pay no current interest. When they mature, the holder receives the full face amount.

↻ 𝒞AUTION

You might want to purchase municipal bonds or bond funds in your own name if you are uncertain whether your child will spend those funds for college.

CHILD CARE CREDIT

The child or dependent care credit was designed primarily to help parents defray the cost of child care. Generally, the credit may be taken by single parents who work outside the home or by married couples (who must file a joint return) if both the husband and wife are employed outside the home.

To qualify you must meet certain requirements. The expenses you incur must be necessary for you to be employed or actively seek employment away from home.

Also, you must bear financial responsibility for maintaining your household, and you must spend money for the care of any of the following dependents while you are on the job:

- Children under 13 who are dependents.
- Dependents who are physically or mentally incapable of caring for themselves—a person with Down's syndrome, for example.

The child care credit ranges from a low of 20 percent to a high of 30 percent of expenses paid during the year. The percentage is based on your

AGI. If your AGI comes to $10,000 or less, the 30 percent credit applies; if it exceeds $28,000, the 20 percent credit applies.

If your income falls between $10,000 and $28,000, the 30 percent credit is reduced by 1 percent for each $2,000 of AGI in excess of $10,000. For example, a person with an AGI of $14,000 would qualify for a 28 percent credit.

The credit applies only to employment-related expenses of up to $2,400 for one dependent and $4,800 for two or more dependents—so the maximum credit is $1,440 (30 percent times $4,800), a dollar-for-dollar reduction of your regular tax liability. The IRS defines employment-related expenses as the cost of hiring people to care for your dependent or to provide household services—cleaning, cooking, and so on.

✪ CAUTION

The child care credit may only be applied to expenses that are equal to or less than your earned income. If you are married, you must use the earned income of the spouse who makes the lesser amount.

◆ EXAMPLE

Assume you earn $2,000 working part-time, and your spouse earns $25,000 working full-time. Also, you and your spouse collect $3,000 in interest from your money market fund. So your joint AGI comes to $30,000. You pay someone $2,400 to care for your child while you are at work.

You may claim only $2,000 worth of child care expenses. Your credit totals $400 (20 percent times $2,000).

◈ TIP

Assume you are married and file a joint return. Because you work outside the home, and your spouse is a full-time student, you pay someone to care for your child. You are entitled to claim a child care credit, even though your spouse is a student and not employed outside the home.

When it comes time to calculate your child care credit, the rules assume that your "student spouse" earned $200 a month for each month he or she attended school full-time. If you claim a credit for more than one child, the amount increases to $400 a month.

✪ CAUTION

If your employer provides a dependent care assistance plan, you may not be eligible for the child care credit. This is because the law says you must reduce the amount of expenses eligible for the credit dollar-for-dollar by the amount excluded from your gross income under the dependent care assistance plan (up to a maximum of $5,000). Doing so may reduce or completely eliminate any expenses you have that would otherwise be eligible for the child care credit.

⊛.𝒯ιp

You must run the numbers to decide whether the child care credit or the dependent care assistance plan provides the greater tax benefit to you.

Usually, if you are in a 28 percent or higher tax bracket, the dependent care assistance plan provides a greater benefit because it reduces not only your taxable income but also your wage base for calculating Social Security taxes.

✪ 𝒞AUTION

The amount you allot in a dependent care assistance plan will be forfeited if not used for the payment of eligible expenses.

⊛.𝒯ιp

To take advantage of either the child care credit or an employer-provided dependent care assistance plan, you must provide your child care provider's Social Security number (or other taxpayer identification number) along with the person's correct name and address, in Part I of Form 2441, "Child and Dependent Care Expenses," which you file with your Form 1040.

Record the necessary information on Form W-10, "Dependent Care Provider's Identification and Certification," which you don't file with your return, but keep for your records to substantiate the information you included on Form 2441.

QUESTIONS AND ANSWERS

Q.   I own my own business and will report my earnings on Schedule C of my 1995 Form 1040. Should I hire my two kids, ages 12 and 13, to help with the filing and cleaning? If so, how will this strategy save taxes?

A.   Hiring your kids will help trim your tax bill in several ways. For starters, you may deduct your kids' salaries on your Schedule C to reduce your business profits. This in turn reduces the amount of income tax you pay on your business's net earnings, which are likely taxed at a rate of 28 percent or more. Reducing your earnings may also reduce the amount of self-employment tax, including Medicare health insurance (HI) payroll tax, you'll owe on your self-employment earnings.

However, the self-employment earnings reductions will not be dollar-for-dollar, since as a self-employed individual you may effectively deduct a portion of your self-employment tax in determining both your net earnings subject to self-employment tax and your adjusted gross income.

In 1995, $61,200 is the maximum earnings subject to the OADSI portion of the self-employment tax, which is imposed at a rate of 12.4 percent, and all of your earnings are subject to the Medicare HI payroll tax of 2.9 percent.

If they have no other wages or earned income to report on their returns, your kids will not pay federal taxes on their earnings from your business, provided the earnings of each are equal to or less than the 1995 standard deduction amount of $3,900. (Even if their earnings are greater than $3,900, they can have taxable incomes of up to $23,350 and still be subject to tax at a 15 percent rate—compared to your rate of 28 percent or more.) Also, neither you, as their employer, nor your children, as your employees, will owe FICA taxes on their wages as long as they are under age 18.

So putting your kids on the payroll helps to reduce your family's tax bill.

Q.   When it comes to a child's income, who is liable for any penalties and interest for failing to file a return or for paying the tax?

A.   The child is responsible. The law says that a child's parents are not responsible for paying penalties and interest or taxes simply because they are responsible for filing the return on their child's behalf.

25

𝒯AX-WISE WAYS TO FINANCE YOUR CHILD'S EDUCATION

- What are some worthwhile strategies for financing your child's education?
- Can you use trusts to shift wealth?
- How are you taxed if you receive a scholarship or fellowship?

A s astronomical as college costs are today, there is no doubt they are going to climb even higher in years to come.

This chapter will help you prepare for financing your children's future education, a process that includes tax planning.

The first section suggests tax-efficient ways to put money aside for college expenses ahead of time. Then we discuss how to get the most out of the cash you set aside for college costs, including minimizing the share that has to go to the IRS.

PLANNING AHEAD

The best way, tax-wise, to finance your child's education depends in large part on whether the child you are saving for has reached 14 years of age. That is because your opportunities to minimize the tax cost are far fewer before your child reaches 14.

The techniques that apply in the case of a younger child are discussed first. Even with the harsher rules, you do have some options when it comes to cutting the tax cost on college savings.

PRE-14 STRATEGIES

Assume you have set aside a few dollars for your child's education, and you want to put them in an investment that pays current income—dividends or interest.

Should you make the investment in your name? Or should you make it in your child's name? If your child is under age 14, it does not much matter tax-wise.

The reason is that a child under age 14 pays taxes on his or her unearned income at the higher of the parents' rate or the child's rate; the parents' rate is almost always higher. (See Chapter 24 for more information.)

The only significant difference is that younger children are not taxed on the first $650 of unearned income, and the next $650 is taxed at their lower 15 percent rate. Given a maximum 1995 tax rate of 39.6 percent, this small break could yield a tax saving of up to $417 each year.

However, because of the impact of the limit on certain itemized deductions (see Chapter 4 for details) and the phase-out of personal exemptions when income falls between certain levels (Chapter 3), some higher-income taxpayers will find themselves paying tax at a higher marginal rate. Thus, for these people the tax savings could come to a bit more each year.

These savings help, but not to a great degree.

Therefore, about the best tax strategy you can use when putting aside education money for younger children is one that involves tax deferral—delaying the tax until the child reaches 14. After that point, more tax saving is possible.

For information on how to defer taxes, refer to the strategies in Chapter 24 suggested for the under-14-year-old. They include buying:

- Series EE U.S. savings bonds.
- Low- or nondividend-paying growth stocks.
- Appreciating property.

Remember one other idea—which we also covered in the preceding chapter—for your under-14-year-old child. Parents who are business owners can shift some of their income to their younger children by putting them to work.

MINORS' TRUSTS

Minors' trusts allow you to make, free of gift tax, one or more gifts to a child, subject to the usual $10,000 per person per year limit—the annual gift tax exclusion.

This rule means that you and your spouse can add up to $20,000 a year to each of your children's trusts without incurring a federal gift tax. (Check with your tax adviser for the rules governing gift taxes levied by your state.)

The principal and earnings that accumulate remain in the trust until the trustee—who may be anyone you would like—distributes them.

The trust document, which creates the trust, must specify that the trustee has the discretionary power to distribute the property and income for the child's benefit until the child reaches age 21. You are free to specify how and when you want the assets distributed, but unless the trust document grants the trustee the authority to carry out your wishes, the gift tax exclusion does not apply.

✪ 𝒞AUTION

It is not a good idea to name yourself as trustee. If you do, the assets of the trust would be included in your taxable estate in the event of your death.

The income earned by the property in the trust is taxed each year but at a partially reduced rate as long as you allow earnings to accumulate within the trust.

The reason is that the trust is taxed, not the recipient. In 1995, the first $1,550 of income in a minor's trust is taxed at only 15 percent; income between $1,550 and $3,700 is taxed at 28 percent; income between $3,700 and $5,600 is taxed at 31 percent; income between $5,600 and $7,650 is taxed at 36 percent; the rest is taxed at 39.6 percent.

The potential annual tax savings is $868—that is, the difference between the first $7,650 of trust income being taxed to the trust at rates of between 15 and 36 percent versus being taxed at a potential rate of 39.6 percent to the individual recipient.

Income distributed from the trust, on the other hand, is taxed under the so-called "kiddie tax" rules.

✪ 𝒞AUTION

Because the highest trust rate of 39.6 percent begins at a relatively low level ($7,650), using a trust may not result in tax savings if the parents' or child's rate is lower. Consult your tax adviser to see if a minor's trust can benefit you.

Another tax advantage of a minor's trust is that the rules allow you to specify when a child is to receive the dollars in trust. If you want to ensure that a child spends his or her money on college, pick 18 or 21 as the age for distribution of the funds.

➤.𝒯IP

When income and principal are eventually distributed to a child, there is no need to recalculate the tax on that income to account for the period of accumulation. With other types of trusts you might have to perform this complicated recalculation (known as the throwback rules).

The minor's trust you establish does have to comply with two major conditions.

- All of the assets in the trust must be distributed to the beneficiary by the time he or she reaches age 21.
- Should the child die before reaching age 21, the trust document must provide for the assets and accumulated income to be paid to his or her estate or be subject to the child's general power of appointment—this means that the child must have the right to name the recipient of the balance in the trust in the event of his or her death.

Is a minor's trust worth the trouble—and the expense? Remember, you are going to have to pay administrative fees to a bank or other institution that acts as trustee. (These fees typically range from 0.5 to 2 percent of the trust's principal.) The answer is: Probably, if you have a lot of money—$10,000 a year or more, say—to put into it.

◆ EXAMPLE

You and your spouse together give your child $20,000 each year for three years, beginning with the child's first birthday.

Assume the trust fund earns income at a 6 percent annual rate and taxes are paid using the trust income tax rates for 1995 (discussed earlier in this chapter).

By the time the child reaches 18 and the tuition bills begin to come due, the trust will have grown to $121,858. If you simply saved the money and paid taxes at your normal 36 percent rate, the fund would have grown to only $109,696. You have accumulated $12,162 more by having set up the trust fund. The savings will be somewhat smaller if you are in a lower tax bracket, but it will be larger if you are subject to the 39.6 percent rate.

Remember to offset this amount by the administrative costs of the trust. These charges vary from institution to institution. Ask your bank or trust company about the charges it imposes.

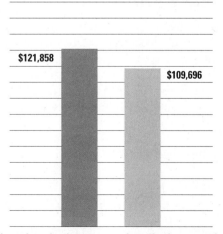

$121,858

$109,696

Investing using minor's trust   Investing in your savings account

✿ CAUTION

If the income from the trust is used to support your child, it is taxable to you. The laws defining legal support vary from state to state.

CRUMMEY TRUST

There is another type of trust that can also be useful. Called a Crummey Trust after the court decision that recognized it, this trust basically allows the distribution of principal and income at the trustee's discretion but does not require the mandatory termination of the trust when the child reaches 21. Instead, the trust document may allow distribution of the principal in stages.

The requirement, however, is that the trustee must notify the beneficiary child annually of his or her right to withdraw over a reasonable period—usually 30 to 60 days—any gifts made to the trust each year.

Whether the child actually withdraws anything from the trust, he or she will be taxed each year on the amount of the trust income that *could* have been withdrawn.

✿ CAUTION

Income that accumulates above this amount is subject to recalculation of income tax under the complex throwback rules.

Since Crummey Trusts are complicated, and because under some circumstances they may actually increase the overall tax liability of a child older than 14, consult your tax adviser before creating one.

BACCALAUREATE BONDS

Another idea worth considering is purchasing so-called baccalaureate bonds. These bonds are a special type of zero-coupon municipal bonds offered by some states.

These bonds are safer than many other types of municipal bonds because they are backed by the full faith and credit of your state.

In addition, income from these bonds is exempt from federal tax. The same is true for state and local taxes as long as you continue to live in the state that issued them. Also, baccalaureate bonds are less likely than other municipal bonds to be called early.

STRATEGIES FOR THOSE 14 AND OLDER

Just because your child has reached age 14 does not mean that it is too late to start saving for college. You just do not have as much time to accumulate assets when your child is this old.

On the other hand, it is only when the child reaches 14 that the IRS truly becomes your partner in the savings effort. From this point on, the child's unearned income will be taxed at his or her rate, not yours.

Therefore, at this point you can begin to do some income shifting—transferring income on which you would pay a high tax rate to your now lesser-taxed child.

Usually you shift income by using gifts. To make sure your kids do not spend their college money on something you would consider foolish, you will probably want to use the Uniform Gifts to Minors Act (UGMA) or the Uniform Transfers to Minors Act (UTMA), discussed in Chapter 24.

WHAT TO DO WHEN SAVING TIME IS OVER

Your child is a high school senior and ready to choose a college. The time for long-range planning is over. Either you have earmarked money for covering college expenses or you have not. In either case, you now have to come up with the money.

You have three options, which you will probably want to use in some combination. You can tap your capital, including whatever assets, if any, you or your child have been accumulating against this day. You or your child can borrow money. Also, you can always apply for financial aid from the government or from the school.

TAPPING CAPITAL

If you have specifically put aside some savings or assets as college money, you will have no reluctance to liquidate them when the bills arrive.

However, even if you have not had such foresight, you can nevertheless tap some of your assets and still get a bit of tax help from the IRS.

Assume that you own stocks or bonds that have appreciated in value over the years. You might think of selling some of them to raise college cash. But if you sell in 1995, you're going to be taxed on the gain that you realize at a maximum 28 percent tax rate.

A better strategy may be to give the stocks or bonds to your college-bound child. (Remember, you and your spouse each may make up to $10,000 worth of gifts annually tax-free. Even if you give more, your gift tax liability will typically be covered by the unified gift and estate tax credit.)

Your child will have to pay the taxes on the appreciated value of the securities.

But he or she will pay taxes only at the 15 percent rate—as long as his or her gain plus other taxable income doesn't exceed $23,350, which is the limit in 1995 for single people paying at the 15 percent rate. When you give him or her the assets to sell, there is more after-tax money left to pay the college bills.

◆ EXAMPLE

A stock you bought many years ago has appreciated in value by $15,000. If you sell it, you receive the $15,000 appreciation minus $4,200 ($15,000 times 28 percent capital gains rate) in taxes. In other words, out of the $15,000 gain, you get to keep $10,800.

If you give the stock to your child and he or she sells it, his or her tax bill will add up to just $2,250 ($15,000 times 15 percent). Your child gets to keep $12,750 of the $15,000 gain. When you give the stock to your child, he or she will have $1,950 more to put toward tuition.

✪ CAUTION

Remember that your child may choose not to sell the stock. Once you give it to him or her, you have lost legal control over what he or she does with it.

BORROWING POWER

If you have to borrow to finance a child's education, probably the best way is through a home-equity loan. The reason is that the interest is probably deductible. (You may not write off the interest you pay on a student loan unless it is secured by your home and meets certain requirements.)

You may generally deduct interest on a home-equity loan of up to $100,000 no matter how you use the money. That fact makes home-equity loans very attractive for financing education costs.

✪ CAUTION

Your kids can always borrow some or all of the cash they need for college from you, provided you have it to lend, but use caution.

You must be careful to treat the transaction in a businesslike manner or the IRS might consider the loan a gift. So make sure to draft a promissory note that states the amount your child borrowed, the interest rate, and the repayment schedule.

✪ CAUTION

Zero-interest loans are not looked upon favorably by the IRS, which will impute (meaning attribute) interest income to you and interest expense to the borrower.

Furthermore, whether it is a zero-interest loan or one made at fair market rates, you actually incur a tax disadvantage when you lend money to your children. These loans result in greater income to you, the higher-bracket taxpayer, and they do not result in a deduction to your child, the lower-bracket taxpayer, since the interest is non-deductible personal interest.

SCHOLARSHIPS AND FELLOWSHIPS

Degree-seeking candidates who are awarded scholarships or fellowships may exclude from their income much of the money they receive. It makes no difference whether they are in graduate or undergraduate school.

If your son, for instance, is in a degree-granting program, he may exclude from income amounts he uses for tuition and books, equipment, supplies, and other course fees. But amounts that are earmarked for room, board, or other living expenses are fully taxable.

Also, he must pay tax on wages he receives for research, teaching, or other services that the school may require as a condition of receiving the scholarship or fellowship.

✪ 𝒞AUTION

The IRS has issued proposed regulations that strictly define course-related expenses. To be considered related expenses, the fees, books, supplies, and equipment must be required of all students in the particular course of instruction.

Say your child uses part of his or her scholarship to buy a word processor because a professor suggested it might be useful. The professor did not, however, require that your child use the word processor as part of the course. In this case, the amount your child spends is not considered part of the tax-free scholarship. Instead, it is treated as taxable income.

➲.𝒯IP

If your child receives a scholarship or fellowship, it is a good idea to keep records that prove that the money covered qualified expenses.

For example, he or she should hold on to copies of bills, receipts, canceled checks, or other documents that verify how scholarship proceeds were spent. In addition, the student should retain documents that list study aids—a calculator or personal computer, say—that are required for each course.

QUESTIONS AND ANSWERS

Q. I have heard a lot about prepaid tuition plans. What are these plans and are they a good idea?

A. Prepaid tuition plans actually come in two general types, each with some potential variations.

With the first type, you pay all four years of tuition when your child becomes a freshman. Since you pay at the first-year price, you are protected against future increases.

These plans may be a good idea under two conditions: You can afford the hefty up-front cost, and you are fairly certain your child will not want to transfer. In any case, it makes sense to check whether your money is refundable if your son or daughter does switch schools.

The second type of prepaid plan that has been established by some colleges and at least one state lets you pay four years' tuition at a steep discount when your son or daughter is a toddler. When your child is old enough to enter college, his or her tuition is already paid, presumably at a price far below current levels.

One drawback is that if your child decides against the college you have paid for, or if that institution closes its doors, you may lose your money entirely. Alternatively, the college or state may refund only the amount you have paid in—with no allowance for many years' interest on your money.

Some schools are forming umbrella plans that allow your child a choice of institutions. However, there is no guarantee that any of these colleges will appeal to your child.

These plans may have tax-related drawbacks. In one case, the IRS found that the plan created by the Michigan legislature triggered three tax liabilities.

First, it triggered a gift tax to the parent when he or she purchased the contract. Furthermore, the IRS said, the $10,000 annual gift tax exclusion did not apply in the case of prepaid education programs.

Second, the plan created a tax liability for the trust in which the funds were deposited on the amount of the trust's earnings. (A recent Court of Appeals decision reversed this IRS position; however, the IRS has not indicated whether or not it will follow the decision with other programs.)

Third, the prepaid plan also triggered a tax liability for the child when he or she began school. The amount taxed is the difference between the annual tuition cost and one-quarter of the cost of the tuition contract (assuming that the contract covered four years of tuition). This means that the income earned by the original purchase price of the contract is actually taxed twice—once when it is earned by the trust and then again when the child receives the education. (If you consider the fact that the original gift was probably made from after-tax dollars, the gift, in effect, has been subject to yet another tax.)

The IRS ruling on the Michigan plan means that its only real savings (if any) to the individual who buys it is the difference between the future value of the current price paid and the actual tuition charge when the child enters school. You will also want to determine whether the income earned by a prepayment trust in your state is subject to state as well as federal taxes. If it is, that is another reduction of overall savings.

However, for many taxpayers these programs are one way to ensure that their children will not be denied college because of lack of funds.

Q.   My parents have offered to pay for my daughter's schooling. Are there any tax implications I should know about?

A.   Generous grandparents (or anyone else) may pay your child's educational expenses and still make other tax-free annual gifts of up to $10,000 each ($20,000 as a couple) per recipient.

The only qualification: They must pay the college or university directly, so make sure they write their check to the school—not to you or your daughter. Otherwise, the IRS will consider the amount of the payment as a gift to which the $10,000 annual exclusion will apply.

Q.   My son was planning to live in a dorm, but friends tell me that it may be better to buy a small condominium for him to live in instead. Do you agree?

A.   There certainly can be tax advantages to seeking alternative housing for your son.

Say you buy an off-campus apartment. You may, under the tax law, treat this unit as your second home and deduct mortgage interest and property taxes. (The IRS allows you to deduct interest expense on your principal residence and one other house; property taxes are deductible on any home(s) you own.) Meanwhile, your son has a free place to live.

Or you could rent the apartment to your son and deduct—subject to the passive loss rules—mortgage interest, property taxes, maintenance, utilities, depreciation, and other expenses associated with maintaining rental property. If you end up with a loss, you may be able to use it to offset your regular income.

However, the laws in this area are complex.

First, the IRS requires that the house be your son's principal residence. Also, you must charge him and any of his friends a fair market rent. And you must actively manage the property yourself—that is, you must participate in collecting rents, authorizing repair work and maintenance, and so on.

If your adjusted gross income (AGI) is $100,000 or less, you may deduct from your income up to $25,000 in losses from rental real estate in which you actively participate each year. But this cap is gradually phased out if your AGI falls between $100,000 and $150,000. When your AGI reaches $150,000, you are entitled to use the losses you incur, but only against other passive income. (However, losses may be allowed if material involvement and time commitments are demonstrated. See Chapter 19.)

When your child graduates, you can sell your property. You may now deduct any losses you were unable to take while you owned the property. In addition, with luck, your property will have appreciated in value.

There is also a tax bonus to setting your son up with a place he can share with friends: You may hire him to manage the property.

Your son can earn up to $3,900 tax-free, provided he has no other income, and you can write that off against the rent his friends pay you. Just make sure that the amount you pay your son for this job is reasonable, or the IRS may challenge the arrangement.

Q.   I plan to claim a dependency exemption for my son, who is 25 and a full-time student. May I?

A.   No, you may not claim a dependency exemption for a student who reaches the age of 24 before the end of the year.

There is an exception to this rule for students whose gross incomes add up to less than the exemption amount—$2,500 in 1995.

However, even if you can't claim an exemption for your child on your tax return, your child may claim an exemption on his or her own return.

26

ITHHOLDING AND ESTIMATED TAXES

- When should you file a new withholding certificate (Form W-4)?
- Are you required to make estimated tax payments?
- How can you avoid penalties for underpayment of estimated tax?

Most taxpayers pay taxes through *payroll withholding.* Thus, they never see the money employers send to the IRS on their behalf.

Taxpayers who are *self-employed* or who have substantial nonwage income—dividends, for example—usually must make *estimated tax* payments four times a year.

It makes no difference whether you make tax payments yourself or rely on the company paymaster to withhold them for you. The IRS still holds you responsible for making sure the taxes you pay throughout the year are adequate according to the law. Indeed, the IRS penalizes taxpayers who underpay their estimated taxes.

This chapter covers the rules governing withholding and estimated taxes. (A calendar of some important tax dates may be found in the Appendix.) The methods available for calculating the required estimated payments and what happens if you do not make adequate estimated payments are also discussed.

Finally, this chapter explains strategies for keeping your estimated tax payments, as well as any penalties, to a minimum.

WITHHOLDING TAXES

Most of us pay taxes on our earnings through payroll withholding. Our employers deduct the money from our paychecks and forward it to the IRS.

The amount of income tax employers withhold from paychecks depends on two factors: the level of earnings and the information provided on the Form W-4, "Employee's Withholding Allowance Certificate."

When you begin a new job, you must fill out a Form W-4 and return it to your employer. If you do not fill out a W-4, the law requires your employer to withhold taxes at the highest rate—that is, as a single taxpayer with no allowances for dependents.

After your Form W-4 takes effect, you can use IRS Publication 919, "Is My Withholding Correct for 1995?" to compare the dollar amount you are having withheld to your estimated total annual tax.

If you found that you paid too little or too much in withholding taxes when you filed your return last year, you should fill out a new W-4 in the current year. That way the amount withheld from your pay will more accurately reflect the tax you expect to owe the IRS.

When you fill out the worksheet provided with the W-4 to figure the number of allowances you may take, you must take into account not only your income but your spouse's income and any nonwage income, such as interest or dividends, that the two of you earn.

Also be aware that the value of certain fringe benefits is subject to withholding.

If you paid too little in withholding taxes last year, consider reducing the number of allowances you take compared to the number you claimed previously. (The number of allowances you claim for withholding purposes does not affect the number of exemptions you may claim on your 1040.) The sooner you revise your W-4, the more your withholding will approximate your actual tax liability for the current year.

If the number of withholding allowances to which you are entitled decreases from the number you have previously claimed on your W-4, you must file a new W-4 within 10 days of the event that led to the decrease in allowances—you and your spouse divorce, for example, or you no longer furnish more than half of the support of a dependent you had previously claimed.

Also, if you claim more than 10 withholding allowances, your employer must send copies of your W-4 to the IRS and you may then be asked to verify your allowances.

The IRS wants to make sure you fill the W-4 form out correctly. So it may fine you $500 if it discovers you deliberately filed, with no reasonable basis, a Form W-4 that results in your having less tax withheld than you should.

However, the IRS has stated that taxpayers who make honest mistakes in calculating their withholding will not be assessed the $500 penalty.

The law also imposes criminal penalties—of $1,000 or a year in jail or both—if you willfully supply false or fraudulent information or fail to supply information that might require an increase in your withholding.

If you have more than one job, or if your spouse works, the total number of allowances you are entitled to claim is figured by combining the income from all jobs and calculating the total allowable exemptions just once. Then you may claim all of your allowances on the W-4 for one job or you may claim some on the W-4 for each job. However, you may not claim the same allowances on the W-4 for both jobs.

For example, you spend your days working for XYZ Corp. and your nights for ABC Co. You claim your four withholding allowances—for your four children—when you fill out your Form W-4 with XYZ. When you file a W-4 with ABC, you must then claim no withholding allowances for your children.

➣.🖋P

If both you and your spouse are employed, the IRS recommends that the spouse with the higher salary take all of the withholding allowances. That way, withholding will more closely approximate the actual tax liability. The same holds true if you have more than one job—take all of the withholding allowances on the higher-paying job.

➣.🖋P

As soon as you discover your employer has withheld too much tax, you should immediately file a new W-4 claiming as many exemptions as allowable.

This strategy makes sense only if you discover the overwithholding before the end of the year. You should periodically review your pay stubs to make sure you are not giving the government a float—that is, an interest-free loan—on your overpaid tax dollars.

Also, make sure you take into account a new marriage, a new child—whether by birth or adoption—or a new house. These changes may increase the number of withholding allowances you are able to claim.

CHILDREN AND WITHHOLDING TAX

Your children are completely exempt from withholding if they paid no income tax last year and expect to pay none this year.

➣.🖋P

This rule is a plus for those children who file returns just to collect a tax refund. However, this exception applies only to income tax, not Social Security.

To claim this treatment, your children must give their employers a completed Form W-4. This treatment is good for only one year.

Therefore, if your children paid no income tax in 1995 and expect to pay none in 1996, you should make sure they file a new Form W-4 by February 15, 1996. If they work "summers only," they should file a W-4 as soon as they begin their summer jobs in 1996. Otherwise, they will be subject to income tax withholding on their wages for the entire year.

Also, if your children have no tax withheld this year but expect to pay income taxes next year, a new W-4 should be filed by December 1 of the current year for the following tax year.

❷ 𝒞AUTION

If you claim (or can claim) your children as dependents on your return, they may not claim personal allowances for themselves on their W-4s.

This rule translates into more kids having taxes withheld from their pay because a child loses the personal exemption when the parents are entitled to claim it (regardless of whether they do). The child can earn only up to $3,900 in 1995—the amount of the standard deduction—without paying income tax and without having to file a return unless Social Security self-employment taxes are due.

❷ 𝒞AUTION

If your child reports any combination of earned and *unearned* income greater than $650, he or she is not exempt from withholding and must file a return.

If your child works only part-time or summers, his or her employer may overwithhold because the amount of withholding is based on the assumption that a worker's pay continues for the entire year.

❷.𝒯IP

Your child should request that the employer use the part-year method to withhold taxes. The result? Your child will not end up making an interest-free loan to the IRS in the form of extra withholding. Rather, he or she will pocket more after-tax dollars in each paycheck.

To qualify for the part-year method, your child must:

- Be a calendar-year taxpayer—that is, he or she must pay taxes on a 12-month year that runs from January 1 to December 31 (almost every child meets this requirement), *and*
- Expect not to be employed more than 245 days during the year, including the first day he or she starts to work and stopping on his or her last day of employment.

Your child then must request in writing that his or her employer use the part-year method of withholding. This request must state that the child passes the two tests; and if the child worked for another employer during the calendar year, he or she must include the date of his or her last day on the job.

QUARTERLY ESTIMATED TAX PAYMENTS

If you are self-employed or you report income beyond wages and salaries, you must generally make your tax payments in the form of estimated taxes.

The IRS expects to get your estimated tax payments once a quarter. For calendar-year taxpayers, the due dates are:

Estimated Tax Payments	
Quarter	Due Date
1	April 15
2	June 15
3	September 15
4	January 15

If the due date falls on a Saturday, Sunday, or legal holiday, your payment is considered on time if you make it on the next business day.

The IRS considers the postmark on the envelope the date of payment—as long as the envelope is postmarked by the U.S. Postal Service, not by a private postage meter. You might want to send your payment by registered or certified mail to have proof positive—via your receipt—that you mailed your estimated tax on time.

The tax law provides that you may skip your January estimated tax payment if you file your return and pay your tax bill in full on or before January 31st.

*☊ ℭ*AUTION

If you extend the filing of your 1995 tax return, this does not extend your first 1996 estimated tax payment. Regardless of the reason for extending the filing date of your return, your first estimated payment for 1996 is due on April 15, 1996.

*☊.𝒯*P

Taxpayers who make their living farming or fishing get special treatment under the tax law. They need to make only a single estimated tax payment of two-thirds of their estimated current year's liability. That payment is not due until January 15 of the following year.

In addition they need to make no estimated payments at all if they file their tax returns and pay their full tax bills by March 1.

*☊.𝒯*P

Also exempted from the quarterly payment requirement are individuals whose estimated current-year tax liability—after credit for taxes that are withheld by their employers—is less than $500. Teenagers often fall into this category.

Excluded, too, are people who owed no tax last year. (These individuals must be U.S. citizens or they must have been U.S. residents for the entire previous 12-month period.)

DO YOU HAVE TO PAY ESTIMATED TAX?

The following provides a convenient "road map" to help you determine whether you must pay estimated tax.

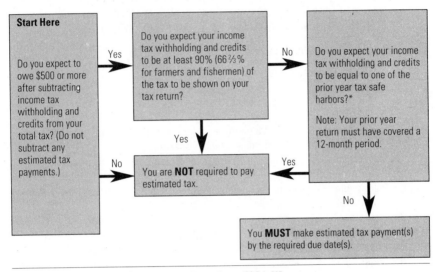

* See discussion under "High-Income Taxpayers" in this chapter. Source: IRS Pub. 505.

FIGURING YOUR PAYMENT

The tax law generally requires that your four quarterly payments total either:

- 100 percent (or 110 percent if your prior year's AGI exceeded $150,000) of the tax you paid during the previous year—that is, the amount of tax shown on your previous return, assuming you had a 12-month taxable year, *or*
- 90 percent of the tax that you will owe in the current year—that is, the amount listed on the tax return you file for the current year.

The IRS thus gives you an option as to determining your payment, which you may use to your advantage.

The amount of AMT you might owe counts when it comes to determining the estimated tax you must pay. Also, the amount of Social Security self-employment tax that you may owe on, say, fees you receive as a freelance consultant must be considered.

◆ ℰXAMPLE

Last year your tax liability came to $35,000 and your AGI did not exceed $150,000. This year you estimate your tax will total $40,000. How much should you pay to the IRS in quarterly payments during the current year?

You may send the IRS either $35,000—100 percent of last year's tax—or $36,000—90 percent of the $40,000 you estimate you will owe this year.

Obviously, paying the $35,000 is a better option.

So far we have discussed estimated payments only on an overall basis. However, note that the government generally requires that *each* of your quarterly payments equal or exceed 25 percent of either:

- The applicable prior year's tax liability safe harbor, or
- 90 percent of the current year's tax liability.

◆. 𝒯IP

The law provides an alternative method—the **annualized income installment method**—that you may use for determining what you owe.

This method is used primarily by self-employed people with seasonal or fluctuating incomes. With this method you may pay installments that actually reflect the income you earn in the period immediately before the installment is due.

If your annualized tax installment for any quarter is less than you would pay under the alternatives we just described, you may pay it without being underpaid in your estimated taxes. But you must attach Form 2210, "Underpayment of Estimated Taxes by Individuals and Fiduciaries," to your Form 1040 to show that you are not subject to the penalty.

To help you annualize your income and figure your adjusted self-employment income for each quarter, the IRS provides worksheets in IRS Publication 505, "Tax Withholding and Estimated Tax," and in the instructions to Form 2210.

HIGH-INCOME TAXPAYERS

All taxpayers are entitled to use an estimated tax "safe harbor" method. If your AGI from the prior year was $150,000 or less, your estimated tax payments may be based on 100 percent of your prior year tax liability. If your prior year AGI was greater than $150,000, your estimated tax payments may be based on 110 percent of your prior year tax liability. Depending upon your AGI, you may use either of these "safe harbors" to avoid underpayment penalties.

◆. 𝒯IP

No matter what your income level, individuals may continue to make estimated payments based on 90 percent of the tax owed in the current year or by using the annualized income installment method (discussed above).

THE PENALTY FOR UNDERPAYMENT

If you underpay your quarterly estimated tax payments, the IRS will impose a penalty on the amount of the shortfall. The percentage amount used to calculate the penalty varies—it rises or falls with current interest rates. (As a guide, the rate was 9 percent for the first quarter, 10 percent for the second quarter, and 9 percent for the third and fourth quarters of 1995.)

If you borrow money to pay your estimated income taxes, the interest you pay on the loan is not deductible. This interest is classified as personal interest (see Chapter 5).

So should you borrow to pay your estimated tax and avoid the penalty?

It depends. Since neither personal interest nor the underpayment penalty is deductible, you might want to borrow to pay your estimated taxes if the interest rate on the loan is lower than the rate used to determine the underpayment penalty. Also factor in the administrative costs and paperwork involved in obtaining the loan, particularly where the penalty amount is minimal.

⊛.🎯P

Instead, consider borrowing via a home-equity loan. That way the interest may be fully deductible so the after-tax costs of borrowing are less. For example, if the interest rate on the home-equity loan is 9 percent (the same as the rate currently charged on the underpayment penalty), the after-tax borrowing cost (assuming a 36 percent tax rate) comes to only 5.76 percent (9 percent x [1 minus .36]). This is considerably lower than the underpayment penalty rate. (The IRS imposes a few restrictions on the deductibility of interest on home-equity loans. These rules are discussed in Chapter 5.)

✿ CAUTION

Remember that it's *your home* you are putting up as **collateral** for the loan.

✿ CAUTION

There may be administrative costs and paperwork in obtaining the loan. So make sure the dollar savings are great enough to justify a home-equity loan.

⊛.🎯P

Employ this same strategy to pay an underpayment penalty. The penalty is nondeductible, but you may be able to write off the interest on the money that you borrow to pay it.

When any single quarterly payment falls short—even if you make up the shortfall in a subsequent payment—the IRS maintains you underpaid and will impose a penalty. This rule holds true even if you eventually receive a tax refund when you file your 1995 return.

◆ ℰXAMPLE

Your tax last year added up to $40,000 and this year it will total $80,000. Assuming you are not subject to the rule for high-income taxpayers discussed above, your quarterly payments are either $10,000 (one-quarter of $40,000) or $18,000 (one-quarter of $72,000, which is 90 percent of $80,000).

Assume you pay $10,000 for each of the four quarterly installments. If you make those payments on time, the IRS will not impose an underpayment penalty, even though your estimated payments amount to only half of your current year's tax liability. Of course, you will have to pay the $40,000 unpaid balance when you file your tax return.

On the other hand, assume that money is tight and that you pay only $4,000 in each of the first three installments. Although you have underpaid each installment by $6,000 ($10,000 less $4,000), the IRS will first apply your estimated tax payment to any underpayment in the order in which such installments were required to be paid. The IRS starts the penalty clock on each underpayment on the date the installment was due.

◆ 𝒯IP

You can limit the amount of the penalty. If on the fourth installment you pay $28,000 to the IRS (the $10,000 due on the fourth installment plus the $18,000 you underpaid on the first three installments), the penalty clock stops running.

You still owe a penalty, the size of which depends on current interest rates, but you have put a cap on the time period that it applies.

◆ 𝒯IP

You could eliminate the penalty altogether—provided you are drawing a salary that is subject to tax withholding. The IRS simply totals all your payroll withholding of income tax at the end of the year. Then it credits one-fourth of the total to each of your four quarterly installments.

Therefore, you may ask your employer to increase the amount of your tax withholding at the end of the year by simply filing a new Form W-4 and claiming fewer or even zero allowances and requesting that an additional amount be withheld. That way you can make up the shortfall from earlier underpayments of estimated quarterly payments.

To see how this strategy works, take the last example and assume that you made those three quarterly estimated tax payments on income that you earn from freelance consulting. You are also employed as an executive of a large oil company, and you usually receive a holiday bonus. You claim no withholding allowances on your W-4. Even so, you calculate that you are still underpaid by $18,000 for the first three quarters.

To eliminate the underpayment penalty you have incurred on your freelance income, you simply have your company withhold an extra $28,000 ($18,000 in underpayments plus the final $10,000 installment) from your year-end bonus check. As long as the extra payroll withholding is done before the end of the tax year, you do not owe a penalty.

However, suppose the situation is different. Suppose you do not want the IRS to credit your withholding equally to all four quarterly installments.

Instead, you want the IRS to credit the amount withheld in the quarter in which the withholding actually happened. This could be useful in minimizing the penalty.

◆ ✐XAMPLE

Assume that you quit your job on April 1. For the first three months of the year your withholding from salary and bonuses totals $24,000.

Because you have investment income, you calculate you are required to pay $40,000 in taxes, or $10,000 per quarter. Because cash is short, you do not make the quarterly payments.

Later you receive some money, and you want to stop the underpayment penalty that has been accruing. So you make one estimated tax payment of $16,000 on January 15. If the IRS prorates your withholding as it normally would, it would credit $6,000 ($24,000 divided by four) to each quarterly installment and you'd then be penalized for being underpaid during the first three quarters.

But if you could claim credit for the $24,000 withheld from your salary and bonus on the dates it was actually withheld, the IRS would consider your first two $10,000 installments paid in full. You would have underpaid the third installment by just $6,000—that is, the $10,000 due minus $4,000 remaining from your withholding. Since you made up for this underpayment with the $16,000 that you sent the IRS in the fourth installment, you have minimized your penalty.

To claim credit for the amounts you had withheld on the actual dates of the withholding, retain proof—such as copies of paycheck stubs—of the dates of the actual withholding. Show the amounts of withholding on Form 2210 according to the dates actually withheld, and include the completed Form 2210 with your 1040.

AMENDING ESTIMATED TAX PAYMENTS

If your tax liability changes during the year—your income goes up, for example, or your expenses decrease—you should amend your estimated tax payments for the remaining installments and make a "catch-up" payment for the shortfall in any prior installment(s) to minimize your underpayment penalty. Likely, the only exceptions to the underpayment penalty that may apply are if you base your installments on one of the prior year safe harbors or you use the annualized income installment method. (In limited circumstances, you might be able to satisfy the IRS that you are entitled to a waiver—a subject we will discuss shortly.)

Assume, for example, you don't use a safe harbor or annualized income method and your income tax estimate increases after you made your first installment. In this case you should amend your remaining three installments to reflect the income tax increase, plus your second installment should include a catch-up payment equal to the shortfall in your first installment. Without the catch-up payment, underpayment penalties on the first installment shortfall will continue to accrue after the second installment due date of June 15.

◆ ✐XAMPLE

Assume your tax liability last year came to $70,000. This year you estimate that you will owe $40,000 and the annualized income method does not apply to you.

Therefore, you base your estimated tax installments on 90 percent of $40,000, or $36,000, and each of your quarterly payments comes to $9,000.

On June 15, however, you revise your expected tax liability for the current year to $60,000. So you must revise the estimated tax you owe to $54,000 ($60,000 times 90 percent) and each of your quarterly payments now comes to $13,500.

Because your first payment fell short by $4,500 ($13,500–$9,000), the IRS will penalize you unless your withholding is enough to cover the shortfall or a waiver applies.

To minimize the underpayment penalty accruing on the shortfall of $4,500 in the first installment, your June 15 installment should include an additional $4,500 catch-up payment—resulting in a June 15 total payment of $18,000. In this way the penalty for the first installment will cease to accrue as of June 15. Your September and January payments will be $13,500 each.

◆.✐ıₚ

If you were able to apply the annualized income installment method, you might be able to minimize or eliminate the penalty for the first installment. You must run the numbers in this case.

Follow similar rules as illustrated above if your estimated income tax liability increases after the second or third installment.

If your income decreases, calculate your expected tax liability and subtract the tax payments you have already made. You may find you have already paid the required amount.

✿ ✐AUTION

If you are entitled to a refund, you must wait until you file your current return to receive it.

◆.✐ıₚ

If you are in fact due a refund, file your return as early as possible to get your refund and minimize your interest-free loan to the IRS.

WAIVER OF THE PENALTY

Although the underpayment penalty is mandatory in most cases, the IRS may—but is not required to—waive it in three situations where it would be unfair.

There is one condition, though: You must file Form 2210 with your return and attach an explanation of the circumstances with supporting documentation entitling you to a waiver. The three situations are:

- Your underpayment is due to a disaster or a casualty.
- It is the result of "unusual circumstances"—a phrase that the IRS has not defined.
- You retired after reaching age 62 or became disabled in the current or previous tax year, and your underpayment is due to reasonable cause, not willful neglect.

APPLYING OVERPAYMENTS

If you overpay your taxes in one year, consider applying the overpayment to your estimated tax bill for the following year.

If your overpayment is approximately the same as you will owe on your first installment, it is usually a good idea to apply your overpayment because your first installment is due April 15, and there is little sense in writing a check to cover an amount that the IRS already has.

If the overpayment substantially exceeds the amounts you owe in the first and second quarters, apply the overpayment to your first and second quarter installments, then request a refund of the remainder. Of course, if you anticipate a significant drop in income for the year, and you expect to pay little or no estimated tax, request a refund for the full amount of the overpayment when you file your return. Once you request that an overpayment be applied to your estimated tax, you cannot change your mind.

⊛.𝒯ıᴘ

To speed receipt of your tax refund, ask your tax preparer if you can file your return electronically—that is, via computer.

The IRS says it will forward refunds from these electronically filed returns within 21 days. The agency normally requires four to eight weeks to process refunds from traditional paper returns. (See Chapter 29 for more information on electronic filing.)

BACKUP WITHHOLDING

Under certain conditions you may be subject to so-called backup withholding on some types of income on which taxes are not ordinarily withheld.

That is because the IRS wants to collect all of the tax that is due. Income that falls into this category includes interest and dividends, rents, profits and other gains, commissions and fees earned by independent contractors, payments by brokers, and royalties.

A business, bank, or other institution must withhold as income tax a flat 31 percent of the amount you are paid if any of the following applies:

- You do not provide the payer with your Social Security number (or other taxpayer identification number, or TIN).
- The IRS notifies the payer that the number you provided is incorrect.
- You fail to certify that you are not subject to backup withholding, even though you are required to.
- The IRS notifies the payer to begin backup withholding because you have underreported interest or dividends on your 1040. (Before taking this action, the IRS will have mailed you four notices over a 120-day period.)

✪ CAUTION

Make sure you provide a correct Social Security number to payers to avoid backup withholding.

Be especially careful when you open bank accounts for children who have not yet applied for or received their Social Security numbers. Note: this would apply only to children under one year old. Children age one and over must have a Social Security number. You will be asked to sign a certificate stating that backup withholding does not apply to your children because you are waiting to receive their numbers. Then you have 60 days to report the numbers. If you do not, the payer will begin withholding taxes on your children's earnings.

➤ TIP

To stop backup withholding once it starts, provide the payer with your Social Security number or other taxpayer identification number and certify that it is correct. The IRS will not automatically pay you back the amount already withheld. You will have to file a return to claim it.

You need to do more, however, if the withholding was triggered by your underreporting income. In this case you must request a determination from the IRS to stop the withholding and you must establish one of the following:

- No underreporting occurred.
- You have a bona fide dispute with the IRS as to whether or not you actually did underreport.
- Backup withholding will cause or is causing you undue hardship, and you are unlikely to underreport interest and dividends in the future.
- If you had not previously filed a return, you corrected the underreporting by doing so and by paying all taxes, penalties, and interest you owed for any underreported interest or dividend payments.

Then if the IRS agrees with you, it will notify the payer to stop withholding tax.

✪ CAUTION

You can be assessed a $500 civil penalty if you give false information to avoid backup withholding. The IRS can also impose a $1,000 fine or up to one year of imprisonment or both.

QUESTIONS AND ANSWERS

Q. My AGI is pretty high in 1995, and I'm worried about underpayment penalties for 1996. Are there any special requirements for payment of my 1996 estimated taxes?

A. Because of recent tax law changes, your calculation of 1996 estimated taxes is a lot easier than it would have been. If your 1995 AGI is $150,000 or less, your 1996 estimated tax payments must be based on either 100 percent of your 1995 tax liability or 90 percent of your 1996 tax liability to preclude imposition of the underpayment penalty.

If your 1995 AGI is more than $150,000, your 1996 estimated tax payments must be based on either 110 percent of your 1995 tax liability or 90 percent of your 1996 tax liability.

Q. Which return does the IRS use to determine how much estimated tax I owe and whether I must pay an underpayment penalty?

A. The IRS uses the last return you mail on or before the due date for filing for that tax year. Say you file an amended return before the due date for filing your original return (including extensions). In this case the IRS considers the amended return your return for the taxable year.

What is more, it uses the amount of tax you owe on this amended return to calculate any underpayment of estimated tax.

You may be able to avoid the underpayment penalty by carefully timing when you file an amended return.

Say you file your return on April 1. On April 10 you receive a K-1 statement that shows partnership income you forgot to include on your original return.

Now, say you file an amended return by April 15, 1996.

The IRS will use your increased tax liability shown on your amended return to determine if you have underpaid your estimated taxes. But if you wait one day after the due date to file your amended return, the IRS uses your April 1 return to calculate whether you owe the underpayment penalty.

Do not make the mistake some taxpayers do of waiting too long after the original due date to file your amended return. Granted, you avoid the underpayment penalty, but you still will pay interest on the amount by which you underpaid your tax.

The interest rate on underpayments and the rate charged as the underpayment penalty is the same—three points over the federal short-term rate, adjusted quarterly, and the interest begins to add up starting with the original due date of the return.

Also, if you understated the tax on your April 1 return by more than $5,000 or 10 percent, whichever is greater, you could face a penalty of 20 percent of the amount by which you underpaid.

The law also makes an exception to the rules on amended returns for some married people filing jointly.

Say you are married and file an amended joint return after the filing due date to replace separate returns that you filed before the due date.

In this case the IRS uses the tax shown on the amended joint return to determine whether you underpaid your estimated tax, even if the amended return is filed after the original filing due date. The reason is that the IRS wanted to help married taxpayers minimize their liability.

In analyzing the tax savings of filing jointly or separately, don't overlook underpayment penalties. Also keep in mind that once you file jointly, you cannot subsequently amend your return after the due date to file separately.

Q. If I make a joint payment of estimated taxes with my spouse, must I file a joint return?

A. Making joint estimated tax payments with your spouse does not mean that the two of you must file a joint return. You may still file separately, and you and your spouse may divide up the estimated payments any way you want.

Q. If my spouse and I make separate estimated payments, can we file a joint return?

A. The answer is yes. However, you and your spouse may not file jointly if either of you is a nonresident alien, legally separated under a decree of divorce or separate maintenance, or have different tax years. Also, you and your spouse can file jointly even if you are not living together—if you have a "commuter marriage," for example.

If you and your spouse file separate estimated tax payments and separate returns, you cannot use an overpayment by your spouse to offset your under-payment, or vice versa.

However, the rules are different if you file separate returns and live in the community property states of Arizona, California, Idaho, Louisiana, Nevada, New Mexico, Texas, Washington, or Wisconsin.

In this case you and your spouse must each report half of the income from all of your community property in addition to reporting your own separate income. And each of you takes credit for half of all taxes withheld on your community income.

27

$\mathcal{A}$VOIDING $\mathcal{I}$RS PENALTIES

- When will IRS penalties apply?
- What strategies minimize penalties and interest?
- Does the IRS ever waive penalties?

The IRS is fairly industrious when handing out penalties to people who don't live up to the letter of the law.

Carelessness or misunderstanding is no excuse. If you are late with your taxes or don't pay all that you owe, you can expect the IRS to assess penalties. And these fines can add up quickly, especially when coupled with the interest that you'll also owe on the balance of taxes due.

If you find yourself in a situation where you are likely to face a penalty, there are some ways you can at least keep it from growing any larger.

Here we explain how the IRS applies its discipline.

INTEREST OWED AND OWING

If you owe the government money, you must pay interest on the amount due—from the very day that it's due. Filing an extension doesn't change the fact that interest on any unpaid amount that you owe begins to accrue on April 15.

Likewise, you may collect interest from the IRS on overpayments. The rate will be lower than the one you would pay if you owed the IRS money.

The rules say the IRS must pay your refund to you within 45 days from April 15 or the date you file your return, whichever is later.

What if the IRS fails to meet this deadline?

It must pay you interest on your refund.

What's more, it must calculate the interest due you from April 15 if you file a timely return (including extensions) or the date on which you file your return if it's a late-filed return.

Both rates—what the IRS pays and what you pay—are compounded daily and are adjusted quarterly based on the *federal short-term rate*. This rate is the average market yield of Treasury bills and other U.S. obligations with terms of three years or less. When the IRS owes you, it pays the short-term rate plus 2 percent. If you owe the IRS, however, you pay the short-term rate plus 3 percent.

Any interest the IRS pays you is taxable as income, but any interest you pay the IRS is considered personal interest and is not deductible. (See Chapter 5 for more information on interest deductions.)

WHAT HAPPENS WHEN YOU FILE OR PAY LATE?

Late filers and late payers are both subject to their respective penalties, and if you're a late filer and a late payer, you're subject to both. The penalties are in addition to interest that's due on the unpaid amounts.

If your return isn't filed by the date it's due (or by the next business day if the deadline falls on a Saturday, Sunday, or legal holiday), the IRS imposes a stiff penalty: 5 percent of the total tax due for each month or fraction of a month that you're late.

There's a cap on this late-filing penalty, though. The penalty may not add up to more than 25 percent of the tax you owe. If, however, the IRS proves that your failure to file was fraudulent or intentional, the penalty increases to 15 percent per month and the cap increases to 75 percent.

What happens if you're just one day late filing your income tax return? You pay the full 5 percent for the first month. If you think the penalty will be small because you owe little or no tax and you file your return more than 60 days late, the minimum penalty you'll have to pay is the lesser of $100 or 100 percent of the tax due.

➲.⁓P

> You can avoid the late filing penalty for your 1995 return by filing an extension request. The request must be filed by April 15, 1996, and must properly estimate your 1995 tax liability (i.e., at least 90 percent of actual tax due).

If you don't owe any tax—say, for instance, your wage withholding more than covered your tax liability for the year—you don't owe a penalty for late filing.

Further, even if your return is mailed to the IRS on time, the IRS may consider it late if it's either unsigned or lacks enough information to compute the tax.

What determines whether your return is late is the postmark on the envelope you mail it in. If you've addressed it correctly, affixed the right postage, and gotten an official postmark that beats the deadline—and if the return makes it to the IRS—it's not late.

If the return never arrives, however, the burden is on you to prove that you mailed it—a difficult task unless you have the receipt from a certified or registered mailing.

✪ 𝒞AUTION

In the eyes of the IRS a postmark from an office postage meter is not official. So think twice before you use your company's meter.

What happens if you file on time but just don't pay the total tax due? More penalties, of course, but late payers' penalties work a bit differently and are assessed at a lower rate.

Initially, the IRS assesses you 0.5 percent of the tax not paid for each month or fraction of a month that the tax remains due.

◆ ℰXAMPLE

You file your tax return on April 15 and it shows you owe $1,000 in tax due, but you don't pay that amount until three months after you file. You would owe a penalty of $15—that is, 0.5 percent times $1,000 times three months.

If you need an extension and you file an extension request on time and properly estimate your actual tax liability, the IRS will accept your request even if you do not pay 100 percent of your estimated tax liability along with the request. However, a late payment penalty will be assessed if you don't pay at least 90 percent of your actual tax liability by the original due date of the return.

You still will owe interest on any tax not paid by the original due date. The IRS will bill you for the interest.

If you cannot pay the tax by the time the extension runs out (usually four months), then you can make arrangements with the IRS to pay the amount due. In this case you will be charged interest and the late payment penalty (0.5 percent per month). See Chapter 30 for more on filing an extension.

What happens if you still don't pay the tax due?

Usually the IRS then sends you four or five notices demanding payment. These letters are mailed to you over a period of six months or so. Then, 30 days before it does so, the IRS lets you know through a levy notice that it intends to file a lien against your assets.

Beginning with the month following the date that is 10 days after the levy notice is given, the penalty rate doubles. From that point on, it's 1 percent of the unpaid tax for each additional month the tax remains unpaid. No matter how late you are in paying, though, the penalty may not exceed 25 percent of the taxes due.

If the late-filing and late-payment penalties both apply for the first five months, the IRS reduces the late-filing penalty by the amount of the late-payment penalty.

In other words, you aren't subject to more than a 5 percent combined penalty in any one month—a maximum of 25 percent during the first five months.

There's only one proven way to avoid the late-filing penalty: File your return on time. Even if you owe the government money and cannot pay it when you file your return, go ahead and file your return by April 15.

The IRS may waive any penalties if you show reasonable cause for not paying or filing on time. Being too busy is not considered reasonable cause. If, however, you are seriously ill, face financial hardship, or if your tax records are destroyed by fire, you may qualify as having reasonable cause. But it is up to you to convince the IRS that what is reasonable to you should also be reasonable to them.

Also, in the case of disaster areas, the IRS may announce an automatic extension of time to file for those unfortunate enough to be affected.

REASONS FOR UNDERPAYMENT

What if upon audit or other IRS adjustment you owe more tax than you originally reflected on your return? The IRS may generally assess three kinds of penalties: those related to honest mistakes, the so-called accuracy-related penalty, and fraud penalties.

What is the difference? An honest mistake is, well, just that. You added five and three on your return and got four. If you make an honest mistake, the IRS will give you 10 days from the day it notifies you of the underpayment to pay up. If you don't pay within 10 days, the penalty is 0.5 percent per month of the amount you have not paid. This penalty may not exceed 25 percent of the underpayment.

The second kind of penalty, the accuracy-related penalty, applies in cases of:

- Negligence,
- Substantial understatements of income tax,
- Substantial valuation misstatement,
- Substantial overstatement of pension liabilities, *or*
- Substantial estate or gift tax valuation understatement.

If any one of the above applies to you, you could be subject to a penalty equal to 20 percent of the underpayment. However, if you get caught in more than one accuracy-related penalty, you are still subject to only one 20-percent penalty.

Negligence includes acts of omission and commission. The most common is keeping inaccurate or inadequate books or records, or having no books or records at all. No longer will you *automatically* be considered negligent if you fail to include on your return an amount that was shown on a Form W-2 or 1099, but the IRS will *usually* consider it negligence if you fail to do so. Other examples of negligence include taking clearly improper deductions, making substantial errors in reporting income, continuing to deduct items that were held to be nondeductible in previous years, or failing to offer any explanation for understatements of income.

Whether something constitutes negligence may depend on a taxpayer's circumstances. For example, whether your books are adequate depends on the size and complexity of your business. The IRS generally holds a highly educated person to a stricter standard than one who is less educated.

If you rely on a tax professional for advice or preparation of your return, you probably will not be found negligent—unless, of course, you negligently failed to supply your accountant or tax preparer with adequate records.

The IRS's finding of negligence is presumed correct. In other words, in the case of an error that results in an underpayment, the burden falls on you to prove that you were not negligent.

A *substantial understatement* is not so subjective. You're guilty of substantial understatement when the amount of tax shown on your return falls short of the tax you should have listed by $5,000 or by 10 percent of the correct tax, whichever is greater.

◆ *E*XAMPLE

Assume that you're a talent agent who spends lavishly on lunches and dinners in search of contracts for your clients. The tax return you filed showed a total tax of $15,000.

The IRS, in an audit, disallows many of your entertainment expenses. Consequently, you owe the IRS an additional $6,000 in taxes. On top of that you owe a $1,200 ($6,000 times 20 percent) accuracy-related penalty because the shortfall is considered a substantial understatement since it exceeds $5,000 (which is greater than 10 percent of the correct tax of $21,000—$15,000 original tax plus $6,000 assessment).

Original tax	$15,000
Increase from audit	6,000
Tax as adjusted	21,000
20 percent penalty*	1,200
Total tax and penalty	$22,200

---

*$6,000 × 20 percent = $1,200. The penalty is imposed because the $6,000 audit increase indicates that the tax was understated by more than (1) $5,000, and (2) 10 percent × $21,000, or $2,100. Thus, the tax was "substantially understated."

Say you take a position in your return that is not clear under the tax law. There are two ways to avoid both the negligence and substantial-understatement arms of the accuracy-related penalty.

First, you will not be subject to the penalties if you take a position in your return that's based upon "substantial authority." Generally, the law considers substantial authority to exist when the weight of authorities supporting your position is significant when compared to the weight of contrary authorities. For the purpose of this rule, authorities include court cases, regulations, IRS pronouncements, Congressional intent, and other similar sources.

Second, as long as you disclose in your return all the facts of a position that has a reasonable basis, the IRS will not impose the accuracy-related penalty for that position on the grounds that it was negligent or that it created a substantial understatement. A reasonable basis requirement is a relatively high standard compared to the "not frivolous" standard that existed prior to the 1993 Tax Act. The reasonable basis standard would not be satisfied if the position is merely arguable or merely a colorable claim. This new reasonable basis standard makes the disclosure exception effectively irrelevant for purposes of the negligence penalty because you generally would not be considered negligent with respect to a return position if it had a reasonable basis.

However, you cannot bury away a proper disclosure in an obscure place on your return. In most cases you are required to make the disclosure on Form 8275, "Disclosure Statement," or Form 8275-R, "Regulation Disclosure Statement." The IRS devised these forms just for this purpose. However, in some cases disclosure on other portions of your return is sufficient.

In other words, you don't have to be absolutely certain of your position. You only have to either have substantial authority for your position or be honest and alert the IRS to debatable positions in your return.

The other three arms of the accuracy-related penalty are less common for most individual taxpayers.

A substantial valuation misstatement is an overstatement of more than 200 percent, but less than 400 percent of an asset's value that causes an understatement in tax of at least $5,000.

A substantial valuation misstatement might occur, for example, when you make a charitable contribution of property (see Chapter 6). Since a deduction for contributed property is equal to the fair market value of the property, an overstatement of the fair market value would give you a greater deduction and therefore cause a tax underpayment.

A substantial overstatement of pension liabilities applies only when you have a pension plan and the pension deduction is based on actuarial determinations, which is usually the case with defined benefit plans (see Chapter 22).

A substantial overstatement of pension liabilities is an overstatement of more than 200 percent, but less than 400 percent, of the amount determined to be correct that causes an understatement in your tax of at least $1,000.

A substantial estate or gift tax valuation understatement exists when the value of an asset you claim on an estate or gift tax return is less than 50 percent, but more than 25 percent, of the asset's correct value and the claim causes an understatement in your tax of at least $5,000.

In the case of any substantial valuation overstatement or substantial overstatement of pension liabilities that is 400 percent or more of the correct value, or a substantial estate or gift tax valuation understatement that is less than 25 percent of the correct value, the accuracy-related penalty is increased from 20 percent to 40 percent of the understatement of tax caused by the valuation.

Consult your tax adviser and a competent appraiser or actuary when:

- You have a deduction in your income tax return that is based upon the value of an asset;
- You are filing an estate or gift tax return where the value of the estate or gift is based upon an asset valuation; *or*
- You have a defined benefit plan.

If the accuracy-related penalty is assessed, the IRS's finding is presumed true. In other words, if you make an error that results in an understatement and do not properly disclose that error, the burden falls on you to prove that you were not negligent or that you had reasonable cause and acted in good faith.

If, on the other hand, the IRS wants to assess the third kind of penalty for underpayment, a *fraud* penalty, the IRS has the burden to prove with clear and convincing evidence that the underpayment resulted from fraud. Fraud is a deliberate attempt to evade the tax law. If the IRS succeeds in proving that any part of an underpayment is due to fraud, you may be liable for a penalty of 75 percent of the entire underpayment.

What happens when the underpayment is only partially due to fraud and the other part was a simple error? If the IRS concludes that part of the underpayment is due to fraud, you must prove that it was not all due to fraud.

If you're successful, the fraud penalty applies only to that portion of the underpayment attributable to fraud. But the IRS may still conclude that the accuracy-related penalty applies to the remaining underpayment.

However, the fraud and the accuracy-related penalties may not both be applied to the same portion of an underpayment.

Also, you must file a return before the IRS may assess the fraud or accuracy-related penalties. So when you fail to file a return, the IRS can assess only the late-payment, late-filing, and/or fraudulent failure to file penalties.

The IRS levies accuracy-related and fraud penalties as follows.

◆ *E*XAMPLE

The IRS audits your return and finds a $1,000 underpayment. Part of it, $100, was due to a math error. Another part, $200, was the result of negligence. You mixed personal expenses with your business travel and entertainment deductions.

But $700 of the underpayment, the IRS decides, was fraudulent. You deliberately omitted income from your return. You reluctantly agree. How do the penalties apply?

The 75 percent fraud penalty ($525) applies to the $700 omission—that part of the underpayment attributable to fraud.

Assume that you can show that the remaining underpayment was not due to fraud. In this case the accuracy-related penalty applies only to that portion related to negligence—the $200—for a penalty of $40 (20 percent of $200).

If you paid the $100 underpayment stemming from the math error within 10 days from the time the IRS asked for payment, you would pay no penalty.

To further encourage voluntary compliance, the IRS charges interest on the late-filing, accuracy-related, and fraud penalties from the due date of the return rather than from the date the penalty is assessed.

FRIVOLOUS RETURNS

The IRS is a collection agency, not a debating society. People who deliberately use their tax returns to register a protest or make a point about public policy may find their social activism rewarded with a $500 penalty for filing a frivolous return. The IRS may impose the penalty if the person filing the return makes a claim that delays or impedes the processing of the return or the payment of tax that is plainly, and legally, due.

What is frivolous? A position is not frivolous simply because it is novel. Rather, a frivolous claim is one that has been repeatedly rejected as utterly meritless.

Examples include claiming clearly unallowable deductions, such as a discount because the United States is no longer on the gold standard or claiming a deduction for the proportion of taxes that would have gone to support the Defense Department.

The burden of proving your return is frivolous falls on the government, but the $500 fine is based on the irregular return, not on any tax underpayment. So the penalty may apply even if you actually paid the correct amount of tax.

TAX SHELTER PENALTIES

Promoters and investors who don't comply with the laws that apply to tax shelters face substantial penalties.

For promoters, failure to register a tax shelter carries a minimum fine of $500. And the fine can go as high as 1 percent of the total amount invested.

Failure to register a tax shelter partnership that raises $3 million, for instance, can cost the organizer $30,000.

Neglect to maintain a list of those who invest in the tax shelter you have promoted, and the IRS may fine you $50 per name omitted—up to a maximum of $100,000 per calendar year.

As an investor, forgetting to report a tax shelter identification number on your return may subject you to a $250 penalty.

FILING FORMS

The IRS is serious about getting the information it needs to track taxpayers' taxable income. Employers who do not file information returns—Form 1099s—with the IRS or who fail to supply a copy of the form to taxpayers face stiff fines.

If you file correct information returns late but within 30 days of the prescribed filing date, you're subject to a penalty of $15 per return, with a maximum penalty of $75,000 per calendar year.

After 30 days but before August 2 of the calendar year, the penalty increases to $30 per return, with a maximum penalty of $150,000 per calendar year.

Finally, if you fail to comply by August 1, the penalty increases to $50 per return, with a maximum penalty of $250,000 per calendar year.

However, a de minimis exception to these rules applies if you file corrected information returns before August 2 of the calendar year. In this case the IRS treats the original return as if it were filed with all the correct information. The number of information returns that will qualify for this de minimis exception is limited to the greater of 10 returns or one-half of 1 percent of the total number of information returns required to be filed.

Small businesses (defined as companies having less than $5 million in average annual gross receipts for the most recent three tax years) are subject to lower maximum levels for this penalty. The maximum penalty for small businesses is $25,000 (instead of $75,000) for failure to comply within 30 days; $50,000 (instead of $150,000) if the failure to comply is corrected before August 2; and $100,000 (instead of $250,000) for failure to comply before August 2.

Any person who fails to furnish a correct information statement on time to a payee is subject to a penalty of $50 per statement, with a maximum penalty of $100,000. However, if the failure is due to intentional disregard of the requirement, the penalty is increased to $100 per statement, or, if greater, 10 percent of the amount required to be shown on the statement, without limitation.

Business owners must deal with many Form 1099s. For example, the law requires 1099s to be filed for real estate transactions and for royalty payments amounting to more than $10 in any calendar year.

In the case of real estate transactions the person responsible for closing the transaction—usually the settlement agent, buyer's attorney, seller's attorney, or title company representative—must file the form. If those people are not present, then the primary mortgage lender, the seller's broker, the buyer's broker, or the buyer, in that order, must furnish copies of the 1099 to the buyer, the seller, and the IRS.

In the case of royalty payments the person or organization that pays the royalties must fill out the required 1099s.

As should be clear by now, the government is serious when it comes to income taxes, and it backs up its beliefs with hefty penalties if you transgress.

The only way to ensure that you do not get slapped with penalties is to educate yourself about the workings of the tax law. Then check to be sure that you have filed a completely accurate return and paid the full amount of taxes due.

QUESTIONS AND ANSWERS

Q.   I was due a refund of $300. But the IRS sent me $3,000 instead. I deposited the full amount in my checking account. Soon afterward I sent the IRS a check for $2,700 to cover the error. They say I owe interest for the time the money was in my account. Do I have to pay it?

A.   The IRS must reduce your interest liability in the event of an erroneous refund attributable to an administrative error.

If the IRS overpays you by $50,000 or less—in your case sends you a refund of $3,000 instead of $300—interest will not start to accrue on the overpayment until the IRS officially notifies you that you owe it the $2,700.

Another rule may work in your favor.

In an audit, for instance, you might concede that a deduction was a bit aggressive and agree to pay the additional tax. But if it takes the IRS a year to get around to mailing you the bill, the IRS may abate the interest attributable to the one-year delay that was its fault.

If you have paid interest to the IRS in the past that qualifies under these interest abatement rules, you may be due a refund. Check it out. You should know, though, that these rules do not apply to returns on which the *statute of limitations* has expired.

Q.   My return was late. But I had a good excuse. I was in the hospital in a coma when April 15 rolled around. Do I still have to pay a penalty?

A.   The IRS does accept some excuses, and yours probably qualifies. If you can show that your return was late not out of willful neglect but due to reasonable cause, you may escape the penalty.

Q.   I received a notice from the IRS that I failed to report $100 in interest income. I failed to report that amount because I never received a 1099 from

my bank. I do not think I should have to pay a penalty to the IRS. Do I have any recourse?

A.   You certainly do. You can ask the IRS to waive the penalty. Each year the IRS forgives a significant portion of the penalties it assesses.

Explain your situation to the IRS in a letter. Include a copy of the notice that the IRS sent you, plus a check for any taxes and interest you owe. Do not pay the penalty until you receive a reply from the IRS.

28

WHAT TO DO WHEN THE IRS SAYS PROVE IT

- What triggers an IRS audit?
- What should you do when the IRS notifies you of an audit?
- If you disagree with the IRS, do you have any options?

You filed your tax forms, mailed them off with your payment, and the canceled check has come back from the bank. Now you can breathe easy. Right? Wrong.

The fact the IRS cashes your check, or sends you the refund you claim as your due, means that your return wasn't lost in the mail, the IRS computers aren't broken, and you didn't make any obvious math errors on the return.

But it doesn't mean the IRS is necessarily happy with your return or that it won't be asking questions. It doesn't mean, in other words, that you escaped an audit.

If your pulse races at the very thought of an audit, you aren't alone. The unhappy fact is the IRS may audit your return at any time.

You do get one break, though—the tax "statute of limitations." The IRS is prohibited by law from assessing any additional income tax after three years have passed from April 15 or the date you filed your return, whichever is later.

But the law does carve out exceptions to this rule. The statute of limitations doesn't apply if you didn't file a return or you filed a fraudulent return. Also, if you failed to report more than 25 percent of your income, the statute of limitations is extended to six years.

Never been audited before? You're lucky. Chances are you'll face an IRS auditor at least once in your lifetime.

Given that eventuality, we're going to suggest ways to help you get through this unpleasantness when your turn comes. Provided you haven't deliberately tried to evade tax, an audit need not be any worse than unpleasant.

And look on the bright side: If you did make an honest mistake, it may have been in the government's favor. You could get money back as a result of an audit.

Here's something else we think you should know: Taxpayers now have a weapon on their side—a so-called *Taxpayer Bill of Rights.*

Adopted by Congress in 1988, this law requires the IRS to disclose its obligations and your rights *before* it conducts an audit or takes any other action against you.

The IRS must explain to you how to appeal an adverse decision, how to make a refund claim, how to file a complaint against the IRS, and the procedures the IRS itself will follow if it decides to assess and collect additional funds.

The law also excuses you from penalties when you act on erroneous written advice provided by the IRS.

The law also establishes an Office of the Ombudsman. If you're about to undergo a significant hardship at the hands of the IRS, such as having the doors of your business padlocked, you now have someone to whom you can turn for redress.

You can take some comfort that this law exists, but don't flout these rules under the false assumption that you'll now be safe from the long reach of the IRS.

AUDITING FOR GOOD CAUSE

Why does the IRS audit tax returns? Although our system of taxation presumes that every citizen will voluntarily pay the amount of tax he or she owes, the government thinks it sometimes gets shortchanged.

Some disagreements over whether or not a taxpayer paid all he or she should stem from different interpretations of the law—yours and the IRS's.

Others stem from lack of knowledge on the part of taxpayers. And every now and then some individuals deliberately fail to report their income or overstate their deductions so they can pay less tax than they rightfully owe. This is called tax evasion.

An audit gives the IRS the tool it needs to make sure taxpayers are indeed paying the correct amounts. In an audit the IRS gets to scrutinize individual tax returns for errors of omission or commission. Moreover, the knowledge that our returns may be subject to scrutiny tends to make us all a little more scrupulous when we fill out our tax forms.

All told, the government audited about 1,059,000 of the 115 million tax returns filed in 1993. That means the odds of being picked for an audit are about 100 to 1.

But you're much more likely to face an audit if you fall into one of the taxpayer categories that the IRS watches closely or if your return upsets IRS computers.

You're also more likely to be audited if you live in certain states. For example, the least frequently audited taxpayers live in the Middle Atlantic region, while the most frequently audited taxpayers live in 19 states west of the Mississippi.

What specifically triggers IRS scrutiny?

When you mail your completed Form 1040 to one of the IRS's regional service centers, a clerk enters the numbers from your return into a computer. The computer compares your numbers (your deductions, for instance) with the average deductions claimed by other taxpayers.

The computer then assigns a score to your return based on how much greater your write-offs are than the average. And the IRS selects returns for audit on the basis of these scores—that is, it selects all returns above a certain score.

At that point a human takes over again. An IRS employee looks over your return and decides whether an audit might be worth the IRS's time and expense.

How far off the average do your claims have to be before the computer picks out your return for this special attention? Not surprisingly, the IRS won't say. But our experience tells us you can gauge the likelihood of an audit from your answers to the following questions.

How much income did you report? The odds of your being audited go up with your earnings. In 1993 for instance, the IRS examined 0.71 percent of returns with gross income of less than $25,000 but 4.03 percent of returns with gross income of $100,000 or more.

Did you itemize deductions? People who itemize are more likely to be audited than those who claim the standard deduction.

Are you self-employed? Individuals in business for themselves are audited far more frequently than those collecting a salary from someone else. That's because the IRS frequently finds abusers among this group.

Are your travel and entertainment deductions significant? The IRS scrutinizes these write-offs because it has found taxpayers frequently inflate or claim improper travel and entertainment deductions.

Do you pay or receive alimony? The IRS has found that not all alimony recipients report their payments as income. As a result, IRS's offices often match deductions for alimony payments by one former spouse with the alimony income reported by the other.

Are you an investor in a tax shelter? If so, your chances of being audited increase dramatically. Often, the IRS earmarks tax-shelter investors for audit after it has examined the return of the tax shelter or has found recurring problems with the promoter that sold the investment.

You should also know the IRS is under pressure from a deficit-haunted Congress to audit a higher percentage of returns and collect more taxes.

But the fact is, your chances of being audited keep going down. In 1964 your chance of being audited was 5.1 percent; in 1993 it was less than 1 percent.

Of course, during this time, the IRS has gotten better at selecting returns for audit that are likely to result in additional taxes being collected.

Of all the individual returns audited for 1993, only 14 percent resulted in no change, and 7 percent produced refunds. Put another way, four out of five audits ended with taxpayers paying additional tax.

You should also be aware that every few years the IRS chooses a number of individual returns completely at random for audit in connection with its *Taxpayer Compliance Measurement Program (TCMP)*. (A TCMP cycle is scheduled for December 1995.)

The taxpayers who filed the targeted returns must justify every entry, line by line. The government isn't picking on them out of any specific suspicion. It just wants to see, by sampling, what proportion of taxpayers aren't complying with the laws and how they aren't complying.

And if, by the way, just knowing that one might have to endure such an audit helps keep us honest, the IRS considers that a very useful secondary effect.

These random audits are also done on partnership tax returns and on information returns filed by businesses. For example, the IRS may check the accuracy of returns that report the payment of interest income, and these audits may indirectly influence your individual return.

WHEN YOU RECEIVE A LETTER FROM THE IRS

Not every letter from the IRS is cause for panic. The notice of an audit may be, but there's another letter the IRS mails.

It simply says the IRS thinks that you've made a mistake and asks that you send it more money. Don't send the money—at least not right away.

But don't ignore the letter either. If you wait too long before responding, the IRS may pull your return for an overall audit. So get your return out of the file and go over it or have your tax preparer go over it for you.

Did you make a mistake?

The data-entry clerk at the IRS may have typed a number incorrectly, or maybe you just forgot to file a form.

In any case don't assume the IRS is right. Check the letter out. If you do owe the money the IRS claims you do, pay it.

But if after checking, you find you don't owe, or you still don't understand the IRS's claim, write the IRS a letter. Explain why you disagree.

To be helpful, enclose a copy of the correspondence the IRS sent you. That way, the IRS employee who gets your letter doesn't have to search through the IRS files, and he or she has a better chance of matching your response with your IRS file.

➤·𝒯IP

There's no need to panic if you receive a second notice from the IRS on the same issue. The IRS usually issues five notices, one every five weeks. A second notice is sometimes mailed before you have time to respond to the first one.

What if you receive a third notice? Write the Problem Resolution office of your IRS district, and contact your tax preparer.

➤·𝒯IP

Send any correspondence to the IRS by certified mail, return receipt requested. That way, if you're called upon to prove you responded to the IRS in a timely fashion, you can do so.

✿ 𝒞AUTION

You say you overlooked an item of income? Don't wait for the IRS to find you. If you pay the tax before the IRS contacts you, you reduce your interest payments and possibly avoid penalty assessments.

PREPARING FOR THE AUDIT

The IRS doesn't actually use the word *audit* when it writes to tell you that your return is going to be audited. It's much more polite. The letter just says the IRS wants to verify the accuracy of your return and requests a meeting.

Never ignore such a letter. The two most common types of audits, other than audits conducted exclusively through the mail, are *office audits* and *field audits.* If you must be audited, you'd prefer the office audit. It's often less detailed.

In an office audit the IRS asks you to meet with its auditor at a specific time and place. The letter you get will specify the areas of your return the IRS is questioning. It will also ask you to bring records to back up deductions or credits you've claimed, income you've reported, or any other item that has a bearing on the tax you have computed.

The letter also usually asks you to bring along a copy of your tax return for the year in question, plus a copy of your prior year's return.

For the more formidable field audit, however, the IRS will announce it's sending its representative to you. That's probably because the auditor will want to see more records than you can conveniently bring to him or her. The field audit isn't a minor affair.

If the date and time the IRS sets for either a field or an office audit is inconvenient, immediately call the IRS office and ask for a change. Chances are, the agent will accommodate you.

Now start getting ready. Preparation and organization are the keys to getting through the audit as painlessly as possible.

You should have the answers to all questions about which the IRS has indicated an interest, and the records to substantiate your answers.

In either an office or field audit, be guided by this general rule: Provide only the information that is requested and answer only the questions that are asked. Don't raise issues the auditor hasn't raised. Otherwise, the audit may extend into areas you aren't prepared to discuss.

WHO GOES TO THE AUDIT?

The issue of who actually goes to the audit is your decision. If your return is a joint one, you or your spouse or both of you may go. But neither of you is required to attend. You may send your accountant to represent you.

In fact almost anyone who has your power of attorney (use IRS Form 2848) may represent you at an audit.

Theoretically you can go to the audit with your accountant, your attorney, and an army of advisers in tow, but it isn't a good idea.

Too many advisers give the impression that you're worried and have a lot to hide, and all those reinforcements are charging you for their time. Also, most audits are generally routine.

If the matter seems simple, you may—with the right preparation and backup documents—be able to handle the audit yourself. If it's complicated, ask your adviser to be there with you. In any case, discuss the matter with your tax adviser before you decide who should go.

THE BIG DAY

The day of the audit is at hand. How should you behave? To begin with, be prompt. When the audit begins, pay attention to what's going on.

If the person you meet says anything to indicate that the examination of your return is anything but routine—or if he or she is introduced as a "special" IRS agent—stop the proceedings right there and seek legal help. Special agents work for the IRS criminal division, and they don't participate in audits unless you're suspected of serious wrongdoing.

By law a special agent is supposed to inform you before the audit begins that this is something more than a routine check.

But listen carefully for the warning. You don't want to miss it. If in doubt, you can always request to see the person's IRS identification card, and you can copy down his or her name and any other information printed on it.

But assuming that your audit is routine, be pleasant but don't be lulled into letting your guard down. Speak when you're spoken to and answer only the questions you're asked.

Above all don't become abusive, railing against the unfairness of the tax system. Keep your politics to yourself. If you know of a neighbor who's getting away with tax murder, this isn't the time to call attention to him or her. It won't distract the auditor's attention from you.

Listen carefully to the auditor's questions, and consider your answer before making it. IRS employees are skilled. They may probe a bit in hopes of identifying additional problem areas on your return.

In short, stay calm. Don't get flustered. Be patient. It will all be over in time.

STAGES OF APPEAL

When it's over, however, you may not agree with the auditor's finding. What can you do about it? There are several stages of appeal, beginning with the IRS itself and eventually, if it comes to that, the courts.

First: Ask for a meeting with your auditor's supervisor. Perhaps you can persuade him or her of the correctness of your position, or you may receive a more satisfactory explanation for the finding than the auditor gave.

Second: If you're still not happy, ask for a meeting with a representative of the Office of the Regional Director of Appeals. Filing a protest is a formal procedure that you shouldn't attempt on your own. Your tax adviser should get involved if you decide to go this route.

IRS statistics show about 85 percent of cases that go to the Regional Director are settled at that level. Settlement often involves compromise by both the government and the taxpayers. It may be worth your while to go through this process if you've taken a supportable though not necessarily 100 percent correct position on your tax return.

Third: If the appeals process doesn't work, there are always the courts. In fact you can take your appeal to the courts at any time.

Fourth: You don't have to exhaust the IRS's internal appeal steps. But here's a word of caution about court appeals. They are expensive and time-consuming.

If the attorney's fees are going to be greater than the IRS's claims, you may want to swallow your pride and principles and pay the government what it wants.

It could be cheaper in the long run. If you think you want to try an appeal, though, seek qualified counsel.

QUESTIONS AND ANSWERS

Q.   **Any advice on how to avoid an audit?**

A.   Perhaps the best advice we can give you is to fill out your returns as honestly and completely as you can. That way, if an audit does come your way, you know your heart—and your Form 1040—are pure. And that knowledge will help you more than anything else in breezing through IRS scrutiny.

29

$\mathcal{G}$ETTING READY FOR YOUR TAX PREPARER

- When should you organize your tax data?
- What can you do to get ready for your tax preparer?
- Why should you keep detailed income and expense records for your tax preparer?

For most people, the hardest part of their tax year is pulling everything together in preparation for filing. Oftentimes they misplace their tax information, receipts, and so on.

You can fill out the tax forms yourself or pay someone to do it for you. Either way, the IRS holds *you* responsible for the accuracy of the information reported. The IRS will look to *you* for documentary proof of the deductions you claim.

In this chapter we tell you how to get yourself and your records ready for filing time. However, whether you enlist the help of a tax preparer or not, the time to start preparing for tax filing is at the beginning of each tax year. It is too late to make plans, devise a tax-savings strategy, or even start accumulating your records and supporting documentation on the following April 14.

If you do use a tax professional to prepare your forms, do not think of him or her just once a year. Work with your tax adviser before the year starts.

GET ORGANIZED

One of the keys to sound tax planning is good organization. The sooner you begin organizing your tax data, the better off you'll be. As we have seen, to maximize benefits from year-end tax planning, you have to act during the year, not after the tax year ends.

The bottom line: It's never too soon for you and your adviser to start developing tax-savings strategies for the current year.

GOOD RECORDS SAVE TIME AND EXPENSE

All the careful tax planning you have done will count for naught if you cannot produce the records and the facts that you need at tax-filing time.

A tax adviser's main function is to help you make the most of the tax law so you can save money. You do not want to waste your adviser's time—and your cash—sorting through, organizing, and interpreting numerous slips of paper.

Another incentive to early preparation is that many tax preparers will be able to file your 1995 return electronically. The IRS says if your preparer files electronically, you will receive any refund you have coming to you in as little as 21 days. So if your tax data are ready, you could receive your refund much earlier by filing electronically.

In the following pages we have compiled a checklist of the records and information you will want to pull together before you or your tax preparer begin work on your return. By getting started early you might achieve a greater tax savings.

⮞.𝒯ɪᴘ

Many tax preparers send their clients forms listing income and deductions for the previous year and asking for data for the current year. If your preparer sends you such a form, use it in addition to our checklists on the following pages. It may jog your memory for deductions you might otherwise overlook.

RECORDS DETAILING INCOME

You need to gather the following records to account for your income. Keep in mind your employer, bank, broker, or a dividend-paying corporation in which you own stock is required by law to mail W-2s or 1099s by January 31. So if you have not received the information by, say, February 10 (a date that allows for mail delays), start making inquiries.

- *Wages.* Copies of all W-2 forms.
- *Dividends.* All copies of your 1099s.
- *Interest.* Again, all copies of your 1099s. Also include any year-end statements you received for tax-exempt interest income, such as from municipal bonds. If you have made loans to friends or relatives, include information on those loans, too.
- *Self-employment income.* Any 1099s you've received from customers or clients, your checkbooks for the year, any other books you have kept, and your bank statements. Summarize all your receipts and expenses by category on a piece of paper, or, if you use a computer to keep track

of these items, bring a copy of your computer printout and possibly a copy of the computer diskette. Also collect all your travel, meal, entertainment, and automobile records, including your charge card slips.

- *Capital gains and losses.* The purchase and sale transaction slips for any securities you may have sold. Make sure the sales slips agree with the Form 1099-B (or substitute statement) you received from your broker. (The 1099-B may also remind you of what you sold during the year.) Summaries of transactions for the year provided by brokers may also be helpful.

  If you sold your personal residence or any other real estate, you will need your closing statement, receipts for your fixing-up expenses, and information relating to the cost basis including improvements. If you purchased a replacement residence, also bring the closing statement for it.

- *Partnerships, estates, trusts, S corporations.* Schedules K-1 received from any of these entities. The form lists your share of income or credits, deductions, and preference items.

  Also, for partnerships and S corporations, be ready to explain to your tax preparer whether your involvement is active or passive. (See Chapter 5 for more information.)

- *Real estate rental activities.* Supporting documentation for your income and expenses (with bank statements and canceled checks or invoices) for the year. Summarize them by category on a piece of paper or computer printout. If you bought the property this year, bring your closing statement.

  Summarize a list of any improvements made to the property this year. And if you or any family members used the property during the year, know how many days of personal and rental use were involved.

  Also, for all of your real estate rental activities, be ready to discuss with your preparer whether you materially participate and meet other eligibility requirements to exclude these activities from the passive loss limitation rules. (See Chapter 19 for more information.)

- *Other income.* All the other slips of paper starting with a *W* or *1099* that organizations have been sending you. List them on a sheet of paper. For instance, you may have received:

  - State tax refunds.
  - Pensions or annuities.
  - IRA distributions.
  - Unemployment insurance.
  - Proceeds from real estate sales.
  - Alimony.

- Gambling winnings.
- Social Security benefits.
- *Supplemental gains and losses.* If you disposed of or sold a car or other equipment that you used in self-employment or for work as an employee, include any information you have relating to those transactions. You'll also need records from when you purchased the car or equipment and its original cost.

RECORDS DETAILING EXPENSES

Up to this point the records you have been collecting will help you account for your income from whatever sources. Now you want to be sure that you also have the records you'll need to justify the deductions you have coming to you, deductions that will help you offset some of this income for tax purposes.

- *IRAs and Keoghs.* Records of these investments, including the current-year contributions. Under certain conditions your IRA contribution is fully or partially deductible from your gross income. And you may deduct the money you've invested in a Keogh. (See Chapters 22 and 23 for more information about retirement plans.)
- *Moving expenses.* Invoices and cancelled checks for transporting your household goods and family if you moved to a new principal place of work (workplace) within the United States or its possessions. In general, you can deduct qualified moving expenses only if your employer did not reimburse you for the expenses. (See Chapter 9.)
- *Alimony.* Canceled checks as proof of your payments. You may deduct "above the line"—that is, directly from your income—any alimony you pay.
- *Interest you forfeit.* Bank statements listing forfeited interest. Interest you forfeit is also deductible above the line. You have forfeited interest, for example, when you take out a two-year CD at 4.5 percent, a year later interest rates rise to 6 percent, and you cash in your CD prematurely and buy a new one with a higher payout.

  When you do, your bank probably imposes a penalty; you lose, say, three months of interest you have already earned and reported as taxable interest to you. The good news is you may deduct the amount you lose. Your Form 1099-INT given to you by your bank or savings and loan association should show the amount of any penalty you were charged due to withdrawing funds from your time savings deposit before its maturity.
- *Employee expenses.* If your employer provides you with a car and reports the value of your usage of the auto on your W-2, your mileage log and any other documents that pertain to the car. (See Chapter 13.)

Also, if your employer pays you a per diem for your travel and entertainment expenses, bring your records documenting your expenses and the amounts you received. (For more information, see Chapters 10, 11, and 12.)

- *Medical expenses.* If you think your medical expenses will exceed the 7.5 percent floor, all your receipts from doctors, dentists, hospitals, pharmacies, and labs—anything related to your good health and well-being.

  If you had to modify your house for medical reasons, bring the signed statement from the doctor and the receipt for the improvement.

  You are entitled to a deduction for medical mileage. Also do not forget to include information about insurance reimbursements you might have received during the year. (Chapter 7 provides more information about medical expenses.)

- *Taxes.* Canceled checks or validated tax bills. Although sales tax is not deductible, other taxes such as state and local income taxes, real property taxes, and personal property taxes are.

  Bring your payroll withholding statements and canceled checks for current or previous years' state or local income taxes you paid, including amended state or local return payments. If you paid property taxes on a vacation home, include the canceled check or the bill. (See Chapter 8 for more information about taxes.)

- *Casualty and theft losses.* Bring evidence of any casualty and theft losses, including documentation supporting the actual loss occurred (e.g., police report for theft loss, insurance claim, etc.) and support of the amount of loss, including actual cost of the property and decline in value of the property (e.g., appraisal report). In addition, summarize all insurance proceeds received or expected to be received.

- *Contributions.* Canceled checks or the receipts you received for your current year's charitable contributions. If you gave old clothes or secondhand goods to a church drive, say, or Goodwill, bring the list you made or the receipt you received.

✪ CAUTION

If you donated more than $500 worth of used goods during the year, the IRS wants to know how much these goods originally cost you, when you bought them, and how you determined their value when you gave them away.

If you donated stock to your favorite charity, note the day you made the donation, the average high and low selling price on that day (if publicly traded), and the price you originally paid for the securities.

If you donated a highly valued piece of jewelry or other property, you should have an appraisal and an acknowledgment (Form 8283) from the organization to which you made the donation. (See Chapter 6 for more information about charitable contributions.)

♻ 𝒞AUTION

Canceled checks are not sufficient substantiation for separate contributions of $250 or more. To obtain a charitable deduction for contributions of $250 or more, you must obtain written acknowledgment from the donee organization prior to filing your tax return.

In addition, a payment exceeding $75 made partly as a contribution and partly in consideration for goods or services you received (e.g., charity banquet dinner) must be supported by a written statement received from the charity as to the portion deductible as a contribution and the portion attributable to the value of the goods or services.

- *Interest.* Interest deductibility depends on how you use the borrowed money. You should be able to relate each loan to its specific use.

Separate your interest expenses into the following categories:

- Principal residence interest.
- Second residence interest.
- All other residence interest.
- Mortgage points.
- Credit card interest.
- Other personal loan interest.
- Investment interest.
- Business interest.
- Passive activity interest.

Investment interest includes interest on money you borrowed to buy, say, stocks or bonds—margin account interest, for example. Bring broker and any other statements summarizing these interest costs.

If you paid at least $600 of mortgage interest to a financial institution, government agency, cooperative housing corporation, or other entity engaged in a trade or business, you should have received a Form 1098 showing the total mortgage interest you paid. Bring this form with you to your tax preparer.

Because not all mortgage interest may be deductible, you should be able to answer these questions for your tax preparer:

- Have you ever refinanced your original mortgage? If so, when did you refinance?
- What were the terms and conditions of your original mortgage (length, refinancing contemplated at the time it originated, and so forth)?
- What was the amount of your original mortgage?
- What was its balance when you refinanced?
- What was your refinanced mortgage amount?

- What were any excess loan proceeds from the refinance used for?
- Did you pay points on the new mortgage?

Also, if you've sold your house, the records you need to substantiate the amount you paid for your home plus the cost of any improvements.

If you purchased a new home, include your closing documents.

If you have more than two residences, talk with your tax preparer about which one you want to consider your second residence to maximize your deduction.

You'll find more information about interest deductions in Chapter 5.

- *Miscellaneous deductions.* Information on out-of-pocket employee expenses and investment advisory expenses. If you used your car as an employee and the actual expenses exceed the amount you were reimbursed, include those records.

Also bring any receipts for your unreimbursed business meals. (See Chapter 9 for a complete list of these miscellaneous deductions.)

✏ *C*AUTION

Business deductions are no longer allowed for club dues (includes business, social, athletic, airline, hotel, luncheon, golf, and other sporting clubs).

WHY IT'S BETTER TO BE PREPARED

It is important to gather together all of your information because the more organized your data, the easier it is for your tax adviser to efficiently prepare your return and save you tax dollars.

Also, the earlier you start your planning, the better the tax-savings opportunities. *In fact, the best plan is to keep your records organized on an ongoing basis.*

Finally, stay in touch with your adviser as your financial circumstances change (e.g., you get married, you sell your home, or you make a killing in the stock market). Remember, you must invest your time today if you're to save tax dollars tomorrow.

30

WHAT TO DO WHEN YOU NEED AN EXTENSION

- How can you obtain an extension of time to file your tax return?
- What can you do to avoid penalties and minimize interest charges?
- Will the IRS allow you to pay taxes later if you're unable to pay when you file your extension or your return?

As April 15 draws near and you are not ready to file your return, you can obtain a filing extension.

By following certain rules in obtaining the extension, you will avoid a penalty and keep interest charges, if any, to a minimum on any taxes not paid by April 15. In this chapter we tell you how to obtain a proper extension.

HOW TO GET AN EXTENSION

Anyone can get a four-month automatic extension for filing Form 1040. That gives you until August 15 to get your records together and get your tax forms filled out and filed. The extension applies only to filing your tax forms. It doesn't ordinarily apply to the payment of the balance due of your taxes.

The IRS accepts extension requests, even when the taxpayer does not pay 100 percent of his or her estimated tax liability with the extension request, as long as a properly completed extension is filed by April 15 and a proper estimate of the taxpayer's total tax liability is made and reflected on the extension form. Thus, even if you can't pay the balance owed to the IRS by April 15, you should properly estimate your tax liability and file for an extension anyway.

✪ CAUTION

You are still liable for interest and possibly a late-payment penalty (discussed below) on any balance of taxes due.

✪ 𝒞AUTION

Even though you don't pay in the balance of your estimated tax liability by April 15, you must properly estimate your tax liability when requesting an extension. If the tax liability is not properly estimated, the IRS may disallow the extension and assess a late-filing penalty.

In arriving at a proper estimate you must make a bona fide and reasonable attempt to locate, gather, and make use of all of the information that will enable you to estimate your tax liability. The IRS doesn't expect you to calculate your final tax bill to the penny, but the number should be as close to your final bill as possible.

As mentioned above, if the IRS decides that you didn't properly estimate your tax liability, it may deny your extension.

If you can't pay the tax with your extension, you may be able to obtain a *payment* extension or enter into an installment agreement with the IRS. These items are discussed later in this chapter.

A filing extension can be obtained for your 1995 return by filing Form 4868, "Application for Automatic Extension of Time to File U.S. Individual Income Tax Return," by April 15, 1996.

AVOIDING PENALTIES AND MINIMIZING INTEREST

You generally will not incur a penalty after you receive an extension provided you've paid at least 90 percent of the taxes finally due by April 15 and you properly estimated your tax liability.

If your payroll withholding and quarterly estimated payments aren't sufficient to meet this 90 percent requirement, you should make an additional payment by April 15 with your Form 4868 so you will meet it.

If it turns out that you didn't pay 90 percent of your full tax liability by April 15, you will owe the IRS a late-payment penalty.

The late-payment penalty is 0.5 percent per month (or portion thereof) on the total balance due. This penalty begins accruing on April 15 and ends the day you file your return and make your final payment. This penalty is capped at 25 percent.

As discussed above, if you fail to properly estimate your tax liability on the extension, or if you fail to file your return on time, you may also be assessed a late-filing penalty of 5 percent of the tax not paid by the regular due date for each month (or portion thereof) the return is late. This penalty is also capped at 25 percent.

If your return is more than 60 days late, the late-filing penalty may not be less than the smaller of $100 or 100 percent of the tax shown on your return. If, however, you can show you have reasonable cause for this failure and it is not due to willful neglect, you may escape the penalty.

If you are subject to both the late filing and late payment penalties, your late-filing penalty will be reduced by your late-payment penalty.

In addition to the above-described penalties, you'll still pay interest on any balance due when you finally get around to filing. The rate is determined quarterly. The interest charge begins to accrue on the unpaid tax from the original due date of your return (April 15) and ends on the day you file your return and pay the balance.

⊘.*Tip*

To minimize the interest charges on your underpayment, send the IRS as much of the tax you owe as possible. Also, be sure to indicate the tax year to which you want the payment to apply, and file your return as soon as you can.

The interest charge is considered personal interest and is not deductible. Similarly, any penalty charges are not deductible.

(For more information on penalties, see Chapter 27.)

ASKING FOR EVEN MORE TIME

If a four-month extension is not long enough for you, you may ask for two additional months. You need to file Form 2688, "Application for Additional Extension of Time to File U.S. Individual Income Tax Return," by August 15.

Or you may send the IRS a letter detailing your needs. You must mail either the form or the letter no later than the end of the original four-month extension.

In the form or letter you should explain why you're requesting the extension. Also specify the tax year for which the extension applies, the length of time needed for the extension, and whether another extension of time to file was already granted for the tax year.

If the IRS approves your second extension request, you then have until October 15 to complete and file your 1995 Form 1040.

Approval of this additional two-month extension isn't automatic, however. If the IRS doesn't think your reasons are good enough, it will deny the extension.

You'll receive a letter to this effect, and the IRS will give you a 10-day grace period—from the date of the letter or from the end of the four-month filing extension, whichever is later—in which to file your return.

If you are unable to pay any tax owed at the end of the automatic four-month extension period, you should complete Form 1127, "Application for Extension of Time for Payment of Tax," or Form 9465, "Installment Agreement Request" (discussed on the next page).

LIVING OVERSEAS?

If you live and work outside the United States or Puerto Rico or if you're on assigned military duty outside the United States or Puerto Rico, you automatically have two extra months, until June 15 (June 17 in 1996 because the 15th is a Saturday), to file your return and pay any taxes due.

However, even though you don't have to pay your taxes until June 15, when your return and taxes are due, you still must pay interest on the balance due from April 15.

When you do file, simply attach to your 1995 Form 1040 a note explaining why you qualify for this two-month extension—that your home and your abode, or military assignment, were outside the United States or Puerto Rico.

To obtain two additional months in which to file, send the IRS a Form 4868 by June 17, 1996, and write across the top of it: "TAXPAYER ABROAD." This procedure will give you another filing extension until August 15, but not a payment extension. As with a taxpayer not living abroad, the IRS will accept extension requests from an individual living overseas even though he or she does not pay 100 percent of the estimated tax liability due with the extension request without subjecting that individual to the 5 percent late-filing penalty—so long as he or she properly estimates the tax liability on the extension form.

You must have at least 90 percent of your expected tax liability paid in by June 15. If you don't, in addition to interest, you will incur the late-payment penalty of 0.5 percent per month (or portion thereof) on any balance due.

WHAT IF YOU DON'T FILE, DON'T ASK, AND DON'T PAY

If you don't file your tax return by its due date and you haven't followed the procedure for an extension, the IRS will impose a late-filing penalty of 5 percent per month (or portion thereof) of any tax due. (This penalty is capped at 25 percent.)

So even if you can't pay your taxes when they're due, don't let that stop you from filing your return or obtaining a filing extension.

By doing so you avoid the late-filing penalty.

If you can't pay the taxes you owe, the IRS may allow you an extension for payment of income taxes for up to six months. You can request a payment extension by sending the IRS a completed Form 1127. An extension will be granted only if you can show that the payment of tax will result in "undue hardship." The term *undue hardship* means more than financial inconvenience. It must appear that substantial financial loss will result to you from making a payment on the due date.

✪ 𝒞AUTION

Be aware, though, that the IRS doesn't grant payment extensions easily. The government expects its money, even if you have to sell assets to raise the cash. However, the government generally will not require you to sell property at a sacrifice price.

If you do not think you qualify for a payment *extension*, you can enter into an agreement with the IRS to pay your tax liability *in installments*—over a period of time. This procedure allows a taxpayer who is unable to pay the tax owed with the return or at the end of the automatic four-month extension period to request an installment agreement. If you wish to take advantage of this new procedure, file Form 9465 with your tax return or Form 2688 if requesting additional time to file. The IRS will notify you within 30 days whether an installment plan is acceptable or whether additional information (e.g., financial statements) is needed.

✪ 𝒞AUTION

If you enter into an installment agreement with the IRS, you are still liable for interest and any late-payment penalties on the balance due.

➤.𝒯P

With the current IRS interest underpayment rate running at 9 percent and the late-payment penalty at 6 percent annually (i.e., 0.5 percent per month), you will be facing a total financing cost of 15 percent on an annual basis if you enter into an installment agreement with the IRS. Thus, consider a bank loan or other sources of financing for a potentially less expensive alternative to an installment agreement with the IRS.

QUESTIONS AND ANSWERS

Q.   I was unable to pay the taxes due on my return. Will the IRS bill me for the balance due?

A.   Yes, the IRS will bill you for the amount you owe—plus interest and penalties (if any) from the date your return was due. Our advice: If you can't afford to pay the entire balance at once, pay as much as you can as often as you can. That way, you'll minimize the interest and penalty charges.

In addition you may consider filing Form 9465, "Installment Agreement Request."

What if you're without the funds to pay? You may want to consider filing Form 1127, "Application for Extension of Time for Payment of Tax."

Q.   I requested an extension to file my Form 1040. Does that request also extend the time for filing my state and local tax returns ?

A.   Not necessarily. State and local laws vary, so consult your tax adviser for the rules for your state or municipality.

31

*T*AX RULES
WHEN YOU HIRE
HOUSEHOLD HELP

- Who qualifies as a household worker?
- Why is the distinction between an employee and an independent contractor important?
- What are your responsibilities as an employer of a household worker?

This chapter discusses a frequently overlooked and often misunderstood area of tax law—what, if anything, do you need to do if you hire household help?

Who qualifies as a household worker? Au pairs, nannies, cleaning people, maids, butlers, drivers, and babysitters are among those who help make the daily routine of life easier for some. And although you may regard your help as an integral part of your family, you may face a variety of tax responsibilities regarding them. This chapter will summarize the tax rules that may apply to you if your household help are employees.

BASIC RULES

You may have to withhold income tax as well as Social Security and Medicare Tax (FICA) from the wages you pay if your household workers are employees. You may also have to pay your share of FICA taxes on their wages, pay federal unemployment tax (FUTA), make advance payment of the earned-income tax credit (EITC), and be subject to various employer reporting requirements.

Failure to comply with these employer obligations can be costly. Not only may you be liable for the tax itself, but you may also be responsible for interest and penalties.

WHO IS AN EMPLOYEE?

A person performing services for you is considered your employee if the services are under your control as to both what must be done and how it must be done. However, if you have the right to specify the work to be performed but not the means and methods of accomplishing the result, the person performing services for you may be an independent contractor.

It makes no difference that the person works full-time or part-time in determining whether the person is an employee or independent contractor. **The distinction between an employee and an independent contractor is crucial because generally *no* reporting and withholding requirements apply for household workers who are independent contractors.**

WHO IS AN INDEPENDENT CONTRACTOR?

The general rule is that an individual is an independent contractor if the person for whom he or she is rendering services has the right to control or direct only the result of the work and *not* the means and methods of accomplishing the result. People such as contractors, subcontractors, public stenographers, auctioneers, and so on, who follow an independent trade, business, or profession in which they offer their services to the general public are generally independent contractors. However, whether such people are independent contractors or employees depends on the facts in each case.

Direct sellers and licensed real estate agents are two general exceptions to the employee classification and are considered independent contractors if certain qualification requirements are met. Generally, to qualify under one of these exceptions, substantially all payments for the services of the worker must be directly related to sales or other output (rather than number of hours worked) and the services must be performed under a written contract providing that they will not be treated as employees.

EMPLOYEE OR INDEPENDENT CONTRACTOR?

The IRS utilizes a 20-factor test (i.e., "common-law rules") as an aid in determining whether a taxpayer has sufficient control over a worker to establish an employer-employee relationship or if the worker is an independent contractor.

The 20 common-law factors have been developed based on an examination of court cases and rulings considering whether a worker is an employee. The degree of importance of each factor varies depending on the occupation and the factual context in which the worker's services are performed.

Examples of some of the 20 common-law factors indicating a sufficient level of control over the worker to establish an employer-employee relationship are:

Instructions.   A worker who is required to comply with the taxpayer's instructions about when, where, and how he or she is to work is ordinarily an employee.

Training.   Training a worker to perform services in a particular method or manner is a factor indicating control.

Set Hours of Work.   The establishment of set hours of work is a factor indicating control.

Doing Work on Taxpayer's Premises.   Work performed on the taxpayer's premises suggests control over the worker, especially if the work could be done elsewhere.

Payment by Hour, Week, Month.   Payment by the hour, week, or month generally points to an employer-employee relationship.

Examples of some of the 20 common-law factors indicating a lack of sufficient level of control over the worker to establish an independent contractor status are:

Hiring, Supervising, and Paying Assistants.   If the worker hires, supervises, and pays other assistants pursuant to a contract under which the worker is responsible only for the attainment of a result, this indicates independent contractor status.

Significant Investment.   If the worker invests in facilities (e.g., office space from an unrelated third party) used by the worker in performing services and such facilities are not typically maintained by employees, this indicates independent contractor status.

Realization of Profit or Loss.   A worker who can realize a profit or suffer a loss as a result of the worker's services is generally an independent contractor.

Working for More than One Firm at a Time.   If a worker performs more than de minimis services for a multiple of unrelated persons or firms at the same time, this is a factor generally indicating independent contractor status.

Making Service Available to General Public.   The fact that a worker makes his or her services available to the general public on a regular and consistent basis indicates an independent contractor relationship.

If the IRS determines that an employer-employee relationship exists by using the 20-factor test, the taxpayer may rebut this determination by either using the same 20-factor test or establishing that a "reasonable basis" argument exists for treating the worker as an independent contractor. To be successful with a reasonable basis argument, long-standing recognized industry practice for treating the worker as an independent contractor generally must be established. Also, the taxpayer must have consistently treated the worker as an independent contractor. It is presently unclear whether a reasonable basis argument exists and would be successful for treating household workers as independent contractors. This determination must be done on a case-by-case basis. Consult your tax adviser.

◈ *E*XAMPLE

If you employ a worker through an agency or service and you do not directly hire, fire, or pay the worker, the agency or service will be considered the employer with the responsibility of the various duties regarding the worker's taxes and reporting requirements.

◈ *E*XAMPLE

You hire a cleaning service to clean your home once a week. You are billed directly by the service, the workers use supplies provided by the service, and the service arranges for their transportation to your home on a schedule it arranged. The workers provided by the service are not your employees.

However, if an association provides you with a list of workers and you hire from that list, set hours, and pay the worker directly, the IRS will probably regard you as the employer of the worker.

◈ *E*XAMPLE

You hire a nanny through a placement agency to care for your children. You set the hours, pay the nanny directly, and set the hours worked. The nanny probably would be considered your employee, triggering the tax rules discussed in this chapter.

◈ *T*IP

When you hire a household or domestic worker, make sure he or she provides you with his or her Social Security number and name as it appears on the worker's Social Security card. If the worker does not have a Social Security card, require the worker to complete Form SS-5, "Application for a Social Security Card," and submit it to the nearest Social Security office.

FAMILY MEMBERS

You can hire your spouse or your child under age 21 to provide household services without facing liability for Social Security, Medicare, and federal unemployment taxes. If you hire your parents to help, you are not responsible for federal unemployment tax based upon their wages, but you may be liable as an employer for Social Security and Medicare taxes.

SERVICES RENDERED BY INDIVIDUALS UNDER AGE 18

Beginning in 1995, payments for household services are exempt from FICA taxes if performed by an individual who is under age 18 during any portion of the calendar year, unless this is the principal occupation of the employee. Being a student is considered to be an occupation for purposes of this test.

XAMPLE

You employ your neighbor's 16-year-old daughter, a full-time student, to babysit after school and on weekends. Since she is under age 18 and babysitting is not her occupation, the wages paid to her will not be subject to the employer reporting and payment requirements, regardless of the amount of wages paid.

*Ẽ*XAMPLE

Instead of employing your neighbor's daughter as your babysitter, you employ a 17-year-old who left school to become a full-time domestic employee. Since babysitting is her occupation, the wages will be subject to the employer reporting and payment requirements.

FICA WITHHOLDING

The Federal Insurance Contributions Act (FICA) provides for a federal system of old age, survivors, disability, and hospital insurance. This system is financed through Social Security and Medicare taxes.

If you pay a household employee cash wages of more than $1,000 in a calendar year, those wages are subject to FICA.

*Ẽ*AUTION

This $1,000 threshold applies to each household worker you employ.

Payments in kind (meals, clothes, bus tokens, etc.) are not used to arrive at the $1,000 amount or to figure the tax. The employer and employee *each* pay FICA tax at a rate of 7.65 percent. As the employer, you must withhold the employee's share of FICA taxes from wages and must pay an equal amount from your own funds. In 1995, the maximum amount of wages subject to the Social Security portion of the FICA tax is

$61,200. However, all wages and self-employment income are subject to the Medicare portion. (See Chapter 2 for more discussion relating to FICA taxes.)

✪ *C*AUTION

If you pay the household employee's share of Social Security and Medicare tax, that amount is considered additional income to the employee for federal income tax purposes. However, that amount does not count as cash wages for Social Security or Medicare purposes.

✪ *C*AUTION

If the household worker files for Social Security benefits years later when he or she turns 65 and can prove who his or her employers were, the IRS may hold each employer liable for the relevant back taxes, plus interest and penalties in some cases, without any protection under the statute of limitations.

INCOME TAX WITHHOLDING

You are not required to withhold income taxes for a household employee unless the employee requests it and you agree to do so. If you agree, you must withhold an amount from each wage payment based on the information shown on Form W-4, "Employee's Withholding Allowance Certificate," provided by the employee.

REPORTING REQUIREMENTS

During 1994, Congress passed the "nanny tax" bill, which increases the household employee FICA tax threshold and makes other changes aimed at easing the administrative burden of the employer. Effective January 1, 1994, FICA taxes on household employees apply only if wages paid to the employee exceed $1,000 in a calendar year.

Beginning in 1995, if you hire household employees and you pay one or more of them more than $1,000 in the calendar year, you will report and pay FICA or FUTA tax obligations for such wages on your own Form 1040. Also, if the employee asks you to withhold federal income tax and you agree, you will pay the tax with your Form 1040—without incurring a late-payment penalty. You are no longer required to file Form 942, "Employer's Quarterly Tax Return for Household Employees," or Form 940, "Employer's Annual Federal Unemployment (FUTA) Tax Return." If you pay a household employee $1,000 or less, you are not required to pay FICA or FUTA tax.

♦ *Ê*XAMPLE

> You hire a nanny for six months and pay her $250 per week. Since you are paying her more than $1,000 in 1995, you will be required to withhold her portion of FICA from her wages. You will pay the FICA and FUTA with your Form 1040.

♦ *Ê*XAMPLE

> You hire a maid to clean your house and pay her a total of $875 during 1995. Since her pay does not exceed $1,000 in 1995, you will not be required to pay FICA or FUTA.

In addition, a completed Form W-2, "Wage and Tax Statement," must be given to any employee whose pay exceeds $1,000 (or if you withhold income tax) by January 31 of the following year. In general, if an employee stops working for you before the end of the year, Form W-2 may be given anytime after the employment ends but no later than January 31 of the following year. A copy of the W-2 must also be filed with the Social Security Administration.

✪ *Ê*AUTION

> If you have more than one employee during the year, you will also need to file Form W-3, "Transmittal of Income and Tax Statements," with the Social Security Administration by February 28.

FEDERAL UNEMPLOYMENT TAX (FUTA)

The federal unemployment tax system pays unemployment compensation to workers who have lost their jobs. If you pay cash wages of $1,500 or more to household employees in any calendar quarter this year or last year, you are liable for federal unemployment tax (FUTA). The FUTA rate for 1995 is 6.2 percent on the first $7,000 of cash wages you paid to each employee during the calendar year. However, timely payments made to a state unemployment fund may apply as a credit against this tax. The credit cannot exceed 5.4 percent of the wages subject to FUTA. (The maximum credit effectively reduces the FUTA liability to 0.8 percent of the applicable wage base.)

FUTA is the obligation of the employer. You cannot pass it on to your em-ployee. Contact your state employment tax office for various state requirements.

EARNED-INCOME TAX CREDIT (EITC)

Certain low-income individuals are eligible for the earned-income tax credit (EITC). The EITC is available for income up to $24,396 for one-child families and $26,673 for families with more than one child. You must make advance payments of the EITC to any eligible employee who requests it. You may also be required to notify the employee that he or she may qualify for the EITC. Your employee makes the request by giving you a completed Form W-5, "Earned-Income Credit Advance Payment Certificate." Each payday, you make the advance payment to your employee from the FICA taxes and withheld income taxes you would otherwise pay to the IRS. The EITC is also available to certain low-income workers without children with incomes up to $9,230. However, they cannot get advance EITC payments.

QUESTIONS AND ANSWERS

Q.   I have not been withholding and paying employment taxes for my household workers. What should I do about it?

A.   First you should determine whether your household worker is an employee. Before determining whether an employer-employee relationship exists, you should contact your accountant or attorney to help you consider the level of control you have over the worker utilizing the IRS established 20-factor test (i.e., the "common-law rules") and whether a reasonable basis exception exists for your independent contractor classification.

If you determine the worker is an employee, you should consider voluntarily coming forward and paying the taxes and interest you owe. The IRS has recently shown a willingness to waive penalties in other situations where taxpayers voluntarily come forward and pay taxes and interest they owe. If, however, the IRS uncovers the noncompliance first, the penalties might not be waived and can be substantial. Obviously, the various tax withholding, payment, and reporting requirements should be met on all wages paid to household employees in the future.

Q.   Can I claim the child care credit if I have treated my children's nanny as an independent contractor for amounts paid to the nanny?

A.   Yes, just as you may take the credit if you treat your nanny as an employee, you may also take the credit if you treat your nanny as an independent contractor. In both cases you must provide your nanny's Social Security number, along with his or her correct name and address in Part I of Form 2441, "Child and Dependent Care Expenses," on your Form 1040 (see Chapter 24). If you take a child care credit on Form 2441 for a nanny that you treat as an independent contractor, you have provided the IRS the ability to identify and question the independent contractor classification of the nanny.

Q.   If I am an employer and must comply with all these paperwork requirements, am I entitled to deduct my employee's wages from my income?

A.   No. Running a home is not considered a business; therefore, you cannot deduct the wages of your household employees. Additionally, the employer taxes (e.g., FICA, FUTA) are also not deductible when paid for household employees. (See Chapter 8 for discussion on the deductibility of employer taxes.)

GLOSSARY

Accelerated depreciation—a method of writing off the cost of business property in recognition of exhaustion and wear and tear (including a reasonable allowance for obsolescence) over its useful life. It allows you to claim larger depreciation deductions in the early years of ownership. The 150-percent-declining-balance method and the double-declining-balance method are examples of accelerated depreciation.

Acquisition debt—debt incurred to purchase, build, or substantially improve a principal residence or a second home. The debt must be secured by the property.

Active participation—significant involvement in the management of a rental activity. You must own at least a 10 percent interest in the activity to be considered an active participant. Limited partners generally do not qualify as active participants.

Adjusted selling price—the sales price of your home minus any selling costs and fixing-up expenses.

Adjustment items—items that receive different treatment under the regular tax system than under the alternative minimum tax (AMT) system. These items are generally added back to (but in some cases are subtracted from) regular taxable income when calculating AMT income.

Alternative depreciation system (ADS)—a slower depreciation system using the straight-line depreciation method and longer recovery periods than are available under MACRS. This method is required for certain property such as tax-exempt use property.

Alternative minimum tax (AMT)—a separate tax system designed to help ensure everyone pays some tax.

Amended return—corrected tax return.

Annualized income installment method—a way to minimize estimated tax payments if your annual income fluctuates. It allows you to reflect in each installment the income you earn in the period immediately before the installment is due.

Associated meals and entertainment—meals and entertainment that precede or follow a bona fide business discussion.

Bargain element—the difference between the price at which you buy stock under a stock option you exercise and the fair market value of the stock at that time.

Basis—the amount used to calculate your gain or loss when you sell an asset. In most cases your basis is the same as your cost (less any applicable depreciation).

Beneficiaries—people designated as your heirs.

Borderline business trips—trips that, when reviewed by IRS auditors, appear to be primarily personal rather than primarily business.

Business interest—interest on loans incurred to operate or buy assets for a business in which you materially participate.

Business meal—a meal directly related to or associated with the active conduct of your trade or business and, therefore, 50 percent of whose cost is deductible. (Before 1994, 80 percent was deductible.) To qualify, you must actually discuss business before, after, or during the meal.

Business use *(of an automobile)*—the miles you drive your car between two business locations or the miles you drive between your home and a place where you're temporarily working. Commuting miles (i.e., driving between your home and your regular workplace) generally do not count as business use.

Charitable contribution—a contribution or gift to, or for the use of, a qualified organization. Does not refer to gifts to private individuals.

Charitable sporting event—one in which all proceeds go to charity and practically all the labor is voluntary.

Collateral—asset pledged to protect a lender in case of default until a loan is repaid.

Commuting—trips to and from your home and your regular place of business.

Credit—direct, dollar-for-dollar reduction in your tax liability. Differs from a deduction in that a deduction is subtracted from either gross income or adjusted gross income, resulting in a reduction in the amount of income subject to tax.

Defined-benefit plan—retirement plan that allows you or your employer to contribute annually whatever amount is required to fund a specified retirement benefit or payout. Since the payout is fixed, the contribution is based on actuarial tables based upon life expectancy.

Defined-contribution plan—retirement plan that allows you or your employer to contribute some fixed percentage of your earnings (or your employer's earnings) to the plan each year.

De minimis fringe benefit—one too small to really matter. In other words, it costs more for a company to keep tabs on the benefit than it costs to provide the benefit. For example, providing employees with free coffee in the morning is a de minimis fringe.

De minimis loans—loans of $10,000 or less.

Dependent—individual who satisfies various criteria and for whom you are entitled to a personal exemption.

Depreciation—tax deduction you claim for the effects on business assets of exhaustion, wear and tear, and obsolescence.

Direct business expenses—expenses directly attributable to your business, such as wages for secretarial help, photocopying, postage, office supplies, and so on.

Directly related meals and entertainment—any meals and entertainment during which a substantial and bona fide business discussion is conducted that is associated with your active trade or business. Such discussion can also be conducted before or after any meals and entertainment. Your primary purpose must be to conduct business.

Disqualifying disposition—disposal of stock purchased under an incentive stock option before the holding period requirement has been met.

Documentary evidence—any kind of receipt that is corroborated by a third party (for example, a restaurant bill).

Double-declining-balance method—also known as the 200-percent-declining-balance method. This method of depreciation yields depreciation deductions in the first year that are twice the amount you would get using straight-line depreciation.

Effective marginal tax rate—rate of tax paid on your last dollar of income. This rate may be higher than the statutory marginal tax rate (i.e., the actual tax rate specified by the tax law that applies to your last dollar of income) because of the phase-out of personal exemptions and the 3 percent floor on itemized deductions.

Effective tax rate—overall rate at which your income is taxed. You calculate your effective tax rate by dividing your total tax liability by your taxable income.

Employment-related education—training that enables you to maintain or improve your present work skills.

Equity—when used in the context of a personal residence, the fair market value of the residence minus any debt secured by that residence.

Escrow—money or property placed in the hands of a neutral third party.

Estimated tax installments—amount of tax you expect to pay over the tax year separate from any amount withheld by your employer. Payment of estimated tax is made in quarterly installments.

Exercise—to purchase stock under a stock option. The date of exercise is the date you purchase stock under a stock option.

Fair market value (FMV)—the price at which property would change hands between a willing buyer and a willing seller, neither being under any compulsion to buy or sell and both having reasonable knowledge of relevant facts.

Federal short-term rate—the average market yield of Treasury bills and other U.S. obligations with terms of three years or less.

Field audit—IRS audit conducted at your home or place of business. A field audit is more detailed than an office audit (conducted in the IRS office).

Five-year averaging—a method that allows you to reduce the tax rate levied on qualified lump sum withdrawals from retirement accounts. Even though you pay your full tax in the year you receive your lump sum, you calculate the tax separately from the tax on your other income and as if you received the money evenly over five years. Then, it is added to your tax on your other income. The use of this method may result in a smaller tax than you would pay by combining the total taxable amount of the distribution with your other income in figuring your tax.

Fixing-up expenses—maintenance and repair expenses incurred no more than 90 days prior to selling your home and that you pay within 30 days after the sale.

Form 1041 K-1, "Beneficiary's Share of Income, Deductions, Credits, etc."— reports your share of trust or estate income and expenses.

Form 1065 K-1, "Partner's Share of Income, Credits, Deductions, etc."—reports your share of partnership income and expenses.

Form 1099-B, "Proceeds from Broker and Barter Exchange Transactions"— reports sales or redemptions of securities, futures transactions, commodities, and barter exchange transactions.

Form 1099-DIV, "Dividends and Distributions"—reports distributions, such as dividends, capital gain distributions, or nontaxable distributions paid on stock, and distributions in cases of liquidations.

Form 1099-G, "Certain Government Payments"—reports unemployment compensation, state and local income tax refunds, agricultural payments, and taxable grants.

Form 1099-INT, "Interest Income"—reports interest income.

Form 1099-MISC, "Miscellaneous Income"—reports miscellaneous income, such as nonemployee compensation, rent or royalty payments, and prizes and awards that are not for services such as winnings on television game shows.

Form 1099-OID, "Original Issue Discount"—reports by bond issuers to purchasers of bonds issued at less than face value.

Form 1099-R, "Distributions from Pensions, Annuities, Retirement or Profit-Sharing Plans, Insurance Contracts, etc."—reports total distributions from retirement or profit-sharing plans, IRAs, SEPs, or insurance contracts.

Form 1099-S, "Proceeds From Real Estate Transactions"—reports gross proceeds from the sale or exchange of most real estate transactions.

Form 1120S K-1, "Shareholder's Share of Income, Credits, Deductions, etc."—reports your share of S corporation income and expenses.

Form 2439, "Notice to Shareholder of Undistributed Long-Term Capital Gains"—reports gains realized by a regulated investment company (but not paid out to you) and the related tax credit.

Form SSA-1099, "Social Security Benefit Statement"—reports Social Security benefits you receive.

401(k) plan—retirement plan created and administered by your employer. With a 401(k), you put away a portion of your salary or wages and pay only Social Security tax or such portion; no income taxes are paid on that amount or any earnings that accumulate until the money is withdrawn, usually at retirement.

Fraud—a deliberate attempt to evade the tax law.

Half-year convention—a rule that applies in determining the depreciation of many types of property. During the first year an asset is placed in service, the rule requires you to treat that property as depreciable for just half the taxable year. The deduction you may take this first year is therefore one-half the amount you would take for a full year of depreciation.

Hobby loss—loss from an activity not engaged in for profit. You may deduct hobby losses only to the extent of your hobby income.

Home-equity debt—debt other than acquisition debt incurred that is secured by your home. You may deduct interest on only your first $100,000 of home-equity debt.

Home-equity loan—a loan secured by your home, in addition to your first mortgage.

Home office—an office you maintain at home that qualifies as your principal place of business and must be used regularly and exclusively for business if it is to qualify for tax write-offs.

Home office expenses—expenses attributable to your home office, not including direct business expenses.

Incentive stock option (ISO)—a type of stock option where no regular tax is due until you eventually sell or exchange the stock obtained with the option, and only if it is sold or exchanged at a profit. Different tax consequences apply for the alternative minimum tax (AMT).

Individual retirement account (IRA)—a retirement plan you create and to which you can contribute. Contributions to an IRA are deductible only if neither you nor your spouse is covered by a qualified tax-deferred retirement plan or your adjusted gross income (AGI) does not exceed a certain level.

Insider—an officer or a director of a public company.

Investment interest—interest incurred when you borrow to make investments as, for example, interest on a stock margin account.

Itemize—to list deductions on Schedule A of your Form 1040 rather than claim the standard deduction.

Keogh—a type of retirement plan for self-employed people.

Lease—a legal agreement that allows you to use an item—for example, a car—for a specified period of time in exchange for rental charges, generally monthly.

Limited partnership—a partnership that limits the liabilities of designated partners to the amount they have invested or promised to invest.

Loan origination fees—see *Points.*

Log—a diary where you record all your business engagements.

Long-term capital gain or loss—profit or loss from capital assets held for more than one year.

Lump sum—withdrawal of total amount from a retirement account.

Margin account—see *Stock margin account.*

Marginal tax rate—statutory tax rate on your last dollar of earnings (see also *Effective marginal tax rate*).

Market price—the last reported price at which an asset is sold (i.e., for stocks and securities, the price on an established market).

Material participation—participation by a taxpayer in a trade or business that meets one of the tests classifying the activity as not a passive activity.

Medical expense—amounts paid for the diagnosis, treatment, or prevention of disease or for treatment affecting any part or function of the body.

Midmonth convention—a depreciation rule under which real estate is depreciated from the midpoint of the month the property is placed in service.

Midquarter convention—a rule that assumes you placed your assets in service halfway through the quarter in which you actually put them into use. You must use the midquarter convention if certain kinds of assets you place in service during the last quarter of the year top 40 percent of the cost of assets placed in service during the year. With the midquarter convention, you may end up in the first year with a smaller total depreciation deduction than under the half-year convention.

Minimum tax credit (MTC)—a credit that recognizes that the alternative minimum tax (AMT) can result in prepayment of regular tax. A credit carryforward is generated by deferral preferences and adjustments that accelerate the recognition of income under the AMT system. The credit may be used to reduce regular tax liability in future years.

Money-purchase plan—a type of defined-contribution retirement plan that requires an annual contribution of a fixed percentage of income.

Mortgage—a loan secured by real property that requires periodic payments.

Mortgage interest—interest on loans secured by your home(s), part or all of which may be deductible as acquisition or home-equity interest.

Negligence—a term that includes acts of omission and commission. Keeping inaccurate or inadequate books or records qualifies as negligence. So does failing to include on your return an amount shown on a Form W-2 or 1099. Other examples include taking improper deductions, making substantial errors in reporting income, continuing to deduct items that were held to be nondeductible in previous years, or failing to offer any explanation for understatements of income.

Nonqualified stock option (NQOs)—a type of stock option that triggers taxes when you exercise the option as well as when you sell the stock at a profit.

Office audit—IRS audit conducted at the office of an IRS agent. An office audit is less detailed than a field audit. See *Field audit.*

150-percent-declining-balance method—a depreciation method that yields deductions in the first year that are one and one-half times the amount you would get using the straight-line method.

Option price—price you pay for the stock under a stock option. Also may be referred to as the exercise price.

Original issue discount (OID)—the difference between the price paid for a bond on issue and the amount you receive for the bond at maturity.

Original issue discount (OID) bond—a type of bond that is sold to the first buyer at a discount.

Paper profit—gain calculated by comparing the current market price of an asset with its basis (typically its cost).

Partnership—two or more parties who agree to engage in business with each other. Profits and losses of the partnership are reported on the income tax returns of the partners. Partnerships pay no separate federal income tax.

Passive activity—a trade or business in which you do not materially participate or a rental activity where you do not provide significant services or meet certain other requirements.

Passive activity interest—interest incurred on a loan used to invest in a business in which you do not materially participate or a rental activity that is deemed a passive activity.

Passive income—income generated from a trade or business or rental activity that is deemed a passive activity.

Passive investment—a trade or business in which you don't materially participate in management or a rental activity that is deemed a passive activity.

Passive loss—a loss incurred from a trade or business or rental activity that is deemed a passive activity.

Payroll withholding—income taxes deducted from your pay by your employer.

Per diem arrangements—a flat allowance paid by an employer to an employee. This method is used instead of reimbursing employees for actual expenses.

Personal exemption—a fixed deduction (subject to phase-out for higher income taxpayers) normally allowed for yourself, your spouse, and qualifying dependents.

Personal interest—interest on a loan used to acquire personal items such as an automobile or a vacation.

Personal property—assets other than real estate. Personal property includes furniture, machinery, and equipment.

Points—the additional amount paid to a lender when a mortgage loan is closed. One point is one percent of the amount of your loan.

Portfolio income—income from investments that is in the nature of interest, dividends, and royalties. Portfolio income also includes gains from the disposition of assets that generate interest, dividends, and royalties.

Preference items—items that receive favorable treatment under the regular tax system but not under the alternative minimum tax (AMT) system. These items are added back to regular taxable income when calculating AMT income. See also *Adjustment items.*

Principal residence—your primary home. The fact that you own a house does not make that house your principal residence. You must actually live in the house for it to qualify as your principal residence.

Private-activity bonds—bonds issued by state and local governments to raise money for private enterprises. Also known as AMT bonds because they have AMT consequences.

Profit-sharing plan—a type of defined-contribution retirement plan that allows flexibility in the annual level of contribution.

Qualified organization—a nonprofit charitable, religious, or educational group that meets government guidelines.

Real property—a legal term for real estate. Real property may or may not be depreciable. For example, buildings are depreciable; land is not.

Recovery periods—periods of time over which you claim depreciation deductions. That is, the length of time it takes to recover the money you paid for depreciable assets. Different recovery periods apply to different types of assets.

Restricted stock—a stock option where an employee must meet a length-of-service requirement.

Related entity—a member of your family or any entity controlled directly or indirectly by family members.

S corporation—a type of corporation for tax purposes. Shareholders pay taxes in the same manner as sole proprietors and partners—that is, profits and losses are reported on the personal tax returns of the owners, and, with a few exceptions, there are no separate federal business income taxes for the corporation to pay.

Second mortgage—a mortgage that allows you to borrow against the equity in your home. All or part of a second mortgage may qualify as home-equity debt and therefore may be fully or partially deductible.

Self-employed—people who work for themselves and file a Schedule C with their individual or joint tax returns. (Some partners are also considered self-employed.)

Selling costs—the costs of selling your home such as sales commissions, advertising, and attorney fees.

Short-term capital gain or loss—the profit or loss from capital assets held for one year or less.

Simplified employee pension (SEP)—a retirement plan similar to an IRA. An employer, rather than maintaining its own pension fund, makes contributions to the IRAs of its employees.

Single-sum expenditure—a flat charge that includes all expenses—meals, lodging, gratuities, and so on.

Small business stock gain—gain on the sale of stock of a qualified small business C corporation with $50 million or less capitalization issued to an individual or other pass-through entity (e.g., partnership or S corporation). Fifty percent of any gain from qualifying stock is excluded from taxable income if held for more than five years. With the maximum long-term capital gains tax rate of 28 percent, the gain is subject to an effective maximum federal tax rate of 14 percent.

Small business stock loss—loss on the sale of stock of a corporation issued to an individual or partnership where the capital of the corporation is less than or equal to $1 million and the corporation meets other qualifications. Losses on such stock may be ordinary (as opposed to capital) losses.

Standard deduction—the amount you may claim on your tax return in lieu of itemizing your deductions on Schedule A of your Form 1040.

Standard rate—a flat amount determined by the IRS and allowed for each business mile you drive.

Statute of limitations—the amount of time that must elapse before the tax year is considered "closed" (i.e., the IRS generally is not allowed to make adjustments to your income for closed tax years, nor can you by amending your return). The statute of limitations is generally three years for income taxes.

Stock appreciation rights—the right to participate in the appreciation of a company's stock without actually purchasing the stock.

Stock margin account—a brokerage account that allows you to buy securities with money borrowed from the brokerage firm.

Stock option—the right to buy a specific number of shares of a company's stock at a specific price within a specific period of time.

Straight-line method—a depreciation method that produces the same write-offs from year to year except in the first and last year of depreciation (i.e., the deduction is taken ratably over the life of the asset).

Substantial understatement—when the amount of tax shown on your return falls short of the tax you should have shown by $5,000 or by 10 percent, whichever is greater.

Surtax—a tax, in addition to the regular tax, imposed on taxpayers in certain income ranges that has the effect of eliminating either favorable rates or deductions.

Taxable income—the amount of income on which your income tax is calculated. You determine taxable income by subtracting your allowable deductions from your income from all sources.

Taxpayer Bill of Rights—legislation adopted by Congress in 1988 that requires the IRS to disclose its obligations and your rights before it conducts an audit.

Taxpayer Compliance Measurement Program—a program that chooses random tax returns for a very detailed audit.

10-year averaging—a method that allows you to reduce the tax rate levied on qualified lump sum withdrawals from retirement accounts. Even though you pay your full tax in the year you receive your lump sum, you calculate the tax separately from the tax on your other income and as if you received the money evenly over 10 years. Then, it is added to your tax on your other income. The use of this method may result in a smaller tax than you would pay by combining the total taxable amount of the distribution with your other income in figuring your tax. Only taxpayers born before 1936 may be eligible for 10-year averaging. Others may be able to use five-year averaging. See *Five-year averaging.*

200-percent-declining-balance method—see *Double-declining-balance method.*

Unearned income—income from sources other than wages, salaries, tips, and other employee compensation (for example, dividends, interest, and rent).

W-2, "Wage and Tax Statement"—reports wages, tips, bonuses, the value of taxable fringe benefits, withheld income taxes, FICA taxes, dependent care benefits, and other elective deferral amounts (e.g., 401(k) amounts).

W-2G, "Statement for Recipients of Certain Gambling Winnings"—reports gambling winnings.

Wash-sale—a sale of stock either 30 days before or after your purchase of the same stock. Losses incurred on wash-sales are not deductible.

Zero-coupon bond—a type of original issue discount (OID) bond sold at a deep discount from face value that does not pay interest currently. Zero-coupon bonds are issued by the U.S. Treasury, government agencies, municipalities, and corporations. The tax consequences of these bonds depend on the issuer.

APPENDIX

Here is a calendar of important tax dates for year-end 1995 and for 1996 if you figure your taxes on a calendar-year basis.

Year-End 1995

December 15	Year-end transactions should be identified to make sure they are completed by December 31. This will ensure they are reported as 1995 transactions.
December 31	Marital status on this date determines your filing status for the tax year.
	Self-employeds must set up Keogh plans by this date.

1996

January 15	Final payment of 1995 estimated tax is due unless you file your 1995 income tax return by January 31 and pay tax balance due at that time.
January 31	Due date for your 1995 income tax return and final payment of 1995 tax balance due to avoid late payment penalty *if* you postponed January estimated tax payment past the regular January 15 deadline.
	W-2 and Form 1099 information statements from your employer, bank, broker, etc. should be received by this date.
April 15	Individual income tax return (Form 1040, 1040A, and 1040EZ) for 1995 with payment of tax balance due. If an extension is required, you must file your extension request (Form 4868) by this date.
	Deadline for making 1995 IRA contributions.
	Last day for making 1995 Keogh contributions to existing accounts.
	Gift tax return for 1995 is due.
	First installment of your 1996 estimated tax is due.
June 17	Second installment of your 1996 estimated tax is due.
August 15	If you filed for an automatic extension of the April 15 deadline, you must file your 1995 return, unless you obtained an additional extension.
September 16	Third installment of your 1996 estimated tax is due.

October 15	Income tax return for 1995 due if you were granted a second extension of the filing deadline. This is the final deadline.
December 15	Year-end transactions should be identified to make sure they are completed by December 31. This will ensure they are reported as 1996 transactions.
December 31	Marital status on this date determines your filing status for the tax year. Self-employeds must set up Keogh plans by this date.

2. Annual Lease Value Table*

Fair Market Value			Annual Lease Value	Fair Market Value			Annual Lease Value
$ 0	to	999	$ 600	22,000	to	22,999	6,100
1,000	to	1,999	850	23,000	to	23,999	6,350
2,000	to	2,999	1,100	24,000	to	24,999	6,600
3,000	to	3,999	1,350	25,000	to	25,999	6,850
4,000	to	4,999	1,600	26,000	to	27,999	7,250
5,000	to	5,999	1,850	28,000	to	29,999	7,750
6,000	to	6,999	2,100	30,000	to	31,999	8,250
7,000	to	7,999	2,350	32,000	to	33,999	8,750
8,000	to	8,999	2,600	34,000	to	35,999	9,250
9,000	to	9,999	2,850	36,000	to	37,999	9,750
10,000	to	10,999	3,100	38,000	to	39,999	10,250
11,000	to	11,999	3,350	40,000	to	41,999	10,750
12,000	to	12,999	3,600	42,000	to	43,999	11,250
13,000	to	13,999	3,850	44,000	to	45,999	11,750
14,000	to	14,999	4,100	46,000	to	47,999	12,250
15,000	to	15,999	4,350	48,000	to	49,999	12,750
16,000	to	16,999	4,600	50,000	to	51,999	13,250
17,000	to	17,999	4,850	52,000	to	53,999	13,750
18,000	to	18,999	5,100	54,000	to	55,999	14,250
19,000	to	19,999	5,350	56,000	to	57,999	14,750
20,000	to	20,999	5,600	58,000	to	59,999	15,250
21,000	to	21,999	5,850				

*IRS table used to determine the amount of annual compensation to include as income, based upon the fair market value of the automobile provided as of the first day the automobile is made available to any employee. For new automobiles provided to employees, the fair market value consists of all amounts attributable to the purchase of an automobile, including sales tax and title fees as well as the purchase price. Special rules apply in determining the fair market value for leased automobiles, so consult with your tax adviser on these rules.

For vehicles having a fair market value in excess of $59,999, the annual lease value is equal to: (0.25 times the fair market value of the automobile) plus $500.

3. Business Mileage Log

Month of: _____

Date	Destination & Purpose	Business Miles	Personal Miles	Commute Miles	Business Tolls & Parking

Total _____

Odometer Reading — Beginning of Month _____

Odometer Reading — End of Month _____

Total Monthly Miles _____

4. Formula for Determining the Dollar Limits of Deductible IRA Contributions*

Upper phase-out limit (adjusted gross income):

Married filing jointly or qualified widow(er)	$50,000	
Married filing separately	10,000	
Other returns	35,000	_____

Less:	Adjusted gross income before IRA deduction	_____
Equals:	Amount below the upper phase-out limit (if zero or less, stop, no amount is deductible)	(_____)
Divide by:	$10,000	_____
Equals:	Percentage of the maximum contribution that can be deducted (not more than 100%)	_____ %
Times	$2,000 ($2,250 spousal)	_____
Equals:	Deductible limit before rounding and minimum limit	_____
	(If the deductible limit is not an even multiple of $10, round down to the next $10)	_____
	(If the deductible limit is less than $200, increase the amount to the minimum limit of $200)	_____

*The formula is used to determine deductible IRA contributions when a taxpayer (or spouse) is an active participant in a qualified retirement plan. See Chapter 22.

INDEX

How Price Waterhouse Can Help You and Your Business Succeed

Today's executives and employees continually face demands in both their personal and professional lives to make financial decisions with often unexpected but potentially far-reaching tax ramifications.

On the home front, saving for your children's education, evaluating executive compensation or retirement plans, or determining the right asset allocation for investments can be confusing and time-consuming. Price Waterhouse professionals can help you resolve these and other issues in an effective manner, enabling you to attain your personal financial goals while minimizing taxes.

As for your professional life, many decisions you make may affect your company's tax bill, and minimizing taxes obviously enhances the profitability of your business. Price Waterhouse advisers can keep you informed of legislative and regulatory developments that affect your company's taxes and help identify advantageous tax strategies.

To respond to the wide-ranging tax needs of businesses, Price Waterhouse has developed specialized tax expertise. Some of those capabilities include:

- **Employee Benefits Services (EBS)**—EBS helps companies design and implement compensation and benefits programs that are both cost- and tax-effective and competitive so businesses can attract, motivate, and retain valued personnel.
- **International Assignment Services (IAS)**—IAS helps companies address the complex tax, compensation, and administrative issues encountered as they move employees around the world.
- **International Tax Services (ITS)**—ITS helps multinational companies and others meet the changing corporate tax challenges of their international operations.
- **Multistate Tax Consulting (MTC)**—MTC helps companies minimize state and local taxes and develop efficient administrative systems for doing business in multiple jurisdictions.

- **Personal Financial Services (PFS)**—PFS helps senior-level executives, closely held business owners, and wealthy individuals take control of their financial futures through a full range of services ranging from education funding to retirement planning. Close personal attention and implementation assistance are the hallmarks of this service.
- **Personal Financial Products (PFP)**—Economic pressures, layoffs, and the increasing corporate shift away from traditional pensions guaranteeing retirement income have made PFP a popular flexible option for all employee levels. Through easy-to-read personal plans, interactive software, focused workshops, and proven follow-up techniques, PFP helps assure companies that employees participate in the program *and* take action on financial planning with confidence.
- **Tax Technology Group (TTG)**—TTG helps corporate tax departments get the most from technology by offering a full range of advanced products and services designed to assist with many tax compliance and planning issues.
- **Valuation Services (VS)**—VS helps companies and individuals make objective determinations of the current value of assets, stock, and business interests that are crucial to effective tax and business planning.
- **Washington National Tax Service (WNTS)**—WNTS, under the direction of former Congressional tax officials and senior IRS personnel, monitors tax developments at the international, federal, state, and local levels and assists both growing enterprises and multinational corporations in complying with new tax laws and developing appropriate tax strategies.

This list highlights only some of the tax services offered. Price Waterhouse tax professionals provide comprehensive tax planning advice to reduce federal, state, local, and foreign taxes. They assist with administrative procedures involving the Treasury or IRS such as obtaining private letter rulings and reviewing technical and policy issues that cannot be satisfactorily resolved at the audit or appeals level. They prepare economic studies of the impact of proposed legislation on businesses, industries, and federal and state governments. In addition, Price Waterhouse tax professionals consult on a wide variety of tax issues affecting acquisitions, mergers, closely held businesses, trusts and estates, and the selection of tax accounting methods.

Further, Price Waterhouse, as a leading business advisory services firm, offers a wide range of professional services provided by accountants, auditors, and management consultants. To learn about these or any of the firm's tax services, please contact the Price Waterhouse office nearest you. For your convenience, we have provided a listing of Price Waterhouse offices in the United States, along with telephone numbers.

SECURE YOUR future

Do you have a financial plan?

If so, is it up-to-date?

Don't reach for the aspirin. Financial planning does not have to be a headache, and you don't have to have a lot of money to have a plan.

The process just got easier with financial planning tools from Price Waterhouse.

Each of our goals are different. We need personalized planning from someone who is unbiased and objective. Price Waterhouse does not sell investments, and is not associated with anyone that does. Financial planning is provided to help you determine, clarify, and reach your financial goals. All information is kept strictly confidential.

We have personalized reports and interactive software that addresses *your* goals and *your* situation.

Take advantage of this opportunity to learn more about what the financial planning program has to offer.

The first step to securing your future is having a plan. Call us for more information:

1-800-752-6234

Corporate programs are also available.
Call (312) 368-6519 for details or send e-mail to:
Mark_Ward@notes.pw.com@Internet.

Price Waterhouse LLP
Retirement and Financial Education Group

Thank you for choosing Irwin Professional Publishing for your information needs. If you are part of a corporation, professional association, or government agency, consider our newest option: Custom Publishing. This service helps you create customized books, manuals, and other materials from your organization's resources, selected chapters of our books, or both.

Irwin Professional Publishing books are also excellent resources for training/educational programs, premiums, and incentives. For information on volume discounts or custom publishing, call 1-800-634-3966.

Other books of interest to you from Irwin Professional Publishing and Price Waterhouse ...

Secure Your Future
Your Personal Companion for Understanding Lifestyle & Financial Aspects of Retirement
Price Waterhouse LLP
A Money Book Club Selection!

Secure Your Future shows you how to approach retirement as a multifaceted process, not a singular event. The professionals at Price Waterhouse have teamed up with Helen Dennis, a leading expert on aging issues, to provide sound advice on a full spectrum of financial *and* psychological issues involved in retirement. *Secure Your Future* presents a fresh approach that will help you create the retirement lifestyle of your dreams.

Using effective four-color graphics, *Secure Your Future* helps you determine where you are now with regard to retirement, where you want to be, and how to get there. Most importantly, you will learn how to avoid financial shortfalls later in life.

ISBN: 0-7863-0526-6

The Price Waterhouse Personal Financial Adviser
Price Waterhouse LLP

This practical guide helps readers face their financial reality and plan for the financial impact of life events such as marriage, children's education, divorce, disability, and retirement. Numerous Price Waterhouse examples, stories, and cases will help readers see how other people have benefitted from solid financial planning.

ISBN: 0-7863-0461-8